Bounded Disciplines and Unbounded Problems

The Clarendon Lectures in Management Studies are jointly organized by Oxford University Press and the Saïd Business School. Every year a leading international academic is invited to give a series of lectures on a topic related to management education and research, broadly defined. The lectures form the basis of a book subsequently published by Oxford University Press.

CLARENDON LECTURES IN MANAGEMENT STUDIES:

The Modern Firm
Organizational Design for Performance and Growth
John Roberts

Managing Intellectual Capital
Organizational, Strategic, and Policy Dimensions
David Teece

The Political Determinants of Corporate Governance
Political Context, Corporate Impact
Mark Roe

The Internet Galaxy
Reflections on the Internet, Business, and Society
Manuel Castells

Brokerage and Closure
An Introduction to Social Capital
Ronald S. Burt

Reassembling the Social
An Introduction to Actor-Network-Theory
Bruno Latour

Science, Innovation, and Economic Growth
Walter W. Powell

The Logic of Position, the Measure of Leadership
Position and Information in the Market
Joel Podolny

Global Companies in the 20th Century
Leslie Hannah

Gatekeepers
The Role of the Professions in Corporate Governance
John C. Coffee

Material Markets
How Economic Agents are Constructed
Donald MacKenzie

Corporations in Evolving Diversity
Cognition, Governance, and Institutions
Masahiko Aoki

Staying Power
Six Enduring Principles for Managing Strategy and Innovation in an Uncertain World
Michael A. Cusumano

The Entrepreneurial Firm: Strategy and Organization in New Markets
Kathleen M. Eisenhardt

Doing New Things in Old Organizations
The (Business) Challenge of Climate Change
Rebecca M. Henderson

Maverick Markets
The Virtual Societies of Financial Markets
Karin Knorr Cetina

Disruptive Innovation and Growth
Clayton Christianson

The Architecture of Collapse
The Global System in the 21st Century
Mauro F. Guillén

The 99 Percent Economy
How Democratic Socialism Can Overcome the Crises of Capitalism
Paul S. Adler

Work and Technological Change
Stephen R. Barley

Selves at Work
Herminia Ibarra

Bounded Disciplines and Unbounded Problems
A Vision for Management Science
Baruch Fischhoff

Bounded Disciplines and Unbounded Problems

A Vision for Management Science

Baruch Fischhoff

Great Clarendon Street, Oxford, OX2 6DP,
United Kingdom

Oxford University Press is a department of the University of Oxford.
It furthers the University's objective of excellence in research, scholarship,
and education by publishing worldwide. Oxford is a registered trade mark of
Oxford University Press in the UK and in certain other countries

© Baruch Fischhoff 2025

The moral rights of the author have been asserted

All rights reserved. No part of this publication may be reproduced, stored in a retrieval system, transmitted, used for text and data mining, or used for training artificial intelligence, in any form or by any means, without the prior permission in writing of Oxford University Press, or as expressly permitted by law, by licence or under terms agreed with the appropriate reprographics rights organization. Enquiries concerning reproduction outside the scope of the above should be sent to the Rights Department, Oxford University Press, at the address above

You must not circulate this work in any other form
and you must impose this same condition on any acquirer

Published in the United States of America by Oxford University Press
198 Madison Avenue, New York, NY 10016, United States of America

British Library Cataloguing in Publication Data

Data available

Library of Congress Control Number: 2024945801

ISBN 9780198893905

DOI: 10.1093/9780191997266.001.0001

Printed and bound by
CPI Group (UK) Ltd, Croydon, CR0 4YY

Links to third party websites are provided by Oxford in good faith and
for information only. Oxford disclaims any responsibility for the materials
contained in any third party website referenced in this work.

The manufacturer's authorised representative in the EU for product safety
is Oxford University Press España S.A. of el Parque Empresarial San
Fernando de Henares, Avenida de Castilla,
2   28830 Madrid (www.oup.es/en).

Dedicated to the lives and memories of my students, friends, and colleagues, Stephanie Byram (1963–2001), who lit a path through adversity, and Victor Louis Rodriguez (1995–2023), who brought science and people together.

Preface

Relations between academia and society have long been fraught, dating back at least to the town–gown riots that sped the establishment of Cambridge University by refugees from Oxford. These tensions deny academia and society the support that each needs from the other. Today's public scorn for "elites" limits academia's ability to provide the expertise that society needs to address complex problems, such as climate change, arms control, homelessness, biodiversity loss, pandemic disease, and political repression. It also prompts reciprocal scorn for the public, which academics can conveniently dismiss as irrational and anti-science.

To some extent, these tensions are out of academia's control, reflecting collateral damage from broader social conflicts. Whatever we, as academics, do will be held against us by pundits and politicians who need a convenient foil and hope to delegitimize any expert whose inconvenient evidence might challenge their claims. Academia is mysterious enough to most people that many charges about its failings might seem true. Those charges might even be welcomed as comeuppance for today's experts, who were yesterday's teachers' pets. Whatever the case, it behooves us academics to consider how we might be failing (or at least acting in ways that make things easier for our critics). The first lecture examines how disciplines' heuristic ways of thinking produce both insights and blinders. The second lecture illustrates these processes in one consequential domain, claims about other people's decision-making competence. The third lecture proposes a strategy for enabling scientific disciplines to work their heuristic magic, while reducing the blinders that can make them part of the problem for civil society rather than part of the solution.

The lectures focus on the disciplines that I know best, psychology and management science, and their intersection in the discipline now called decision science (or behavioral decision research). I draw on my own experiences, allowing me to discuss issues that do not make it into published papers. I have not tried to situate my observations in the literatures on intra-, inter-, multi-, and transdisciplinary research, where I lack even advanced amateur standing. I assume that those studies face the same challenges as the disciplines I know: How to be useful, while maintaining necessarily narrow disciplinary standards.

My lectures embrace the normative-descriptive-prescriptive arc of decision science, asking, in turn, how to conceptualize decisions formally, how people approach them intuitively, and how we can help people—by improving either their understanding or their options. The "people" here include not just those we study, but also ourselves, as we choose problems, formulate studies, and interpret results. The lectures illustrate these imperfect processes with decision science, emphasizing its shared roots with other management sciences. The lectures conclude by proposing a shared future, in which disciplines collaborate with one another, prompted by the practical need and intellectual value of serving others.

The message of the lectures is simple. Each discipline has its own internal logic, emerging from its members' interactions, creating and interpreting evidence in terms that they consider legitimate. Following that internal logic gives scientists a distinctive ability to get to the bottom of narrowly defined questions. However, the long-term intellectual health and social value of any discipline depends on transcending those boundaries by interacting with other disciplines and with people who need their help.

Management science can play a central role in making these interactions happen. Its analytical methods can accommodate results from other scientific disciplines, stretching to include indigenous knowledge and perspectives from the humanities. Its behavioral methods can identify ways to bring scientists together with one another and with decision makers. Its engagement methods can structure those interactions. The lectures propose a strategy for employing these capabilities that serves both science and society. That strategy uses graphic templates as platforms for bringing together diverse preferences, forms of evidence, and decision makers—and for evaluating its success. This book lays out the strategy proposed in the lectures.

Chapter 1, *Bounding Complexity: The Wisdom of Conscious Blinders*, describes the kinds of complexity that take decisions outside the scope of any single discipline. Using Herbert Simon's *bounded rationality* as an organizing framework, the chapter discusses the potentially vital roles of internecine conflicts within disciplines and the potentially destructive roles of imperial conflicts between disciplines. It concludes with management science's potential role in fostering fewer, but better conflicts within and between disciplines.

Chapter 2, *Sciences (in)Action: A Success and a Failure in Confronting Complexity*, describes two case studies illustrating the complexity of the kinds of fateful decisions that disciplinary scientists might hope to inform: climate change and equitable allocation of COVID-19 vaccine. With the former, management science has underperformed for decades, through both some, and no, fault of our own. With the latter, we played an essential role. The chapter concludes by contrasting these two high-stakes enterprises, with lessons for what follows.

Chapter 3, *Decision Science: Boundedly Rational Study of Rationality*, describes the boundedly rational discipline that studies how people make decisions in terms comparable to idealized models of how they should make them. The chapter shows the potential benefits and risks of the discipline's focus on a small set of clearly defined concepts (e.g., probabilities, preferences). The benefits include opportunities to identify general patterns; the risks include undisciplined generalization and restricted forms of evidence. The chapter concludes by discussing how decision science exemplifies the promise and perils of disciplinary science.

Chapter 4, *Questions of Competence: Disciplined Empathy*, considers the ethics of decision science's fundamental perspective, contrasting observed behavior and an idealized standard. It discusses the risks of both over- and underestimating people's decision-making competence, both for those people and for scientists studying them. It illustrates the versatility of the analytical standard and the challenges of applying it. It concludes by discussing incentives that misalign the interests of decision scientists and those they study, and proposes a model of slow decision science that can realign them.

Chapter 5, *Slow Science (Beliefs)*, describes how decision science can assess and inform decision makers' beliefs, using methods that run at different speeds. These include the interaction between fast responses to surveys, with little time to reflect on questions or possible answers, and the slow process of formulating questions and interpreting responses. Those interactions protect against the rush to judgment feared in Chapter 4 by allowing decision makers to inform research about them. The chapter concludes with proposals for slower methods to complement faster ones.

Chapter 6, *Slow Science (Preferences)*, describes how decision science can assess and inform decision makers' preferences, again using methods that run at different speeds. As in Chapter 5, they include slow and fast processes. They largely exclude some common tasks (e.g., importance ratings) that limit people's ability to express themselves in ways that will be interpreted as intended. The chapter concludes with proposals for slower methods to complement faster ones.

Chapter 7, *A Strategy for Bonding Bounded Disciplines*, proposes a strategy for bonding bounded disciplines, using fast and slow decision science to bring them together in solving applied problems. The strategy employs slow decision science to grasp the complexity of decisions and decision makers, and (slowly developed) fast decision science to complete the picture. The chapter concludes with missing links that the humanities can provide.

Chapter 8, *A Vision for Management Science*, considers the institutions that could implement the bonding strategy. It examines the "business case" for making it happen as well as the inertia of the entrenched disciplines. It offers examples of institutions exemplifying the strategy, typically arising in acute crises (e.g., wars). It concludes with proposals for responding to chronic crises like climate change and social polarization.

Chapter 9, *Change (in)Action*, asks how well the proposed bonding strategy captures what went wrong and right with the two cases in Chapter 2, climate change and the COVID-19 pandemic. It concludes with an assessment of the strategy, in the light of these experiences.

Chapter 10, *Management Science as a Bonding Discipline*, describes how schools of management could lead in implementing the bonding strategy, bridging the worlds of theory and practice. The chapter considers current academic incentives that pose barriers and ways to overcome them. It concludes by calling on management schools to lead in bringing together science and society.

Acknowledgments

I am grateful to the Saïd School of Management for the invitation to give the Clarendon Lectures in Management Studies, which gave me a chance to gather my thoughts on issues that have occupied me throughout my professional career and, indeed, when pondering whether to have such a career. I have been fortunate to have worked in places—sometimes by chance, sometimes by design—that have provided opportunities to collaborate with people from other disciplines on problems that needed all our skills, and sometimes more. The strategy for management science proposed here grew out of those attempts to make my management science, behavioral decision research, useful and to use these experiences to advance the science. Those professional homes include the Psychology Department of the Hebrew University of Jerusalem, Decision Research (Eugene, Oregon), the Medical Research Council Applied Psychology Unit (Cambridge), and Carnegie Mellon University. Each place had a deep history of creating the conditions for the collaborations needed to make ourselves useful. One of those conditions was willingness to put basic research on hold when a chance arose for its application. For me, some of the most valuable invitations came from the (US) National Academies of Sciences, Engineering, and Medicine, where I have served on some forty committees, and US federal agencies (notably, the Department of Homeland Security, Environmental Protection Agency, Food and Drug Administration, Nuclear Regulatory Agency, and Office of the Director of National Intelligence). These institutions have enabled me to pursue the vision of management science that impelled me to seek an academic career. That is the vision offered in this book.

I have had exceptional mentors, who gave me intellectual tools for that pursuit, notably Robyn Dawes, David Jonah, Danny Kahneman, Reuven Kaminer, Samuel Komorita, Sarah Lichtenstein, Assaf Orr, Paul Slovic, and Amos Tversky. I have had wonderful colleagues, collaborators, and students, inside and outside academia. I have lived my life in loving families. Who could ask for anything more?

Contents

1. **Bounding Complexity: The Wisdom of Conscious Blinders**   1
   - Confronting Complexity   2
   - Coping with Complexity   3
   - Sciences in Complexity   4
     - Burrowing within Boundaries   5
     - When Details Matter   7
   - Boundary Disputes   9
   - Conclusions   12

2. **Sciences (in)Action: A Success and a Failure in Confronting Complexity**   13
   - Equitable Allocation of COVID-19 Vaccine   14
     - The Complex Problem   14
   - The Disciplines   16
     - Management Science Tasks   20
     - Lessons Learned   23
   - Human Dimensions of Climate Change   25
     - The Complex Problem   25
     - The Disciplines   26
     - Management Science Tasks   29
     - Lessons Learned   32
   - Conclusions   34

3. **Decision Science: Boundedly Rational Study of Rationality**   35
   - Decision Science, Flourishing within Bounds   36
   - Out-of-Bounds Observations   38
   - Pushing Heuristic Bounds   39
   - The Bias Heuristic   42
   - Simple Models or Simple Processes   45
   - Conclusions   47

4. **Questions of Competence: Disciplined Empathy**   48
   - Avoiding a Rush to Judgment   49
   - The Discipline of Decision Science   50
   - Structured Empathy   51
   - "Literacy" Tests   53
   - Individual Differences   54
   - Merchants of Bias?   58

xii   Contents

    Scientists Are People, Too 60
    Conclusions 61

5. Slow Science (Beliefs) 62
    What Are We Asking? The Face Validity of Questions 63
    What Are They Telling Us? The Face Validity of Answers 67
    How Much Do People Think about the World? 70
    What Do Experts Believe? 74
    Conclusions 79

6. Slow Science (Preferences) 80
    Ostensibly Simple Tasks 80
    What Are We Asking: The Face Validity of Questions 81
        Defining Risks 81
        Defining Benefits 85
    What Are They Telling Us? The Face Validity of Answers 88
    If We Have Questions, Do They Have Answers? 92
    Might They Have Answers, If We Slowed Down? 94
    Conclusions 95

7. A Strategy for Bonding Bounded Disciplines 96
    Barriers to Bonding Bounded Disciplines 97
    A Strategy for Bonding Bounded Disciplines 98
        Staffing: Are the Right People Involved? 100
        Internal Consultation: Are Those People Talking
          to One Another? 105
        External Consultation: Are Those People Talking with
          Stakeholders? 108
    Conclusions 110

8. A Vision for Management Science 112
    Management Science as General Contractor 112
    Creating an Intellectual Commons 114
        Methods for Assessing Experts' Beliefs 114
        Methods for Assessing Nonexperts' Beliefs 115
    Creating Communities 116
        Methods for Creating Shared Ways of Thinking 116
        Methods for Creating Respectful Ways of Interacting 119
    Creating Incentives 120
    Boundary Organizations for Bonding Bounded Disciplines 122
    Conclusions 125

9. Change (in)Action   **126**

    COVID-19   127
        Vaccines   127
        Face Masks   129
        Movie Studios   131
    Climate Change   132
        Better Story Telling   134
        Better Stories   137
        Reflection   142
    Conclusions   143

10. Management Science as a Bonding Discipline   **144**

    Decision Science   145
    From a Multidisciplinary Field to an Interdisciplinary Platform   146
    An Interdisciplinary Platform in a Multidisciplinary World   148
        Psychology   149
        Economics   151
        Management Science   152
    Strategic Gambles   154
    Conclusions   157

Index   159

Chapter 1
Bounding Complexity

The Wisdom of Conscious Blinders

The world is awash with problems. Climate change, political polarization, inequality, alienation, anxiety, biodiversity loss, child abuse and neglect, pandemic disease—and more. Legions of researchers have dedicated their professional lives to addressing these problems. Yet something is not working. We experts are not always quick to respond when problems arise. We are not always asked to help. We are not always the best helpers. We move too haltingly for people passionate about problems. We are not always heeded. We are not always liked.

There are always other people we can blame. Practitioners are too set in their ways to bridge the "valley of death" separating them from our wisdom. Some politicians use us as convenient foils for populist rhetoric. Other politicians exploit us, imploring people to "follow the science" when it points in directions that they favor. Nonexperts misunderstand our science. Merchants of doubt prosper from belittling us.[1] News media sometimes find us boring, sometimes sensationalize our results.

Those obstacles all exist. Nonetheless, it's always worth asking whether we are part of the problem. How real are our proposed solutions? What goals do we pursue, and ignore? What uncertainties do we consider, and ignore? How well can we change course if we falter? Who stands behind our proposals if they fail? Do they crowd out more worthy solutions? Whose authority do they increase, and diminish? Do they elevate our status and power, relative to the people we are advising?

The answers to these questions reflect the ways that we, as experts, cope with the complexity inherent to challenging problems. Disciplines define themselves by their coping strategies, and the constraints that they impose on those schooled in them. This book first considers the benefits and costs of the essential myopia of disciplinary science. It then proposes a strategy for management science to lead in creating the collaborative wisdom that arises when diverse experts and their clients work together.

[1] Oreskes, N., & Conway, E. M. (2014). *Merchants of doubt*. Bloomsbury.

2 Bounded Disciplines and Unbounded Problems

Confronting Complexity

According to Herbert Simon, the great challenge in decision making is not *uncertainty*,[2] which poses clear, if sometimes unwelcome, gambles. Rather, it is complexity, which makes it hard to know what those gambles are. Complexity can arise from each of the three elements of any decision: the *options* that decision makers might choose, the *outcomes* that might follow, and the *events* that determine which outcomes are actually experienced.

Options can be complex because there are many *discrete* ones (e.g., which breakfast cereal, mutual fund, baby name, wording of an apology, or travel destination to choose). Options can be complex because they are *continuous*, without clear delineation. For example, what percentage of a nest egg to put into equities, of income to donate to charity, or of the day to reserve for reflection? How long to exercise, study for a test, or stay as a house guest? Options can also be complex because they are *ambiguous*, and hence open to interpretation. For example, what is meant by "the terms of use" for a website? What does a half-smile say about an invitation?

Outcomes can be complex for the same reasons. There can be many discrete ones (e.g., all the possible side effects rattled off in pharmaceutical commercials,[3] all the career pathways that an undergraduate student might select, all the distributional impacts of an energy policy). They can be continuous, with unclear gradations. For example, when does pain become noticeable, distracting, or unbearable? When does wealth become adequate, comforting, or corrupting? They can be ambiguous, without clear meaning (e.g., what does it feel like to lose someone close, gain an unexpected honor, or face an unfamiliar threat?)

The same forms of complexity can affect the events that link options and outcomes. There may be too many discrete things that could go wrong or right (e.g., competitors' responses to a product rollout, people one might meet at a party, countries that might sign a treaty). There may be complex relationships among continuous variables (e.g., how performance responds to time pressure, plants respond to spring temperatures, stocks respond to inflation expectations). The relationships may be ambiguous, making connections unclear (e.g., the effects of climate change on terrorism, terrorism on climate change, or parenting style on sociability).

In the thicket of such complexities, it can be hard to know where to focus when thinking about the decisions that one might choose or be forced to make.

---

[2] I will follow the convention of italicizing technical terms (or jargon) when first used.
[3] Only the US and New Zealand allow such ads.

Coping with Complexity

Herbert Simon famously distinguished two strategies for dealing with complexity: *bounded rationality* and *satisficing*.[4] The former entails looking for the perfect solution to a simplified (bounded) version of a problem. The latter entails looking for an adequate solution, accepting that better ones may be missed.

The success of either strategy depends on decision makers' *heuristics* for implementing it.[5] For bounded rationality, those rules of thumb might determine which discrete options to consider (e.g., only things that you have done before), how to discretize continuous options (e.g., never invest more than you can afford to lose), or how to reduce ambiguity (e.g., only invest in firms whose products you have used). Analogous heuristics could bound complex outcomes or contingencies.

Once these bounds are applied, they leave, in effect, a matrix whose rows are options, whose columns are outcomes, and in which each cell entry is the expected outcome if the corresponding option is chosen. The smaller the matrix, the more feasible it is to examine each cell thoroughly enough that further examination would not affect the choice, thereby achieving bounded rationality. Conversely, the smaller the matrix, the greater the risk that relevant options, outcomes, or relationships will fall outside its bounds.

Satisficing heuristics are holistic and often harder to describe. They include the forms of pattern recognition that physicians use in performing trauma triage, dealers use in selecting art, and DJs use in creating mixes. Each involves picking options worth evaluating. These options may exist already (e.g., new cars, college courses, vacation destinations) or may be created (e.g., logos, legislation, book outlines). A heuristic evaluation process then asks whether the options produced by the heuristic search process are good enough to stop searching. That assessment depends on both the options and the expectations for finding better ones. Evaluation heuristics might include: "If I'm hungry for ethnic food and see a place full of 'ethnics,' that's good enough for me." "Let's run the study. We're not going to know what's wrong with the design until we collect some data." "Let's keep haggling. I sense that the merchant believes that we know about alternatives."[6,7]

---

[4] Simon, H. A. (1957). *Models of man.* John Wiley & Sons—work that won him the 1978 Nobel Prize in Economics.

[5] Georg Polya made heuristics a centerpiece of his approach to teaching mathematics (Polya, G. (1945). *How to solve it.* Princeton University Press). Allen Newell described its contribution to his work with Herbert Simon: Newell, A. (1981). The heuristic of Georg Polya and its relationship to artificial intelligence. In Groner, R., Groner, M., & Bischoof, W. F. (Eds.), *Methods of heuristics* (pp. 195–244). Lawrence Erlbaum.

[6] The poet Paul Celan once wrote "Poems are never finished, only abandoned."

[7] Optional stopping algorithms formalize these decisions in boundedly rational terms. In one version of what was once called the "secretary problem," a manager decides at the end of each interview whether

Both of Simon's strategies are *consequentialist*. They consider only the expected outcomes (or consequences) of choices, not the process for getting to them. Thus, it would not matter whether a choice is induced by a manipulative nudge, reached by trial and error, or inferred by thoughtful deliberation. Nor would it matter how the decision-making process affected decision makers' understanding of the world, sense of self-efficacy, or autonomy—unless that process affected an outcome (e.g., people who choose 11-point Calibri are seen as unthinking Word users).

Sciences in Complexity

Researchers face the same forms of complexity in selecting the problems that they study. Researchers interested in human behavior face a multitude of individuals, settings, forcing events, endogenous developments, mechanisms, outcomes, time horizons, cultures, incentives, and constraints to study, among other things, along with the interactions among these factors. These researchers can characterize each factor in different ways. They might identify individuals by demographics, personality tests, or physiological measures. They might summarize outcomes by means, variances, or equity. They might represent theories in a variety of constructs. And so on.

A heuristic way of thinking about scientific disciplines is that each deals with complexity through its own form of bounded rationality, followed by its own form of satisficing. The first step drastically reduces the set of possible research questions to the subset that is legitimate within the bounds of the discipline. The second step determines whether specific studies addressing those questions satisfice, and could withstand the rigors of disciplinary peer review.

That strategy shapes disciplinary mentoring. New students learn the bounds of their discipline, the conventions of their field, and perhaps the confines of their mentor's "lab." Within those constraints, they learn the satisficing tools of the trade, such as the measures and analyses most likely to produce reviewer-resilient results. Their apprenticeship includes mastery of the trial and error of study design, which proceeds until a satisficing rule deems it "good enough," given the constraints of time, material resources,

to offer the candidate the job. Each interview incurs a cost (for the manager), while yielding information about the candidate pool. The algorithm calculates how many interviews to conduct before the manager knows enough about the distribution to recognize a candidate who is good enough that it is not worth looking further. The manager recognizes that there are better candidates "out there," but chooses to satisfice.

and new ideas. When designing his first empirical study, Barry Dewitt, a graduate student with previous degrees in pure mathematics, described it as a Zeno paradox-like process, gradually approaching the perfect study, but never getting there.

Box 1.1 lists heuristics for disciplinary science that I attribute to Amos Tversky, one of my primary mentors. He is no longer with us for me to check their accuracy, but I hope that he would approve. One corollary, which I remember him saying, is that successful scientists are no smarter than successful businesspeople or military leaders. However, we can exercise greater control over how we spend our time. If we cede that control, then we have forfeited our strategic advantage.[8]

Box 1.1 Heuristics for Disciplinary Science

Have hypotheses clear enough to be wrong and be willing to admit it.
Want to get it right.
Protect the time to think.

Amos Tversky (attributed)

It is that relentless burrowing which distinguishes scientists, trying to get it right, from consultants, trying to get it done. It leads to disputes among scientists that represent intellectual vigor for those content to live within disciplinary bounds, and tempests in teapots for those with other event horizons. An example may give a feeling for disciplinary work, and its essential tensions.

Burrowing within Boundaries

A critical task for any organism is learning the frequency of events in its environment. One subfield of cognitive psychology examines how people perform that task. It typically bounds its studies to tasks that exclude prior observation, consultation with others, instruction, or expertise. The results

---

[8] By way of contrast, Lee Sproull once mentioned to me that, in her observations of how business leaders spend their time, she found that, on the rare occasions when they had an unprogrammed block of time, they found someone to talk to rather than spending it in contemplation. They had lost, or perhaps never had, the ability to use unstructured time well.

of those studies might be extrapolated most directly to real-world settings with similar constraints, such as landing at an unfamiliar website, visiting a foreign country, or learning a new language. The purpose of that artificiality is to examine these cognitive processes in isolation. In perhaps the earliest such study,[9] people were asked to write down as many examples as they could of categories like quadruped mammals, US cities, fellow college students, and words that could be made from the letters ONDTERH. It found that the production rate decreased predictably over time, reflecting some combination of exhausting the people or their memories. The authors went to some lengths to explain the logic of the exponential function predicting those rates, perhaps a first in psychology.

Studies in this vein have found that people have a remarkable ability to learn frequencies—so great that it appears to be an automatic process. Thus, the mind is counting, even when people are not paying overt attention.[10] Within that constraint, a battle has raged between two theories. One holds that the brain records each observation separately; when people estimate frequency, they tally the observations (or *tokens*). The second theory holds that there is a single memory *trace* for each *type* of event, which each observation strengthens; when people estimate frequency, they assess the strength of that trace.

The science progresses by devising new tasks, where researchers claim that the competing theories make different predictions. Those claims rely on heuristic *auxiliary assumptions* about how people perform them. One task in a set of studies asked people to produce rhymes for a series of words and then surprised them by asking how many words began with each letter (even though they had been focusing on the ends of the words).[11] The studies' auxiliary assumptions were strengthened by drawing on research from two other fields, each with its own bounded rationality: how people process a stimulus when they focus on its sound (acoustics) or meaning (semantics).[12]

To an outsider, the intensity of these debates over such ascetic issues may seem misplaced. However, the two theories reflect fundamentally different accounts of how the brain encodes experiences. Everyday life is too

---

[9] Bousfield, W. A., & Sedgewick, C. H. W. (1944). An analysis of sequences of restricted associates responses. *Journal of General Psychology, 30*(2), 149–165.

[10] Hasher, L., & Zacks, R. T. (1981). Automatic processing of fundamental information: The case of frequency of occurence. *American Psychologist, 39*(12), 1372–1388.

[11] Jonides, J., & Naveh-Benjamin, M. (1987). Estimating frequency of occurrence. *Journal of Experimental Psychology: Human Learning and Memory, 13*(2), 230–240.

[12] The authors concluded that each theory explained some results better.

complicated to distinguish the two accounts, but the bounded reality of experiments offers some hope. Realizing its potential requires meticulous attention to detail in experimental design. The wisdom of experimental research, like that of all disciplines, lies in its mastery of those details—which people without researchers' specialized training might miss or misinterpret. The folly of any discipline lies in exaggerating the importance of those details.

In 2010, Saul Perlmutter gave a Dickson Prize lecture at Carnegie Mellon University, where he demonstrated the part played by meticulous measurement in distinguishing the roles of dark matter and dark energy in the evolution of the cosmos.[13] Those roles were still unresolved (although he had his hunches), spurring new research and the search for research in adjoining fields that might prove useful. Perlmutter observed, though, that despite the intensity of physicists' internecine debates, the predictions of the competing models were within the width of the line depicting the relationship between the distance of celestial bodies from earth and the red shift of waves coming from them.

When Details Matter

The debate over frequency encoding received added impetus from its part in Amos Tversky and Daniel Kahneman's account of the central role of heuristics in judgment. The *availability* heuristic holds that people judge the relative frequency of events by how easily examples come to mind.[14] The automaticity of frequency encoding makes availability a plausible heuristic. If people unconsciously track relative frequency, why wouldn't they consult those mental records when they need that information?

The usefulness of the availability heuristic depends on how well the events that people notice represent the universe of events—and how well they can correct for the bias in unrepresentative samples. Sometimes, people are aware of bias and can correct for it. "My child shares all his problems; my mother shares none. I can tell what they're feeling from what they're saying and not saying." Sometimes, people are aware, but can't correct. "I know I'm in an echo chamber on politics (or sports or investments). However, I don't know

---

[13] https://www.cmu.edu/dickson-prize/past-winners/index.html (accessed August 16, 2024). Sadly, I could find no recording.
[14] In memory research, availability is sometimes used to denote whether information is in memory, and *accessibility* to denote whether it can be retrieved. The availability heuristic includes elements of both processes.

8 Bounded Disciplines and Unbounded Problems

what is echoing in the other chambers." Or sometimes people are unaware, but still correct. "I stopped listening to them. I'm not sure why, but they upset me."[15] Sometimes, they have no idea; then marketers and propagandists succeed.

Availability is compatible with either the trace or the token representation of frequency. Indeed, one hotly contested theoretical issue, with potential practical implications, is whether probabilities or frequencies are the more natural way to think about risks. Arguably, the former is more compatible with traces and the latter more compatible with tokens. As with all experimental research, there are many ways to translate these general constructs into specific terms. For example, displays may be written (e.g., "0.1 percent" or "1 in 1,000") or graphic (e.g., a slice of a pie chart or a subset of stick figures). Research on the question is vast[16] and, to this observer at least, strangely acrimonious.

The depth of such debates depends on the maturity of the science, within its accepted bounds. The tenor of the debates depends on the civility of the participants. In this debate, one local maximum was found in studies refining the Drug Facts Box for communicating the risks and benefits of pharmaceuticals.[17] Initial versions of the Box offered both percentages and frequencies, not knowing which was better. Eventually a study reduced the clutter, by finding that percentages worked better in this context.[18]

That result from a decision science study could inform memory researchers, if they can extract its implications from the complex applied context. However, memory researchers might conclude that responses to a Drug Facts Box could be colored by emotion, unlike responses to banal categories and innocuous words (as in the examples above). If so, then they have little to learn from studies using the Box.

Later chapters describe two other internecine battles that have shaped the discipline of decision science. One was abandoned as unproductive. It asked whether people were "conservative Bayesian updaters" because they "misperceived" or "misaggregated" new evidence (terms explained later). The second continues. It asks whether researchers can interact with the people whom they study or must remain passive observers of their behavior.

---

[15] Holman, E. A., Garfin, D. R., & Silver, R. C. (2014). Media's role in broadcasting acute stress following the Boston Marathon bombings. *Proceedings of the National Academy of Sciences, 111*(1), 93–98.
[16] Peters, E. (2020). *Innumeracy in the wild*. Oxford University Press.
[17] Schwartz, L. M., & Woloshin, S. (2013). The drug facts box: Improving the communication of prescription drug information. *Proceedings of the National Academy of Sciences, 110*(Suppl. 3), 14069–14074.
[18] Woloshin, S., & Schwartz, L. M. (2011). Communicating data about the benefits and harms of treatments. *Annals of Internal Medicine, 155*(2), 87–96.

Boundary Disputes

The contentiousness of these squabbles arises, in part, because the parties cannot walk away from one another. As members of the same discipline, they publish in the same journals, review one another's work, compete for the same research funds, and want their theory to prevail. Sometimes, judicious editors mediate disputes and elicit accounts that satisfice for some parties. Other times, warring parties censor one another's work or force mumbled compromises, blurring rather than sharpening the issues.[19] The "Limitations" sections that conclude articles offer a place to acknowledge other interpretations of their evidence.[20] Occasionally, the parties engage in *adversarial collaborations*, seeking evidence that each would consider definitive.[21]

Members of different disciplines, though, can choose to ignore one other, even when ostensibly studying the same phenomenon. The standard strategy is to place the other discipline's work outside the bounds of one's own science (or perhaps even acceptable science). Sociology and psychology have long housed separate fields of social psychology. The former studies how people interact, the latter how people think about interactions. The former finds little value in research without behavior revealing the results of those thought processes. The latter finds little value in research without evidence regarding the thought processes that could produce behavior.

Economists and psychologists interested in decision making have often treated one another's work as outside their bounds. Economists generally insist on observing behavior "in the wild," as people choose among actual options. They assume that they know how people think, rationally, in order to infer what they think about.[22] Psychologists typically insist on observing behavior in the lab, where they can control the wild of everyday life. They assume that they know what people are thinking about—the features explained clearly in their tasks—in order to learn how they think about it.[23]

Over time, some economists moved in the psychologists' direction, creating the field of experimental economics. Sadly, in my view, they have often chosen to do this on their own, ignoring the century of experience conveyed

---

[19] Some journals offer the option of avoiding a small number of possible reviewers, typically no questions asked.
[20] A more forward-looking, and ego-protective, term than limitations is needed future research.
[21] Kahneman, D., & Klein, D. (2009). Conditions for intuitive expertise: A failure to disagree. *American Psychologist, 64*(6), 515–526.
[22] Historically, economists have assumed that people were rational actors, implicitly calculating the expected utility of their choice options. More recently, some have assumed that people follow some alternative behavioral calculus.
[23] Choices in economics and psychological studies are sometimes called revealed and expressed preferences, respectively, even when the latter involve actual choices for the small stakes in most studies.

in experimental psychologists' apprenticeship. As a result, their experiments can seem so ham-handed that psychologists may feel like they can learn little from them. For example, experimental economists typically insist on *incentive-compatible* tasks, designed so that rational research participants will reveal their true preferences.[24]

However, psychologists know how hard it is to convey abstract incentives for unfamiliar tasks and how important it is to include *manipulation checks* to determine how well people have mastered the instructions (and are, in fact, performing the intended task). For example, studies looking into how quickly people make decisions may instruct participants to "try to get everything right." However, response times can be very sensitive to whether people interpret the desired *speed–accuracy trade-off* as a 1 percent or 3 percent error rate, and to how accurately they estimate their error rate.[25] In the 1970s, attempts to improve probability judgments with incentive-compatible *proper scoring rules* foundered when researchers realized that the rules were too hard to understand or use.[26]

Experimental economists are smart, dedicated, and well resourced. Over time, they have constructed a largely parallel research universe, independently discovering some results of psychological research, and some new ones. Still, they might have gone faster and further had they collaborated more fully with their psychology cousins. A potentially productive road not taken was sketched by two of the earliest psychology-curious economists. David Grether and Charles Plott created a matrix (Box 1.2) summarizing studies possibly demonstrating one form of nonrational behavior.[27] Its columns were studies. Its rows were factors that might affect results (including whether a study was conducted by psychologists or economists). Each cell entry indicated whether the study's results supported the explanation.

---

[24] They are typically assumed to have veridical beliefs, an assumption that is rarely tested. More on all these issues in later chapters.
[25] Wickelgren, W. (1977). Speed–accuracy tradeoff and information processing dynamics. *Acta Psychologica, 41*(1), 67–85.
[26] The Brier Score is the best-known proper scoring rule (Mellers, B., Ungar, L., Baron, J., Ramos, J., Gurcay, B., Fincher, K., Scott, S. E., Moore, S., Atanasov, P., Swift, S. A., Murray, T., Stone, E., & Tetlock, P. E. (2014). Psychological strategies for winning a geopolitical forecasting tournament. *Psychological Science, 25*(5), 1106–1115). Perhaps because they were chastened by the high penalty for errors, participants rewarded by a proper scoring rule expressed less confidence than participants just asked to think hard. That response coincidentally reduced overconfidence, creating an illusion of learning.
[27] Grether, D., & Plott, C. (1979). Economic theory of choice and the preference reversal phenomenon. *American Economic Review, 67*(4), 623–638. The behavioral anomaly in question involved gambles with similar expected value (probability times monetary outcomes), where preferences were reversed when people were asked how much they would pay to play each (which focused them on the outcomes) and when they were asked which they preferred to play (which focused them on the probabilities).

Box 1.2 Bounded Accounts of Preference Reversals

	Theoretical criticism and/or explanation	Lichtenstein & Slovic (1971) experiment			Lichtenstein & Slovic (1973)	Lindman (1971)	Slovic (1975) experiment				This study experiment	
		1	2	3			1	2	3	4	1	2
	Economic theory											
1	Misspecified incentives	I	I	I	N	I	I	I	N	I	N	N
2	Income effects	N	N	E	?	N	N	N	E	N	N	N
3	Indifference psychological	N	I	I	I	I	I	I	I	I	N	N
4	Strategic responses	E	E	E	E	E	N	N	N	N	E	N
5	Probabilities	I	I	N	?	N	N	N	N	N	N	N
6	Elimination by aspect	N	N	N	N							N
7	Lexicographic semiorder	N	N	N	N							N
8	Information processing: decision costs	E	E	E	?	E	E	E	E	E	N	N
9	Information processing: response mode, easy justification experimental methods	E	E	E	E	E	E	E	E	E	E	E
10	Confusion and misunderstanding	N	N	N	N	N	N	N	N	N	N	N
11	Frequency low	N	N	N	N	N	N	N	N	N	N	N
12	Unsophisticated subjects	?	?	?	N	?	?	?	7	N	N	N
13	Experimenters were psychologists	I	I	I	I	I	I	I	I	I	N	N

I = The experiment is irrelevant to economics because of the reason or theory.
N = The experimental results cannot be explained by this reason or theory.
E = The experimental results are consistent with the reason or theory.
? = Data insufficient.

Source: Grether, D., & Plott, C. (1979). Economic theory of choice and the preference reversal phenomenon. *American Economic Review, 67(4),* 623–638. Used with permission of the authors.

Empirical methods are ultimately matters of taste, reflecting the compromises that satisfice for a discipline. So, too, are statistical methods. Advanced econometrics are the lingua franca of economics. Although psychologists learn regression methods, they rarely achieve the mastery needed for economics journals. Indeed, many psychologists have a taste for simple statistical methods, hoping to reduce the risks of burying assumptions or torturing data to achieve desired results.[28] As a result, economists may find psychologists' analyses unsophisticated, while psychologists find economists' analyses obscurant. Thus arise disciplinary barriers between near neighbors.

Conclusions

Scientific disciplines cope with complexity through bounded rationality: sweating the details on issues within their bounds, ignoring those outside. When successful, they discern details that outsiders miss, through what can look like overblown squabbles to those without that disciplinary background. When the bounds of disciplines overlap, as they sometimes do for psychology and economics, there can be uncomfortable and unproductive conflicts, as theparties struggle to discern what they can compromise without losing their integrity and cohesion. When fields deny one another's legitimacy, the result can be the *normalized pathology* of imagining that a discipline's bounded domain is all that matters. When disciplines acknowledge one another's legitimacy, the contrast can inform the self-reflection needed to recognize the bounds to their own form of rationality.

When disciplines get too settled within their bounds, scientists bear the direct cost of investing their life's energies ineffectively. Those who depend on them bear the opportunity costs of receiving less valuable knowledge than they would, were the disciplines better able to work together. Chapter 2 describes two cases where the public needed disciplinary collaboration. In one case, that need was met; in the other, it was not. The difference was, arguably, whether there was an integrative approach, grounded in management science.

---

[28] Ward Edwards described strong results as achieving the "interocular traumatic effect": they hit you between the eyes. Edwards, W., Lindman, H., & Savage, L. J. (1963). Bayesian statistical inference for psychological research. *Psychological Review, 70*(3), 193–242.

Chapter 2
Sciences (in)Action

A Success and a Failure in Confronting Complexity

By their very nature, individual scientific disciplines cannot solve complex problems. Disciplines solve bounded subproblems of complex ones. In order to be useful, their expertise needs to be coordinated with the expertise of other disciplines. That coordination reveals, and sometimes stretches, a discipline's bounds.

In some domains, there are established patterns for coordination. Construction projects have architects who create overall plans, subject to review by licensing authorities, insurers, lenders, and others. They have general contractors who recruit subcontractors with requisite skills, ensure the supply chain, and follow blueprints circumscribing the parties' roles and interactions. In bridge construction, that role might include coordinating expertise in the tensile strength and corrosion resistance of cables. In home construction, it might include coordinating expertise in installing solar panels, electrical wiring, permitting, and tax incentives.[1]

With novel complex problems, there are no general templates to adapt to specific cases. Project leaders must start from scratch in identifying the requisite expertise,[2] recruiting people who have that expertise, coordinating their work, and ensuring that it meets practical needs. This chapter offers my personal experience with two such problems. In the first case, equitable allocation of COVID-19 vaccine, the challenge was largely met, showing that it can be done and demonstrating the benefits of success. In the second case, response to climate change, the challenge has largely not been met, showing the costs of failure and raising the question of whether more could have been done with better mobilization of disciplinary scientific expertise.

The chapter proposes five factors that determine the success (or failure) of such ventures. It also proposes that management science, broadly defined,

---

[1] Policies on "net metering" will determine whether homeowners can sell excess capacity into the grid, thereby reducing their costs or perhaps even turning a profit.

[2] Ashby described "requisite variety" as having complexity matching that of problems. Ashby, W. R. (1956). *An introduction to cybernetics*. Chapman & Hall.

could play a leadership role in satisfying them. In that vision, my discipline, decision science, provides one essential component, bridging analytical and behavioral approaches to problem solving. Chapter 3 describes decision science in those terms. The next three chapters describe the insights and oversights arising from the bounded rationality of decision science, in three domains critical to complex problems: assessing and supporting decision makers' competence (Chapter 4); describing and informing decision makers' understanding of their options (Chapter 5); and eliciting and aiding decision makers' choices among those options (Chapter 6). The concluding chapters (7 to 10) offer a shared vision for decision and management science, encompassing additional disciplines brought together by the demands of complex problems.

These accounts draw heavily on my personal experience. Those experiences provide backstory, not found in the research literature, regarding who is invited and who is heard when complex problems arise. However, as oral history, they reflect the limits to my powers of observation, memory, and reporting. These issues have been on my mind throughout my professional career, and my decision to follow this career—so I hope to get it right. Nonetheless, they are doubtless colored by many things, including my fluctuating levels of optimism.

Equitable Allocation of COVID-19 Vaccine

The Complex Problem

The COVID-19 pandemic set off a multilane race to develop a vaccine.[3] Its urgency was so great that investments were made in manufacturing capacity and distribution channels while candidate vaccines were still in clinical trials, not knowing which, if any, would be successful. Even with these investments, it was immediately clear that any vaccines would be in great demand and short supply.

At the time, Spring 2020, COVID-19 vaccine politics in the US were not as polarized as they would become. Indeed, even with the later rise in anti-vax sentiment, it would be a long time before supply outstripped demand. However, pandemic politics were already intense and public health officials were

---

[3] NASEM (2020). *Framework for equitable allocation of COVID-19 vaccine.* National Academies Press.

already losing trust, through both forced and self-inflicted missteps, such as confusing reversals on the origins of the pandemic and the efficacy of face masks.[4]

Moreover, COVID-19 showed every sign of extending the long-standing legacy of health inequities. Members of historically disadvantaged groups were more likely to work in jobs with high risk of exposure (slaughterhouses, hospital intake, food service) and to have less access to personal protective devices. They were more likely to have comorbidities that increased the severity of disease for those who contracted it. They were more likely to live in congregate living settings, with greater risk of transmission. They were less likely to have access to treatment and resources to pay for it.

In response, the heads of the National Institutes of Health (NIH) and the Centers for Disease Control and Prevention (CDC) requested a consensus report from the National Academies of Sciences, Engineering, and Medicine (NASEM), advising them on "Equitable Allocation of COVID-19 Vaccine." They wanted the Academies' authority, as well as their wisdom, expecting that some of the public would not trust recommendations that NIH or CDC produced on their own.[5]

The vaccine equity committee first met on July 22, 2020, and reported on October 2, 2020, a month before results from the first vaccine clinical trial were announced. In early September, the committee conducted a public consultation on its preliminary conclusions. It received 1,400 written comments over a period of three and a half days, followed by a Zoom meeting with forty-eight five-minute presentations. Formally, the committee advised CDC's Advisory Committee on Immunization Practices (ACIP), whose recommendations advised the state, tribal, local, and territorial (STLT)[6] authorities that ultimately set and implemented vaccination policies. CDC and other federal bodies exerted indirect control over these decisions through the resources that they provided.

The National Academy of Sciences (NAS) was chartered by President Lincoln to provide independent scientific advice to the federal government. Academy legend has it that its first two assignments led to fixing the compasses on Union (North) Monitor-class ironclad ships and a

---

[4] COVID Crisis Group (2023). *Lessons from the COVID war: An investigative report.* Public Affairs. (Philip Zelikow was the lead author.) Oversold science helped to dig this hole.

[5] July 24, 2020. https://www.nationalacademies.org/our-work/a-framework-for-equitable-allocation-of-vaccine-for-the-novel-coronavirus (accessed August 14, 2024).

[6] This order, the preferred one at the time of the committee, reflects one position on the sovereignty of the four classes of authority.

recommendation that the US adopt the metric system. Ideally, committee members are also Academy members. However, the disciplinary success required for election to NAS typically pulls scientists away from engagement in public policy, however public-spirited they might be.[7] Committee members serve without pay. However, NASEM has large operating expenses, hence is largely constrained to answer questions that funders ask.[8] In principle, that dependence might create institutional incentives to produce recommendations that please clients, for the sake of repeat business. In practice, though, my observation, from serving on some forty committees, is that NASEM treats the integrity of its reports as its primary asset. Under the Federal Advisory Committee Act (FACA), NASEM invites public comment on potential committee members. Those chosen must file and discuss discuss potential conflicts of interest. Draft reports are reviewed anonymously by individuals who could have constituted an equally qualified panel.[9] All comments receive written responses, although they need not be accepted. Sponsors have no interaction with the committee until the report is finished, when they may receive a briefing just prior to its release.[10]

The Disciplines

Box 2.1 shows the members of the vaccine equity committee. Even from these brief descriptions, their personal and professional diversity is apparent.[11] There is no substitute for having diverse views at the table when solving complex problems.[12] Otherwise, people who are at the table must rely on

[7] The National Academies of Engineering and Medicine are more likely to honor practical contributions. My section of NAS, Human Environmental Sciences (64), is more likely than most to reward policy engagement. It includes geography, one of two social science disciplines at the time of NAS's founding. The second, anthropology, has its own section.

[8] It also has a small reserve fund for independent inquiries.

[9] The reviewers' identity is revealed when their contributions are acknowledged in the final report. A review coordinator selects them and approves the committee's response to their reviews. A review monitor checks the review coordinator's work.

[10] That said, the system can be gamed, as when consulting with NASEM is used to delay a policy decision or slow walk its implementation. For example, during the late Clinton administration, I was on a committee examining the evidence related to the Occupational Safety and Health Administration's ergonomic standard. Meant to reduce work-related musculoskeletal disorders, it had some strong industry opponents whose political allies hoped to delay implementation until a hoped-for Republican administration would scrap it. When the first committee concluded that the evidence was strong (https://nap.nationalacademies.org/catalog/6309/work-related-musculoskeletal-disorders-a-review-of-the-evidence (accessed August 14, 2024)), those allies reworded the question in a way that NASEM felt compelled to address with a new committee (https://nap.nationalacademies.org/catalog/6431/work-related-musculoskeletal-disorders-report-workshop-summary-and-workshop-papers (accessed August 14, 2024)), which ran out the clock until George W. Bush was elected.

[11] Appendix B of the report gives fuller bios.

[12] Dietz, T., & Stern, P. (Eds.) (2008). *Public participation in environmental assessment and decision making* (National Academies Press); Medin, D., Ojalehto, B., Marin, A., & Berg, M. (2017). Systems of (non)diversity. *Nature Human Behavior, 1*(5), Article 0088.

intuition and stereotype when guessing what missing people with other backgrounds know, want, and feel. They need even greater powers of imagination to anticipate the insights that would emerge from interacting with those missing people. The vaccine committee honored the principle of diverse representation to an unusual degree.[13]

Box 2.1 NASEM Committee on Equitable Allocation of COVID-19 Vaccine

WILLIAM H. FOEGE *(Co-Chair)*, Emeritus Distinguished Professor of International Health, Rollins School of Public Health, Emory University

HELENE D. GAYLE *(Co-Chair)*, President and Chief Executive Officer, The Chicago Community Trust

MARGARET L. BRANDEAU, Coleman F. Fung Professor of Engineering, Professor of Medicine (by courtesy), Department of Management Science and Engineering, Stanford University

ALISON M. BUTTENHEIM, Associate Professor of Nursing and Health Policy, University of Pennsylvania School of Nursing

R. ALTA CHARO, Warren P. Knowles Professor of Law and Bioethics, University of Wisconsin Law School

JAMES F. CHILDRESS, University Professor Emeritus, Institute for Practical Ethics and Public Life, University of Virginia

ANA V. DIEZ ROUX, Dean and Distinguished University Professor of Epidemiology, Dornsife School of Public Health, Drexel University

ABIGAIL ECHO-HAWK (citizen of the Pawnee Nation), Director, Urban Indian Health Institute, Chief Research Officer, Seattle Indian Health Board

CHRISTOPHER ELIAS, President, Global Development Division, Bill & Melinda Gates Foundation

BARUCH FISCHHOFF, Howard Heinz University Professor, Department of Engineering and Public Policy, Institute for Politics and Strategy, Carnegie Mellon University

DAVID MICHAELS, Professor, Environmental and Occupational Health, Milken Institute School of Public Health, The George Washington University

JEWEL MULLEN, Associate Dean for Health Equity, Associate Professor of Population Health and Internal Medicine, University of Texas at Austin Dell Medical School

SAAD B. OMER, Director, Yale Institute for Global Health

---

[13] I have been on only one majority-minority NASEM committee, on environmental justice. The committee's composition facilitated site visits hosted by affected communities, with candid sharing of views (e.g., how little scientists were trusted). The composition also meant that many members were new to the NASEM committee process. As a result, its NASEM veterans handled much of the writing of the final report, on behalf of the committee. Institute of Medicine (1999). *Toward environmental justice*. National Academies Press.

DANIEL POLSKY, Bloomberg Distinguished Professor of Health Policy and Economics, Carey Business School and Bloomberg School of Public Health, Johns Hopkins University

SONJA RASMUSSEN, Professor of Pediatrics, Epidemiology, and Obstetrics and Gynecology, College of Medicine and College of Public Health and Health Professions, University of Florida

ARTHUR L. REINGOLD, Division Head, Epidemiology and Biostatistics, Professor of Epidemiology, School of Public Health, University of California, Berkeley

REED V. TUCKSON, Managing Director, Tuckson Health Connections, LLC

MICHAEL R. WASSERMAN, President, California Association of Long Term Care Medicine

Study staff

LISA BROWN, Study Director
BENJAMIN KAHN, Associate Program Officer
ELIZABETH FINKELMAN, Senior Program Officer
AURELIA ATTAL-JUNCQUA, Associate Program Officer
EMMA FINE, Associate Program Officer
REBECCA CHEVAT, Senior Program Assistant
ROSE MARIE MARTINEZ, Senior Director, Board on Population Health and Public Health Practice
ANDREW M. POPE, Senior Director, Board on Health Sciences Policy

Science writer

ANNA NICHOLSON

Source: NASEM (2020). *Framework for equitable allocation of COVID-19 vaccine.* National Academies Press.

The architects of the committee's composition and process were its co-chairs, both physicians. Helene Gayle was then head of the Chicago Community Trust and is now president of Spelman College. William Foege was a leader in the global eradication of smallpox, and later head of CDC. They ran good meetings, making everyone feel respected, facilitating mutual understanding, parceling responsibilities, coordinating the pieces, and maintaining a breakneck pace—with multiple revisions of a long report completed in three months.

Box 2.2 contains the committee's Statement of Task, which required that it conduct some form of public consultation regarding the report's discussion draft (final section). It did not explicitly require the inclusive process that the committee followed, which included inviting public comments on its draft prioritization criteria. In addition to opening an online portal, it invited members of diverse groups to an online workshop with sessions on the concerns of minority communities, state and local government, health and medical organizations, older adults, occupational risk, and special populations (in that order). Each speaker had five minutes, whether representing a large organization (e.g., American Hospital Association, American Dental Association, American Federation of Teachers) or a small one (National Council of Asian Pacific Islander Physicians, Farmworker Justice, Vaccinate Your Family). The online format, mandated by pandemic travel restrictions, allowed participation by people who could not leave their positions (e.g., at a rural Alaska clinic), even if their transportation expenses were paid.

Box 2.2 Statement of Task for Committee on Equitable Allocation of COVID-19 Vaccine

Statement of Task

An ad hoc committee of the National Academies of Sciences, Engineering, and Medicine will develop an overarching framework for vaccine allocation to assist policy makers in the domestic and global health communities in planning for equitable allocation of vaccines against severe acute respiratory syndrome coronavirus 2 (SARS-CoV-2). The expectation is that such a framework would inform the decisions by health authorities, including the Advisory Committee on Immunization Practices, as they create and implement national and/or local guidelines for SARS-CoV-2 vaccine allocation. As part of this effort, the committee will consider the following:

- What criteria should be used in setting priorities for equitable allocation of vaccine?
- How should the criteria be applied in determining the first tier of vaccine recipients? As more vaccine becomes available, what populations should be added successively to the priority list of recipients? How do we take into account factors such as:

  - Health disparities and other health access issues
  - Individuals at higher risk (e.g., elderly, underlying health conditions)
  - Occupations at higher risk (e.g., health care workers, essential industries, meat packing plants, military)
  - Populations at higher risk (e.g., racial and ethnic groups, incarcerated individuals, residents of nursing homes, individuals who are homeless)

- Geographic distribution of active virus spread
- Countries/populations involved in clinical trials

- How will the framework apply in various scenarios (e.g., different characteristics of vaccines and differing available doses)?
- If multiple vaccine candidates are available, how should we ensure equity?
- How can countries ensure equity in allocation of COVID-19 vaccines?
- For the United States, how can communities of color be assured access to vaccination?
- How can we communicate to the American public about vaccine allocation to minimize perceptions of lack of equity?
- What steps should be taken to mitigate vaccine hesitancy, especially among high-priority populations?

As part of the overall study, the committee will produce a discussion draft of the framework for public comment, and hold a public workshop to solicit feedback from external stakeholders.

Source: NASEM (2020). *Framework for equitable allocation of COVID-19 vaccine*. National Academies Press.

The general contractors for executing the committee's architecture were the NASEM staff listed at the bottom of Box 2.1. They recruited the members and speakers, ensured Federal Advisory Committee Act compliance, managed the paper flow, set up the meetings, responded to reviewer comments, deflected pressures, and performed other actions unseen by members. Failure in any of these tasks could have undermined the report's quality and the committee's credibility.[14]

Management Science Tasks

The Statement of Task framing the committee's work, presented in Box 2.2, asks a relatively precise policy question, and one central to management science: how to set priorities that are faithful both to the evidence and to decision makers' values. It requires a methodology robust enough to accommodate the known unknowns of the disease and vaccines. It also requires a methodology whose "achievement of equity" can be communicated to the American public.

---

[14] They received the National Academy of Medicine's staff award for the year.

The committee interpreted its charge as:

> To ensure that the allocation framework is equitable and [can] be seen as equitable, the committee designed its framework so that it (1) can be easily and equally understood by diverse audiences, (2) reflects widely accepted social and ethical principles, (3) can be reliably translated into operational terms, (4) distinguishes scientific and ethical judgments in its application, and (5) does not perpetuate discrimination and inequities.[15]

Recognizing the potential diversity of decision makers' values, the committee included bioethicists, who proposed six broadly accepted principles for fulfilling conditions (2) and (5). Three of those principles involved outcomes: bringing maximum benefit to the public, showing equal concern for all, and mitigating health inequities. Three were procedural: engaging all members of the public equally, communicating transparently, and basing recommendations on evidence.

While powerful, these principles are still quite general. The committee turned to management science to translate them into operational terms. The result was four simple risk criteria, which were meant to satisfice, by capturing the essence of more complex, boundedly rational optimization schemes. These criteria defined COVID-19 risk as (a) the probability of getting the disease, (b) the probability of that illness being serious, (c) the probability of transmitting it to others, and (d) the expected number of people who would suffer if a person were unavailable because of the disease. The criteria were left in vector form, without a formal combination rule, lest the calculations reduce transparency and preempt discussions about how to weigh them in specific settings.

Other committee experts applied health and labor statistics to these criteria, leading to the priorities in Figure 2.1. Each group was characterized as having high, medium, or low risk on each criterion, noting special circumstances, such as group heterogeneity or cases where risks could be reduced without vaccine (e.g., by workplace protections). A management science-framed chapter had sensitivity analyses, working through the implications of scenarios that varied vaccine availability, efficacy, safety, distribution, and uptake. Generally speaking, these changes had little effect on the priorities.

The four risk criteria do not mention historical health inequities directly. They address them indirectly by giving higher priority to groups subject to those inequities. These groups have greater risk, as defined by the

---

[15] Statement of Task for Committee on Equitable Allocation of COVID-19 Vaccine, pp. 5–6.

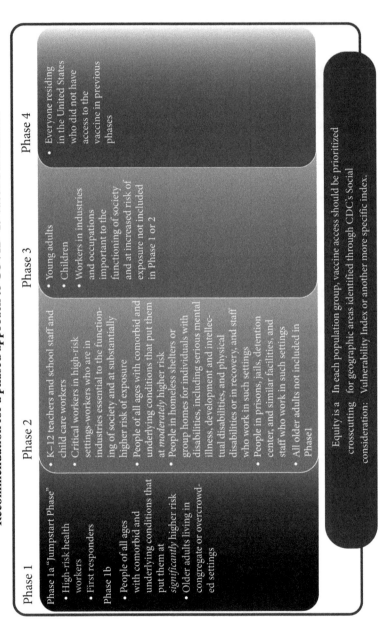

Figure 2.1 Recommendation for a phased approach to COVID-19 vaccine allocation
Source: NASEM (2020), *Framework for equitable allocation of COVID-19 vaccine.* National Academies Press.

criteria (e.g., working in places with high exposure and limited protection; comorbidities that worsen disease outcomes). The fact that the inequities were not addressed directly troubled some committee members, for whom that recognition was vitally important. Other members argued that mentioning them would be a red flag to some political figures, reducing the chances of getting vaccine to individuals in high-risk groups, like those without homes or in prison.

Lessons Learned

By and large, the committee's recommendations met little controversy and framed the policies of state, tribal, local, and territorial authorities. That acceptance was a remarkable achievement, especially at a time of escalating polarization. As best I can tell, the committee made a difference in the world, and the risk criteria, based in management science, helped make that happen. The criteria operationalized the ethical principles in terms that nonexperts could understand, implement, and adapt to local conditions. They allowed relatively objective implementation of the inherently subjective ethical principles. The sensitivity analyses showed how robust the baseline priorities were, when changes would be needed, and how to make them.

Other disciplines made their own contributions. The ethicists identified principles that fit the problem. Occupational and housing experts identified hot spots for disease transmission (the first risk criterion). Physicians identified the factors affecting disease severity (the second risk criterion). Epidemiologists identified the factors affecting disease transmission (the third). Sociologists and economists identified broader impacts of individuals' sickness (the fourth). Public health experts described how to create community partnerships for recruiting and reassuring vaccine candidates.

Reflecting on this experience and others in this book, I believe that the answers to the questions in Box 2.3 go a long way toward predicting the success of any collaboration. The vaccine committee had affirmative answers to them all.[16]

The committee had a common cause. Its urgency impelled members to represent their discipline, and not just their specialty or pet theory. It focused them on being useful rather than getting a piece of the action. It discouraged scientists' natural desire to do more studies, rather than apply what they know, while admitting what they don't.

---

[16] As discussed in later chapters, other committees' foci were less successful, lacking some of these necessary conditions.

Box 2.3 Factors Determining Collaboratory Success

Is there common cause?
Do researchers and practitioners sit at the same table?
Is there a shared problem space?
Is the process deftly moderated?
Do the implementing organizations have absorptive capacity?

Researchers and practitioners sat at the same table (electronically). They listened to one another, knowing that they needed to produce a consensus report. They got to hear and assess one another's expertise, passions, and prejudices. They had opportunities to discuss their way through to joint solutions, which would have been impossible with asynchronous emails and document drafts.

The committee had a shared problem space, defined by its charge and structured by its risk criteria. The simplicity of the criteria, intended to ensure external transparency, also facilitated internal deliberations. Ethicists could assess the fidelity of the criteria to their principles. Physicians could ensure their clinical realism. Analysts could see what data were needed and how to use them.

The committee was deftly moderated. People felt heard and respected. The process was aided by some members having had long histories with one another and, I suspect, some behind-the-scenes work between meetings. Meeting online may have leveled differences, as it did with the public meeting discussing the draft report.[17]

The implementing agencies had absorptive capacity[18] for the report's conclusions. They had staff who could understand its rationale, apply it to their local conditions, and explain it to their publics. There were people like them on the committee, who could see that their concerns were represented. The committee's one notable failure reflected public health agencies' lack of absorptive capacity for implementing its recommendation that they communicate authoritative estimates of vaccine safety and efficacy, separately from their advocacy for vaccine uptake.

When successful, such consultations provide society with a practical return on its investment in the contributing disciplines. The benefits to those disciplines might include recognition (and resources), new ideas (and funding),

---

[17] After the report was released, we had a Zoom "cast party," with games, storytelling, and hand dancing.
[18] The term comes from economics. Cohen, W. M., & Levinthal, D. A. (1990). Absorptive capacity: A new perspective on learning and innovation. *Administrative Science Quarterly, 35*(1), 128–152.

greater appeal to students, and personal gratification. The disciplines may or may not reward individual scientists for work that might bring these collective benefits.

Human Dimensions of Climate Change

The Complex Problem

The "greenhouse gas" effect of CO_2 has been known for a century.[19] So has its primary contributor, burning fossil fuels.[20] The aggregate increase in atmospheric CO_2 concentration has become increasingly apparent with observations like the Mauna Loa time series, beginning in the 1950s. It shows a cyclical seasonal pattern, reflecting greater winter emissions in the more heavily populated and industrialized northern hemisphere. It also shows a secular trend, with steady yearly increases.

Simple calculations found that burning fossil fuels alone could dramatically increase global temperature. Moreover, those changes could not be easily reversed, given the long half-life (dwell time) of CO_2 in the atmosphere—unlike pollutants that settle quickly (causing damage where they fall). However, those simple early calculations could not estimate the effects of potential complicating processes. For example, particulate matter from fossil fuel combustion might dampen the temperature rise (as with the "year without a summer" following the eruption of Krakatoa).[21] Indeed, a new ice age seemed possible, not to mention fears of a "nuclear winter," following a thermonuclear exchange.

Increased computing power created opportunities for increasingly complex models, simulating possible atmospheric futures, with more processes, more inputs, and more elaborate predictions. Additional models studied the effects of CO_2 deposition on ocean chemistry, sometimes coupling heat transfers between air and water. New observations gradually revealed past changes (e.g., Greenland ice cores, paleobotany of tree rings and pollen, reconstruction of Little Ice Age seasons). Predicting the interactions between climate and natural and human systems led to yet more complex models. Even when the models are static, there are always new computer systems and

---

[19] Portions of this section are adapted from Fischhoff, B. (2021). Making behavioral science integral to climate science and action. *Behavioural Public Policy*, 5(4), 439–453.
[20] The release of greenhouse gases from soil (including permafrost), triggered by warming from fossil fuels might provide competition here.
[21] A recent spike in global temperatures may reflect cleaner ship emissions, reducing particulate matter—and pollution.

statistical packages, allowing ever finer and more encompassing estimates. Truly, climate modelers' work is never done.[22]

The Disciplines

In 1979, the then-new US Department of Energy (DOE)[23] commissioned the American Association for the Advancement of Science (AAAS) to help develop a twenty-year plan for its Carbon Dioxide Effects Research and Assessment Program. That effort produced a research agenda[24] and supporting workshop summary.[25] Even then, it was clear that "the probable outcome is beyond human experience."[26] Its steering committee included experts in climate science (Roger Revelle, Stephen Schneider), agronomy (Sylvan Wittwer), ecology (Charles Cooper), economics (Lester Lave), and sociology (Elise Boulding).[27]

The project had five working groups. Three dealt with environmental effects: on the oceans, cryosphere, and ocean biota; on the managed biosphere; and on the less-managed biosphere. Two dealt with human behavior: economic and geopolitical consequences; and social and institutional responses. The breadth of the groups reflects the complexity recognized by the project's leaders and sponsors. So does the groups' acknowledgment of human footprints everywhere on the planet.[28]

I was in the social and institutional responses group. It included researchers from sociology, climate science, anthropology, political science, history, law, demographics, atmospheric science, geography, philosophy, and psychology.[29] It also included two staff members for Rep. George Brown (D-CA), a leading science advocate. Figure 2.2 shows an excerpt from our

---

[22] Echoing my mother's "Mothers' work is never done."
[23] Until 1974, the Atomic Energy Commission had both promoted and regulated nuclear power. Recognition of the incompatibility of these two roles led to its division into the Nuclear Regulatory Commission and the Energy Research and Development Administration, which became the Department of Energy in 1977, with expanded research and development authority.
[24] US Department of Energy (1980). *Environmental and societal consequences of a possible CO$_2$-induced climate change: A research agenda* (DOE/EV/10019-01). DOE, https://www.osti.gov/biblio/6728173 (accessed July 2, 2023); US Department of Energy (1980). *Workshop on environmental and societal consequences of a possible CO$_2$-induced climate change.* DOE, https://www.osti.gov/biblio/6927055 (accessed July 2, 2023).
[25] Department of Energy, *Workshop on environmental and societal consequences.* (CONF-7904143).
[26] Department of Energy, *Workshop on environmental and societal consequences,* p. Intro-1.
[27] At the time, international research was coordinated by the Global Atmospheric Research Program. Coincidentally, the display window of a bookstore near the workshop hotel featured *The World According to Garp* (Irving, J. (1978). *The world according to Garp.* E. P. Dutton). One might have imagined that our message was already a bestseller.
[28] Presaging McKibben, B. (1989). *The end of nature.* Random House.
[29] One member, Haraldur Ólafsson, represented not just his discipline (sociology), but also a European community that had been threatened by climate change (Iceland).

⁰ Panel IV Social and Institutional Responses. The CO_2 issue appears to be a gradually developing problem that is so far proceeding too slowly to attract significant public notice. Yet it does have aspects that are linked to other high-priority social problems, including the development of alternative energy systems and certain environmental threats. Uncertainties inhibit precise definition of the social costs and benefits of CO_2-induced climate change. Impacts of climate change will not be distributed uniformly; consequently, the economic and social effects for each region would vary greatly. Prevention of CO_2 build-up is a global matter, but individual nations or other political units could act independently to adapt to changing climates. As scientific research on CO_2 progresses, information regarding the risks and benefits of climate change should be diffused through the hierarchy of social units -- ranging from individuals, families, and communities to nations and international groups. Institutions then will be better able to identify and implement appropriate strategies for dealing with the situation. Because of the varied geophysical, biological, and societal effects that may result from CO_2 build-up, the problem calls for an unprecedented interdisciplinary research effort. The format used in this undertaking can perhaps be applied to other complex social problems as well.

Figure 2.2 Climate change: 1980 call to action

Source: US Department of Energy. (1980). *Workshop on environmental and societal consequences of a possible CO_2-induced climate change* (CONF-7904143). DOE, pp. vii–viii. https://www.osti.gov/biblio/6927055

report. Except for the first sentence, it could be written today, especially the call for "an unprecedented interdisciplinary effort."

The grand plans of the DOE–AAAS initiative ended with the 1980 presidential election. In the ensuing period, the physical sciences managed to protect enough of their climate-related programs to keep them alive, and then gradually grow. However, the social and behavioral sciences, having no programs to begin with, stayed on the sidelines—for the next quarter century.[30] The period before the DOE–AAAS project had seen active behavioral research on energy conservation, prompted by the 1970s oil crises. However, that research was being wound down, without having created a sustained institutional presence that could pivot to climate change.[31]

---

[30] Economics, with different funding needs and sources, revived somewhat sooner than the other social and behavioral sciences.

[31] Stern, P. C., Aronson, E., Darley, J. M., Hill, D. H., Hirst, E., Kempton, W., & Wilbanks, T. J. (1986). The effectiveness of incentives for energy conservation. *Evaluation Review*, *10*(2), 147–176.

In the mid-1980s, the National Academy of Sciences created a Committee on the Human Dimensions of Global Change, hoping that someone would fund the research opportunities that it identified. It, too, had prominent members of diverse disciplines: economics (Nancy Birdsall, Pierre Crosson, William Nordhaus, Thomas Schelling), law (Edith Brown Weiss), political science (Harold Jacobson, David Vogel), anthropology (Robert Netting), sociology (Thomas Dietz), ecology (Elliott Norse), climate science (Roger Barry, Oran Young), history (William Cronon), geography (Billie Turner), and psychology/decision science (me). The report makes instructive reading, in terms of the questions that were asked way back then and the very limited resources for answering them.[32]

The few behavioral research projects during that period suggest what those sciences might have contributed to understanding, and shaping, human responses to climate change, before the battle lines were drawn.[33] Willett Kempton and colleagues showed how a multimethod approach could capture the richness of diverse groups' climate-related decisions.[34] Ann Bostrom and colleagues studied the mental models that shape the credibility of claims about climate change.[35] Jon Krosnick and colleagues pieced together the closest thing we had to a tracking survey of climate beliefs and attitudes.[36]

As the social, behavioral, and decision sciences did little to help, greenhouse gases continued to accumulate in the atmosphere, where they will take generations to dissipate. Vested interests, opposed to climate-change mitigation policies (e.g., reduced fossil fuel use, tighter control of methane emissions), honed attacks on climate science.[37] Long-term capital investments (e.g., buildings, transportation infrastructure) constrained future action. Development proceeded as though ecosystems would be as resilient in the future as they seemed to have been in the past.[38] Domestic, foreign, and national security policies ignored destabilizing effects of climate change.

---

[32] https://nap.nationalacademies.org/catalog/1792/global-environmental-change-understanding-the-human-dimensions (accessed August 14, 2024).

[33] The climate science community's terms for preventing climate change (mitigation) and reducing its impacts (adaptation) are unfortunate choices for communicating with anyone for whom reducing effects is mitigation—and perhaps emblematic of the climate science community's communication problems, preferring its jargon to everyday use.

[34] Kempton, W. M., Bister, J. S., & Hartley, J. A. (1991). Lay perspectives on global climate change. *Global Environmental Change*, 1(3), 183–208.

[35] Bostrom, A., Morgan, M. G., Fischhoff, B., & Read, D. (1994). What do people know about global climate change? Part 1. Mental models. *Risk Analysis*, 14(6), 959–970.

[36] Krosnick, J. A., Holbrook, A. L., & Visser, P. S. (2000). The impact of the fall 1997 debate about global warming on American public opinion. *Public Understanding of Science*, 9(3), 239–260.

[37] Oreskes, N., & Conway, E. M. (2014). *Merchants of doubt*. Bloomsbury.

[38] At least for those who didn't look too hard at their decline.

Management Science Tasks

At the time of the DOE–AAAS initiative, though, our role seemed so obvious that I wrote what might be the first article on the topic.[39] It posed five management science questions: (a) What's worth knowing, for climate change-related decisions? (b) What are the properties of that information? (c) How well can we convey that information, including its uncertainties? (d) What is our place in the political process, in terms of whose interests we serve? (e) What is our place in the politics of science?

I asked Lita Furby, a developmental psychologist and methodologist with cross-cultural expertise, to help write the workshop report on the psychological dimensions of climate change.[40] Box 2.4 sets out the five projects that we proposed. These, too, still seem relevant today. The path looked bright, for research that would be good for science, as well as for society. The projects all required collaboration among diverse disciplines, who could learn from one another and from diverse publics, who could pose fresh problems and perspectives. However, that was not to be, for reasons that can inform future research.

Box 2.4 Psychological Dimensions of Climate Change: Five Research Projects (1983)

Project 1. Identifying and characterizing subjective aspects of the "facts" of CO_2-induced climatic change

(1) Where do subjective judgments enter into scientific analyses?
(2) How valid are those judgments?
(3) How well are experts able to identify and assess such judgments?
(4) How can we make better use of experts by better understanding the limits to their abilities?

Project 2. Understanding and improving lay decision makers' perceptions of the facts of CO_2-induced climatic change

(1) How do lay decision makers interpret the facts presented to them by experts?
(2) Is this testimony about climate consistent with their direct sensory experience with weather; if not, how are conflicts resolved?
(3) What kinds of information pose particular conceptual problems?

---

[39] Fischhoff, B. (1981). Hot air: The psychology of CO_2-induced climatic change. In J. Harvey (Ed.), *Cognition, social behavior and the environment* (pp. 163–184). Lawrence Erlbaum.
[40] Fischhoff, B., & Furby, L. (1983). Psychological dimensions of climatic change. In R. S. Chen, E. Boulding, & S. H. Schneider (Eds.), *Social science research and climate change: An interdisciplinary perspective* (pp. 183–203). D. Reidel.

(4) How can such problems be remedied, so that decision makers can make the best use of available scientific knowledge and the wisdom of their own experience?

Project 3. Clarifying and enriching the space of possible action options

(1) What options naturally occur to people?
(2) How is feasibility judged?
(3) What consequences (or side effects) tend to be overlooked?
(4) In what ways are decision makers prisoners of their own experience?

Project 4. Understanding how alternative responses to climatic change are evaluated

(1) How do people combine multiple and conflicting risks and benefits of various options into a single decision?
(2) How can people's opinions on these issues be accurately elicited so as to inform government officials?
(3) How can faulty elicitation methods distort the values expressed through them?

Project 5. Anticipating and clarifying conflicts created by the inequitable effects of CO_2-induced climate change: Offering paths of resolution

(1) How will climate change pit nation against nation, group against group?
(2) What commons dilemmas will be created (or exist already)?
(3) What sorts of mistrust and misunderstanding will emerge and can be avoided?
(4) Can frameworks or options be devised for conflict resolution?

Source: Adapted from Fischhoff, B., & Furby, L. (1983). Psychological dimensions of climatic change. In R. S. Chen, E. Boulding & S. H. Schneider (eds.), *Social science research and climate change: An interdisciplinary perspective* (pp. 183–203). D. Reidel.

Often, one discipline owns a problem. That discipline sets research priorities and controls research resources. With climate change, that discipline was the physical science that first postulated greenhouse gas processes and then painstakingly described their extent, drivers, implications, and complications. Those scientists pursued the curiosity-driven problem solving of any normal science, with little perceived need, or capacity, for input from other sciences. Problems were formulated in terms compatible with physical scientists' expertise: analyzing complex, bounded, quantitatively defined problems. The complexity of those analyses means that endless refinements are possible, each needing attention before other disciplines are engaged. Even then, those other disciplines must speak in quantitative, model-friendly terms. Some economists could do that (e.g., estimating aggregate energy production and consumption). Most social, behavioral, and biological scientists could not.[41]

In principle, there are three ways for other disciplines to connect with a model-driven discipline. One is to translate their results into the quantitative terms of those models' conventional inputs. The second is to make those models more useful, by adding decision-relevant concerns that they have missed and by communicating model results to decision makers. The third is to treat modeling as human behavior, asking how experts' judgments affect the definitiveness of their results. These are all management science tasks, reflecting its straddling of the worlds of analysis and observation.

In terms of translating research results into model-friendly terms, management science can help by creating clear, shared definitions of variables, estimating effect sizes, and assessing uncertainty. For example, residential energy consumption is an input to some models, and many behavioral interventions have sought to reduce it. Alex Davis and colleagues translated the results of those interventions into common terms and then adjusted the values observed in field trials to more realistic ones, using correction factors from studies of medical clinical trials.[42] In this case, after those corrections, they found the interventions had no effect on energy conservation and only a modest one for *peak shaving*, reducing use when demand is high (e.g., hot summer afternoons).

In terms of making climate models more useful, the last fifteen years have seen a surge in research on one half of the connection: communicating climate science to decision makers. Some climate scientists have welcomed that help in telling their story, acknowledging that the science has not spoken for itself. The research has revealed some sources of that failure to communicate: nonexperts often use terms differently than experts (e.g., geoengineering, mitigation), lack mental models of physical processes (e.g., how global warming can produce severe winter storms), and struggle to construct stable preferences for novel climate-related decisions.[43] There has been less progress in making the reverse connection,

---

[41] In a current project on engineering options for preserving the Thwaites Glacier in Antarctica, I have heard glaciologists lament the limited resources available for research providing essential inputs to physical models related to sea-level rise and ocean currents. Ecologists and social scientists have analogous concerns about funding for research needed to circumscribe the impacts of climate change, and possible responses.

[42] Davis, A.L., Krishnamurti, T., Fischhoff, B., & Bruine de Bruin, W. (2013). Setting a standard for electricity pilot studies. *Energy Policy*, 62, 401–409. For example, how were impact estimates affected by letting people choose whether they would be in the experimental or control condition?

[43] See Chapter 6.

communicating decision makers' needs to climate scientists, so that they can make their research more relevant to decision makers (and not just other modelers).

In terms of understanding experts' behavior, *expert elicitation* is increasingly used to assess the uncertainty in the bounded rationality of climate models. These in-depth interviews ask experts to reflect on model inputs from different perspectives and then summarize their judgments in probabilities distributions. Experts receive training, based on behavioral research, to improve the precision and reduce the bias in their judgments. Figure 2.3 has an early, influential example, with judgments of mean global temperature accompanying a doubling of atmospheric CO_2. Two experts (#2, #4) have different distributions, depending on whether there is a "state change" or "surprise," like collapse of the Gulf Stream.[44] The figure shows that, while individual experts are highly uncertain, they generally agree (except for one highly certain climate skeptic, #5).

Lessons Learned

However valuable, these behavioral science contributions came long after climate scientists realized the magnitude of the crisis. Our worlds and their world were too far apart to make the needed connections, without greater effort than we (or they) could (or would) make.[45] By the time that the pace of behavioral research picked up, climate science and politics were too ossified to affect either that much. The election of Ronald Reagan doomed the DOE–AAAS twenty-year research program. Its cancellation also revealed fragmentation in the research community that frustrated collaboration later, once it became possible again.

The five questions in Box 2.3 point to the sources of this failure.

The project's members had a common cause. However, it was not urgent enough to impel collaboration across disciplinary boundaries. Given the steering committee's vision, those boundaries might have fallen, had the project happened and the disciplines spent more time together.

Diverse disciplines were at the table in each of the five working groups. However, they did not sit at one another's tables. Although some scientists had

---

[44] Formally, the Atlantic Meridional Overturning Circulation. Neither expert could assess the probability of that happening. Neither would predict the future as the weighted average of the two possible states, given how different they were.

[45] Thirty-plus years ago, Eric Barron, a leading climate scientist, and later President of Penn State University among other academic leadership roles, made a telling comment at a meeting of the NASEM Committee on the Human Dimensions of Global Change. A friend of social and behavioral science, he advised us to band together and create "big science" projects that could engage the physical sciences on more equal terms. He lamented the fractured, insular character of our disciplines.

Surface temperature change

Box plots of probability distributions of climate sensitivity, the change in globally averaged surface temperature for a 2 x [CO,] forcing. Horizontal lines denote range from minimum to maximum assessed possible values. Vertical tick marks indicate locations of lower 5 and upper 95 percentiles. Box indicates interval spanned by 50% confidence interval. Solid dot is the mean and open dot is the median. The two columns of numbers on right side of the figure report values of mean and standard deviation of the distributions.

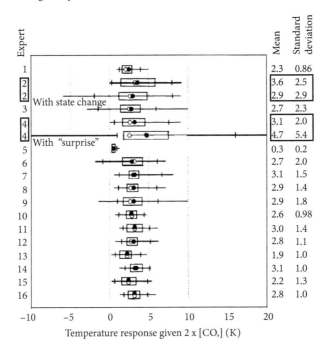

Figure 2.3 Expert elicitation of mean global temperature with doubling CO_2 (1995)

Source: Morgan, M. G., & Keith, D. W. (1995). Subjective judgments by climate experts. *Environmental Science and Technology, 23*(10), 468–476.

practical experience, few practitioners were at any table, beyond the DOE sponsors and two Congressional staffers. Here, too, more time together might have made a difference.

The project had no shared problem spaces, in the sense of specific decisions that it was meant to inform, requiring coordinated contributions. When terminated, the project was still focused on capabilities, creating information that might be useful to someone somewhere, rather than on solutions, delivering useful information to specific decision makers.

The project had gifted leadership, with a broad-minded steering committee, whose members knew many attendees. However, absent resources, those ties could not sustain its momentum.

DOE had staff with absorptive capacity, and plans to hire more. Had the project continued, they might have made the needed connections.[46]

One can only speculate on how different the world and the disciplines would have been had the answers to these five questions been different.

Conclusions

Complex problems require the best available science from multiple disciplines. Whether they get that advice is partly a question of intellect. Can the disciplines see beyond the bounds that define their expertise? Is there a plan whose architecture enables their collaboration? It is also partly a question of motivation. Will experts share resources with one another? Will they put the common good above that of their personal research programs? And it is partly a question of execution. Is there a general contractor who can recruit and coordinate the experts, with one another and with the decision makers who need their knowledge?

As oral history, these two case studies are better guides to the kinds of things that can happen than to what exactly did happen. As told, these stories illustrate the need for affirmative answers to the five questions in Box 2.3—and management science's roles in providing them. Two of those roles are analytical: creating a shared problem-solving space for the experts and characterizing the uncertainty in their work. Two roles are behavioral: communicating decision makers' needs to researchers and communicating research results to decision makers. Decision science is a management science that studies the analytical and behavioral foundations for these roles. Chapter 3 examines the discipline and its evolving bounds and rationality.

---

[46] A DOE staff member required behavioral science involvement in the request for proposals that led to Davis et al.'s analysis of energy conservation interventions (Davis et al., Setting a standard for electricity pilot studies). It was part of an American Recovery and Reinvestment Act program (following the 2008 financial collapse) supporting electricity companies for installing smart meters.

Chapter 3
Decision Science

Boundedly Rational Study of Rationality

Decision science arose as psychology's contribution to a remarkable mid-twentieth-century period, in which scientists and scholars from diverse disciplines collaborated in pursuing issues that had coalesced in von Neumann and Morgenstern's landmark volume defining rational choice theory.[1] In a seminal article[2] and subsequent *Annual Review of Psychology* chapter,[3] Ward Edwards framed the field's commitment to studying tasks, as presented by life or researchers, in tandem with studying responses to them.

In this view, studying a decision has three interrelated steps. *Normative* (or formal) analysis identifies the best possible choice, for a rational individual, given available evidence. *Descriptive* research characterizes actual decision making, in terms comparable to the normative analysis, allowing for flawed beliefs and inconsistent preferences. *Prescriptive* research attempts to close the gap between the normative ideal and the descriptive reality—and to understand the secrets of success, when there are no gaps. When gaps remain, the process repeats, trying to understand the decision and the decision maker better.[4]

---

[1] von Neumann, J., & Morgenstern, O. (1944). *Theory of games and economic behavior*. Princeton University Press. Seminal contributions from Frank Ramsey two decades earlier, and others, laid foundations for their work.

[2] Edwards, W. (1954). A theory of decision making. *Psychological Bulletin, 51*(4), 380–417.

[3] Edwards, W. (1961). Behavioral decision theory. *Annual Review of Psychology, 12*, 473–498.

[4] Edwards initially called the field *behavioral decision theory*. As hopes for an all-encompassing theory faded, the term morphed into *behavioral decision making*, the name of its journal of record. *Behavioral decision research* might be the most commonly used term today, or *judgment and decision making*. However, some people use these terms without the commitment to normative analysis that mostly clearly bounds the discipline, distinguishing it from the many other approaches to studying how people make decisions. Chapter 4 addresses the practical and policy importance of normative analysis.

Bounded Disciplines and Unbounded Problems. Baruch Fischhoff, Oxford University Press. © Baruch Fischhoff (2025). DOI: 10.1093/9780191997266.003.0003

Decision Science, Flourishing within Bounds

The normative[5] model defines sound decision making in terms of the relative desirability of each possible *outcome* of each possible choice *option*, multiplied by the *probability* of that outcome happening, yielding the option's *expected outcome*. Within these bounds, researchers can accommodate a great variety of decisions. They can consider only monetary outcomes, with *values* set by markets, or also subjective *utilities*, set by individual preferences. They can consider only the *statistical frequency* of outcomes, or also *subjective probabilities*, for unique events or ones whose statistical record may no longer hold. They can consider only *compensatory* decisions, which balance good and bad outcomes, or also *noncompensatory* ones, where each outcome must pass a threshold of acceptability or where one outstanding outcome is enough.[6] They can restrict themselves to *repeated* decisions or *unique* ones; to decisions whose track record is *experienced* or *described*; to decisions with *discrete* options (new cars) or *continuous* ones (investment amounts); to decisions involving one or more *players*; to decisions with and without options for gathering more information or delaying.[7]

Within each subset of bounds, researchers have shown great ingenuity in devising tasks that compare behavior to a normative standard for sound decision making. A key research program in the 1960s and early 1970s exemplifies that ingenuity.[8] That program bound itself to tasks like assessing the probability that a series of balls was drawn randomly from an urn with mostly red or mostly blue balls (e.g., 30:70 or 70:30).

Experimentalists working within such a bounded world are fascinated by variations within it. ("What if we vary the number of balls in each draw?") They are adept at drawing real-world analogies. ("Sometimes, reality reveals itself bit by bit; sometimes all at once.") They are attuned to spotting real-world instances where that difference matters. ("See how differently people respond to individual studies of the effectiveness of face masks and meta-analyses, combining studies.")

The theoretical question animating these studies was whether people were "intuitive Bayesians," in the sense of following the rules of *Bayesian inference*,[9] when they processed new information. It followed an earlier research program asking whether people were "intuitive statisticians," in the sense of

---

[5] In this world, the norms are the procedural rules for making decisions, as distinguished from social norms, for following the crowd.
[6] Depending on the formulation, noncompensatory decision rules might violate the *continuity axiom* defining rational choices, whereby, in effect, everything has a price.
[7] The theory is notably silent on where the options, values, and information come from, as discussed in later chapters.
[8] Slovic, P., & Lichtenstein, S. (1971). Comparison of Bayesian and regression approaches to the study of information processing in judgment. *Organizational Behavior and Human Performance*, 6(6), 649–744.
[9] Described below.

being able to do the mental arithmetic needed to calculate statistics (e.g., means), based on experimenter-provided observations.[10] Those conducting these studies were versed in earlier research on how to elicit numbers. That research in turn emerged from *psychophysics*, which studies the psychological equivalents of physical stimuli (e.g., weight, noise, brightness).[11] It has identified many factors that can keep numerical judgments from faithfully representing underlying feelings. For example, *response biases* can lead to a preference for round numbers or avoiding fractions. *Stimulus range effects* can lead to using an entire scale (e.g., 0–10) for whatever stimuli are presented, so that "10" may mean different things.[12]

Bayesian inference differs from classical statistics by allowing probabilities based on judgment, rather than statistical summaries of repeated events.[13] Those judgments may reflect questions about how well the observations represent the underlying universe. Or they may reflect information from diverse sources. Bayesian inference offers normative rules for making consistent (coherent) inferences based on prior beliefs about what might be true, the interpretation of new observations, and the criteria for having sufficient evidence. Bayesian inference is possible when there are no repeated observations for calculating statistics (e.g., the chance of thermonuclear war, the unemployment rate in a profession twenty years hence).

Among researchers working in the teapot of ball-and-urn studies,[14] the key tempest swirled around why people were "conservative," in the sense of not updating their beliefs as much as they should, given new observations. The primary competing explanations were *misperception* and *misaggregation*. Do people extract too little information from new observations or do they fail to combine new and old information properly? In addition to reflecting different theories of behavior, the two accounts lead to different practical interventions. Misperception requires helping people to see the world more accurately. Misaggregation requires helping them with mental arithmetic.[15]

---

[10] Peterson, C. R., & Beach, L. R. (1967). Man as an intuitive statistician. *Psychological Bulletin, 68*(1), 29–46.

[11] Littman, R. A. (1979). Social and intellectual origins of experimental psychology. In E. Hearst (Ed.), *The first century of experimental psychology* (vol. 5, Chapter 2). Psychonomic Society.

[12] Poulton, E. C. (1989). *Bias in quantifying judgments*. Lawrence Erlbaum; Poulton, E. C. (1994). *Behavioral decision making*. Lawrence Erlbaum; Woodworth, R. S. & Schlosberg, H. (1954). *Experimental psychology*. Holt; Tune, G. S. (1964). Response preferences: A review of some relevant literature. *Psychological Bulletin, 61*(4), 286–302.

[13] Edwards, W., Lindman, H., & Savage, L. J. (1963). Bayesian statistical inference for psychological research. *Psychological Review, 70*, 193–242; Fischhoff, B., & Beyth-Marom, R. (1983). Hypothesis evaluation from a Bayesian perspective. *Psychological Review, 90*(3), 239–260.

[14] At the time, the studies were known as bookbag-and-poker chip studies, reflecting an analogous experimental task. Researchers sometimes filed away the tiny point left by the injection mold that produced one color of chip, allowing them to reach into the bookbag and pull out chips in a standard order, for the sake of experimental control.

[15] Edwards, W. (1968). Conservatism in human information processing. In B. Kleinmuntz (Ed.), *Formal representation of human judgment* (pp. 17–52). Wiley.

Out-of-Bounds Observations

Work within these disciplinary bounds produced ingenious experiments, with similar methods being used long past the ball-and-urn era. Researchers' enthusiasm was boosted by having a common enemy, the *frequentists*, who deny the legitimacy of the subjective probabilities central to Bayesian inference, arguing that only observed relative frequencies are meaningful.[16] Eventually the controversy petered out, with realization that both sides were similarly bounded, prompted by the cold shower of results that fit neither account.[17]

For ball-and-urn research, the cold shower was a terminal review by Paul Slovic and Sarah Lichtenstein.[18] It included results like cases where people who saw a red ball increased their probability that the urn had mostly blue balls—explained as "an exception that proved the rule." They also offered a way out: Amos Tversky and Daniel Kahneman's seminal research on heuristics and biases.[19] One prediction from that research is that people misperceive randomness, hence might expect such exceptions.[20]

The heuristics-and-biases framework offered its own rich field for invention. Indeed, researchers are still exploring that space fifty years on. Its endurance is a tribute to the power of its ideas, which reflect a rare synthesis of the three decision science elements. It has robust normative standards, as needed to call behavior "biased." It has descriptive research tasks that seem to evoke natural behavior, while still being insulated enough for experimental research. It reveals biases worth eliminating. It also invokes basic psychological processes (e.g., automatic encoding of frequency, pattern recognition), making the heuristics more plausible and solutions more feasible.

The first published study in the program, "Belief in the law of small numbers," exemplified this synthesis.[21] It documented the flawed judgments of statisticians and mathematical psychologists when asked to intuit solutions to research design problems that could be calculated, if they were given the

---

[16] This dispute is a corollary of the probability versus frequency controversy described in Chapter 1.

[17] Lakatos, I. (1990). Falsification and the growth of scientific research programmes. In I. Lakatos & T. Musgrave (Eds.), *Criticism and the growth of knowledge* (pp. 91–196). Cambridge University Press.

[18] Slovic, P., & Lichtenstein, S. (1971). Comparison of Bayesian and regression approaches; Ward Edwards, their graduate advisor, offered a proud, and deliberately somewhat curmudgeonly, comment. Edwards, W. (1971). Bayesian and regression models of human information processing: A myopic perspective. *Organizational Behavior and Human Performance*, 6(6), 639–648.

[19] Tversky, A., & Kahneman, D. (1974). Judgment under uncertainty: Heuristics and biases. *Science*, 185(4157), 1124–1131.

[20] More specifically, people expect more alternation and fewer runs than random sequences actually have. As a result, a red ball is due after a run of blues from a predominantly blue urn. The gamblers' fallacy, in predicting betting outcomes, is another corollary.

[21] Tversky, A., & Kahneman, D. (1971). The belief in the law of small numbers. *Psychological Bulletin*, 76(2), 105–110.

time and saw the need.[22] The normative answers held for different performance standards (Bayesian and non-Bayesian).[23] The results suggested ways to reduce a known problem, requiring researchers to calculate the *statistical power* of studies, as protection against expecting too much from small samples.[24]

The brilliance of these seminal papers lay partly in the persuasiveness of the experimental tasks. Observers tend to agree about which heuristic people would use for a task, and how they would use it. For example, one task asked questions like, "Is k more frequent as the first or third letter of a word?"[25] It seems natural to think about examples, which seem naturally coded lexicographically in memory.[26] Relying on the availability heuristic in that way means overestimating the relative frequency of k-first words, to the neglect of less available k-third words such as "like."[27]

Such tasks have been used in many studies, reliably producing biased judgments with potentially interesting variations (e.g., time pressure, priming, incentives). The price paid for that reliability is a *research monoculture*, which can produce fragile results that vanish outside its bounds, like an orchid that thrives only at limited altitudes with morning mists and specific pollinators. Researchers have pursued two strategies for escaping those bounds. One is to extend a heuristic's range of observations. The second is to study new heuristics. Both face the challenge of describing behavior in terms comparable to a normative standard.

Pushing Heuristic Bounds

Psychologists use the term *construct validity* to describe the web of assumptions made in interpreting results.[28] The strength of those assumptions depends on the body of relevant research. For example, the availability

---

[22] Ward Edwards was optimistic about people seeing the need for help. Research on calibration of confidence judgments (see Chapter 4) gives reason for doubt, suggesting that people overestimate the need for help in some settings, and underestimate it in others.

[23] When teaching the paper, I direct students to the footnotes, explaining the logic of the normative solutions.

[24] Paradoxically, this bias increases the risk of publishing results that are statistically significant by chance, and is a plausible contributor to the "reproducibility crisis" in psychology and other disciplines, whereby published results fail to replicate. Cohen, J. (1962). Statistical power of abnormal-social research: A review. *Journal of Abnormal and Social Psychology*, 65(3), 145–153.

[25] Collecting data for this study was one of my first tasks in graduate school, taking advantage of my access to English-speaking students at the Hebrew University of Jerusalem.

[26] Consistent with studies like Jonides, J., & Naveh-Benjamin, M. (1987). Estimating frequency of occurrence. *Journal of Experimental Psychology: Human Learning and Memory*, 13(2), 230–240, mentioned in Chapter 1.

[27] Except perhaps for Scrabble, Boggle, and crossword players.

[28] Fischhoff, B. (in press). Heuristic assumptions. *Journal of Risk and Uncertainty*. (special issue tribute to Daniel Kahneman). https://doi.org/10.1007/s11166-024-09437-3.

heuristic relies on assumptions about memory retrieval and storage. Supporting evidence comes from studies finding that people typically produce instances of a category at a decreasing rate.[29] If people rely on availability to estimate category size, then they should overestimate the frequency of events with easily retrieved instances, when they spend just a little time, as was likely with the letter k task. However, if they work harder, they might learn that an initially easy category is readily exhausted, and produce more accurate estimates.

Ruth Beyth-Marom and I tested this web of inferences with a simple study.[30] We gave people[31] either five seconds or two minutes to estimate the relative number of countries whose Hebrew name begins with the letter "yud" (y) or "kuf" (k). The former category has five countries, all easily recalled (Israel, Jordan, Japan, Greece, Yugoslavia), but just those five. The latter has a dozen mostly less salient ones (e.g., Cambodia, Cameroon, Canada, Congo-Brazzaville, Congo-Kinshasa).[32] People given more time had more accurate estimates, affirming the inferences.

In a more ambitious study on a more consequential topic, we looked at whether people rely on availability when they judge the risks of everyday life, as reflected in annual fatalities.[33] If so, then they should have a good feeling for relative risks, unless there is some bias in what they observe. One expected bias involved suicides and homicides. Although the former are more common, we expected people to believe the opposite, because suicides are often hidden, while homicides make the news. Describing some details of our study will give a feeling of the intricacies of this disciplinary science, for those who have not endured its apprenticeship.

Our normative analysis involved identifying consensually defined risks with good statistical estimates. We settled on annual fatalities for forty-one familiar causes of death, ranging in frequency from smallpox[34] and botulism to stomach cancer and heart disease.[35] Our descriptive research

---

[29] See Chapter 1. Bousfield, W. A., & Sedgewick, C. H. W. (1944). An analysis of sequences of restricted associates responses. *Journal of General Psychology, 30*(2), 149–165.

[30] Beyth-Marom, R. & Fischhoff, B. (1977). Direct measures of availability and judgments of category frequency. *Bulletin of the Psychonomic Society, 9*, 236-238.

[31] In the professional literature, the people being studied in behavioral research are varyingly called subjects, participants, respondents, or interviewees. However, as they are typically treated as though they represent people in general, I will use "people," unless clarity demands otherwise.

[32] The study was conducted long enough ago that the last two countries have changed names. That would change the normative standard for accuracy, but judge unfairly people who were good at estimation but poor at current events.

[33] Lichtenstein, S., Slovic, P., Fischhoff, B., Layman, M., & Combs, B. (1978). Judged frequency of lethal events. *Journal of Experimental Psychology: Human Learning and Memory, 4*(6), 551–578. The study is widely cited, although, to the best of my knowledge, no one has pursued the full range of converging tests partially described here.

[34] The study was conducted long enough ago that smallpox was still a threat, even though, by that time, more people in the US died from the vaccine than from the disease.

[35] In our research report, we noted that, "For convenience, these frequencies are referred to in this article as the true frequencies, although we recognize that they are statistical estimates" (Lichtenstein et al.,

recognized that translating a sense of doom into a numerical estimate could be challenging. Drawing on psychophysics, we adopted a multimethod approach, looking for patterns that emerged however the question was asked.

In a pretest, we asked people[36] to fill in a blank with annual fatality estimates. In response, they gave wildly different numbers. Some gave estimates so low that they implied very long lives, with only a tiny fraction of Americans dying each year. Others gave estimates that implied the opposite. Seeing these differences, we realized that few people have any feeling for how many people die (or live) in the US.[37] As a result, we gave hints, telling people in one group that about 1,000 people die annually from electrocution and people in a second group that about 50,000 people die annually in motor vehicle accidents.[38] Such hints have a well-known effect: *anchoring*.[39] People who are unsure what to say may "anchor" on a salient value and then adjust from there. However, anchors can be sticky, leaving final estimates too close to them. Indeed, that's what we found. People who saw 50,000 gave higher estimates than did people who saw 1,000. However, their estimates were only two to five times higher, and not fifty times (the ratio of the two anchors).[40] So people must have known enough not to be entirely at the mercy of our hints.[41]

To test the robustness of these judgments, we asked other people to estimate the relative frequency of paired causes (e.g., how many times more people die of cancer than from tornadoes).[42] Those judgments were similar to the ratios of the estimates for the individual causes (cancer, tornadoes).[43] As another test, we elicited similar judgments for the frequency of words (in written English) and occupations (in the US), and found similar patterns.

Given how sensitive these numerical judgments were to how questions were asked, we looked for reliance on availability in relative, rather than

---

Judged frequency of lethal events, p. 554). Indeed, recording causes of death can be a fraught enterprise (Seybolt, T., Aronson, J., & Fischhoff, B. (Eds.) (2013). *Counting civilian casualties: An introduction to recording and estimating nonmilitary deaths in conflict.* Oxford University Press).

[36] The "people" in these studies were either individuals who responded to ads in the University of Oregon *Daily Emerald* or members of the League of Women Voters. We paid the former the price of a beer and two slices of pizza at Taylor's, a campus bar, for an hour's work. We paid the latter with a contribution to their organization. None of our studies used students participating as a class requirement.
[37] And why should they? Other than game shows, bar bets, and perhaps citizenship exams, why would anyone need them?
[38] At the time, the death penalty was banned in the US, so we did not have to specify "accidental electrocution." The rate of traffic fatalities then was about twice today's rate, despite many more vehicles and miles driven now—a tribute to engineering, seatbelt laws, and graduated licensing for new drivers.
[39] Tversky & Kahneman, Judgment under uncertainty.
[40] 50=50,000/1,000=deaths from motor vehicle accidents/deaths from electrocution.
[41] Merchants know that, when they propose high selling prices to inexperienced customers.
[42] Zur Shapira got similar answers when he asked people to express their confidence in numbers by squeezing a dynamometer (handgrip). Shapira, Z. (1975). Measuring subjective probabilities by the magnitude estimation method. *Organizational Behavior and Human Performance, 14*(3), 314–320.
[43] When judgments are accurate, they are also internally consistent. However, consistent judgments can all be too high, too low, too similar, or too disparate.

absolute, estimates. We found that, for any given statistical frequency, people gave higher estimates for causes of death when they reported direct or indirect experience. A follow-up study, counting deaths in two newspapers (a much harder task then than now), found over-reported causes to be overestimated.[44]

Our intervention research sought to reduce availability bias by telling people about it and suggesting ways to reduce its influence (e.g., "think about deaths that might not get reported"). We failed, as have other researchers who have found that warnings have little effect unless accompanied by useful ways to approach tasks differently.[45]

In many ways, the judgments that we observed were quite good. People had internally consistent beliefs, which roughly followed statistical estimates and deviated from them for predictable reasons (anchoring, availability).[46] This relatively upbeat picture emerged both despite the strangeness of our tasks and because of it. Compared to most studies, our questions were unusually demanding, but also unusually precise. We posed a clear question (annual fatalities), removing the need to guess what we meant and allowing us to evaluate the answers fairly.

The Bias Heuristic

Publication of the causes-of-death study was accompanied by a comment from our friend James Shanteau, who had been one of the paper's reviewers.[47] He accepted our claim of bias, based on comparing judgments and statistics, but challenged our claim regarding availability, arguing that we had no way of knowing what people had actually observed.[48] In his critique, he captured the essential strength and limit to the bounded world of experiments: observations can be controlled, at a price in realism.[49]

---

[44] Combs, B., & Slovic, P. (1979). Newspaper coverage of causes of death. *Journalism and Mass Communication Quarterly*, 56(4), 837–849.

[45] In this case, underestimated causes of death included "quiet killers," such as asthma and diabetes. Debiasing papers. Fischhoff, B. (1982). Debiasing. In D. Kahneman, P. Slovic, & A. Tversky (eds.), *Judgment under uncertainty: Heuristics and biases* (pp. 422-444). Cambridge University Press.

[46] Thus, we took the observation of an expected bias (availability) as evidence that people could use the numbers appropriately.

[47] Reviewers are typically anonymous, or blinded, unless they choose to reveal their identity as Jim did. Some journals offer authors that option as well, although it can be hard to achieve within a field or when papers build on the authors' previous research.

[48] He noted that the judgments of words and occupations were more accurate, consistent with relying on availability in domains with less reporting bias—which he recognized as a speculative inference.

[49] Jonides & Naveh-Benjamin, Estimating frequency of occurrence.

According to Google Scholar (GS), Shanteau's comment has forty-seven citations. Our paper has 2,368. By my reading, few of those citing us cared much about our web of construct validity inferences. Most just noted the gist of the study, finding bias in risk judgments. The most common specific reference is one phrase in our paper's abstract, saying that we had observed "a tendency to overestimate small frequencies and underestimate larger ones."[50] Although our results showed that, they did not mean that. Due to anchoring, our reference numbers (1,000 or 50,000 deaths) pulled up low estimates and pulled down high ones; that meant overestimating low risks and underestimating high ones.[51] In retrospect, we should have said that whether estimates were too high or too low depended on how the question was asked.[52]

I wish that we could take back our misstatement, given its contribution to what Patrick Humphrey and Dina Berkeley called "the bias heuristic": the tendency to observe behavior that doesn't seem quite right and criticize people for it.[53] That tendency has made biases an end in themselves, rather than a means to reveal the heuristics and conditions that produce them. Over time, there has been a vast proliferation of alleged biases, beautifully captured in the Cognitive Bias Codex.[54]

Often, these studies reflect the work of researchers from other disciplines, with insights and imaginative tasks but without the normative analysis to support claims of bias. Seeing the creativity coming from outside decision science, Ruth Beyth-Marom and I tried to make Bayesian reasoning more accessible.[55] In making our case we noted that, without that common framework, the field had used the same term, *confirmation bias*, for two different phenomena and had identified a "bias" that seemed to break no normative rules (the *dilution effect*). We proposed characterizing all biases in terms of the normative rules that they violated. That would, we argued, make the research more parsimonious, by consolidating related effects, and

---

[50] Lichtenstein et al., Judged frequency of lethal events, p. 551 (abstract).

[51] We may also have sold people short with another conclusion: "Unless the true frequencies of a pair of lethal events differed by more than a factor of two, there was no guarantee that subjects could correctly indicate which was more frequent" (Lichtenstein et al., Judged frequency of lethal events, p. 574). A more balanced account would have given people credit for discriminating larger differences, which might be good enough for many decisions.

[52] Poulton, E.C. (1977). Quantitative subjective estimates are almost always biased, sometimes completely misleading. *British Journal of Psychology*, 68(4), 409–425.

[53] Berkeley, D., & Humphreys, P. (1982). Structuring decision problems and the "bias heuristic." *Acta Psychologica*, 50(3), 201–252.

[54] Cognitive Bias Codex: https://commons.wikimedia.org/wiki/File:Cognitive_bias_codex_en.svg (accessed August 13, 2024).

[55] Fischhoff & Beyth-Marom, Hypothesis evaluation from a Bayesian perspective.

more comprehensive, by identifying neglected topics.[56] Box 3.1 contains our proposal.[57]

Box 3.1 A Bayesian Framework for Descriptive Decision Science Research

Potential sources of bias in Bayesian hypothesis evaluation

Task	Potential bias	Special cases
Hypothesis formation	Untestable Nonpartition	Ambiguity, complexity, evidence unobservable Nonexclusive, nonexhaustive
Assessing component probabilities	Misrepresentation Incoherence Miscalibration Nonconformity Objectivism	Strategic responses, nonproper scoring rules Noncomplementarity, disorganized knowledge Overconfidence Reliance on availability or representativeness
Assessing prior odds	Poor survey of background Failure to assess	Incomplete, selective Base-rate fallacy
Assessing likelihood ratio	Failure to assess Distortion by prior beliefs Neglect of alternative hypotheses	Noncausal, "knew-it-all-along" preconceptions, lack of convergence Pseudodiagnosticity, inertia, cold readings
Aggregation	Wrong rule Misapplying right rule	Averaging, conservatism? Computational error, conservatism?
Information search	Failure to search Nondiagnostic questions Inefficient search Unrepresentative sampling	Premature conviction Tradition, habit Failure to ask potentially falsifying questions
Action	Incomplete analysis Forgetting critical value	Neglecting consequences, unstable values Confusing actual and effective certitude

Source : Fischhoff B. Beyth-Marom R. (1983). Hypothesis evaluation from a Bayesian perspective. *Psychological Review* 90(3) 239–260.

---

[56] After reviewing fifty years of publications in the *Journal of Applied Psychology*, Darley concluded that analytical results remained evergreen. However, substantive results tended to repeat every twenty years, with different labels and the theoretical framing of the day. The analogous hope here would be that substantive results will be more robust, if defined in contrast to an analytical model. Darley, J. G. (1968). A journal is born. *Journal of Applied Psychology, 52*(1), 1–9.

[57] For an organizing scheme organized more around processes than task characteristics, see Oeberst, A., & Imhoff, R. (2023). Toward parsimony in bias research: A proposed common framework of belief-consistent information processing for a set of biases. *Perspectives on Psychological Science, 18*(6), 1464–1487.

As mentioned, the magic and impact of the original heuristics-and-bias demonstrations reflect their rare combination of normative analysis, psychological insight, and prescriptive potential. Thus, the work falls at the intersection of disciplines whose bounded rationality specializes in each element. Outside that intersection, researchers may not realize the limits to their hard-won expertise. Researchers grounded in analysis may know what they mean, in normative terms, but not what they are saying, when asking people to interpret their tasks. Researchers grounded in behavioral science may know what they're saying, when creating tasks that people understand as intended, but not what they mean, in normative terms, when evaluating people.

Engaging these boundaries stretches the disciplines involved. Analytical researchers must ponder the normative status of people's responses to behavioral researchers' tasks. Behavioral researchers must employ the structured empathy of analysis when thinking about the decisions that people face. For both, the process slows the rush to judgment that produces unsupported claims of bias. As the constituent disciplines expand and specialize, it becomes increasingly difficult for any individual to master more than one. Indeed, even in the much smaller research world of half a century ago, it took a fortuitous collaboration to give decision science much of its current shape.

Simple Models or Simple Processes

Disciplines that study decisions made by many people (e.g., choices of careers, cars, diets) often rely on *regression models*, interpreting predictor weights as reflecting the relative importance of those variables in the decisions. Complex regression models underlie the *revealed preference* analyses central to economics. Simple versions underlie variants of the *health belief model*,[58] which guides much behavioral research, including the development of medical decision aids[59] and the prominent theory of planned behavior and its offshoots.[60]

Although once common, regression models are now rare in decision science.[61] That absence owes much to the Oregon Research Institute (ORI),

---

[58] Becker, M. H. (1984). The health belief model: A decade later. *Health Education and Behavior, 11*(1), 1–47.
[59] Stacey, D., Lewis, K. B., Smith, M., Carley, M., Volk, R., Douglas, E. E., Pacheco-Brousseau, L., Finderup, J., Gunderson, J., Barry, M. J., Bennett, C. L., Bravo, P., Steffensen, K., Gogovor, A., Graham, I. D., Kelly, S. E., Légaré, F., Sondergaard, H., Thomson, R. … Trevena, L. (2024). Decision aids for people facing health treatment or screening decisions (review). *Cochrane Database of Systematic Reviews, 1*(1), Art. CD001431.
[60] Ajzen, I. (1991). The theory of planned behavior. *Organizational Behavior and Human Decision Processes, 50*(2), 179–211.
[61] Egon Brunswik's followers are an important exception. Brunswik, E. (1947). *Systematic and representative design of psychological experiments.* University of California Press.

which brought together researchers from disciplines with analytical, descriptive, and prescriptive expertise.[62] ORI had the unusual practice of having its dozen scientists review all grant proposals before submission, so that they knew, thought, and talked about one another's work. Some were also graduates of the University of Michigan Mathematical Psychology program, one tributary to the nascent field of management science.[63]

One sustained discussion at ORI concerned a puzzling result from clinical psychology, discovered by Paul Meehl, Lowell Kelly, Donald Fiske, and others.[64] During World War II, regression models had been used as efficient ways to select people for jobs and to diagnose clinical conditions.[65] After the war, researchers asked how good those predictions had been. One recurrent finding was that simple regression models often predicted as well as experts. A second recurrent finding was that simple regression models predicted experts' judgments as well, a baffling result that belied the effort put into those judgments. Lewis Goldberg, a personality researcher at ORI, summarized the puzzle as "Simple models or simple processes?"[66]

Robyn Dawes, a mathematical clinical psychologist at ORI, solved the puzzle.[67] His solution had several pieces. One is that simple models can often predict complex processes for unintuitive statistical reasons.[68] Thus, even if experts were engaged in complex judgments, a simple model might still predict them. Indeed, Dawes showed the value of simply comparing the number of factors favoring and opposing a prediction.[69] A historical example is Benjamin Franklin's *prudential algebra*, which tallies arguments for and against a choice.

The second piece is that predictors are often correlated with one another. Given such multicollinearity, regression weights may not reflect the importance of each predictor. As a result, many models may predict equally well, but tell different stories (in their regression weights). For practical purposes, any

---

[62] They included John Reid, Jerry Patterson, Lewis Goldberg, Robyn Dawes, Richard Jones, and Lita Furby, as well as Paul Slovic, Sarah Lichtenstein, and me.

[63] An intangible factor is that almost all had moved to Eugene for work. Without extended family, many created a community for one another, reinforced by Eugene's counterculture.

[64] Kelly, E. L., & Fiske, D. W. (1951). *The prediction of performance in clinical psychology*. University of Michigan Press.

[65] Not to mention its contributions to training, intelligence analysis, group processes, and equipment design (Lazarsfeld). Lazarsfeld, P.F. (1949). The American Soldier: An expository review. *Public Opinion Quarterly, 13*(3), 377-404.

[66] Goldberg, L. R. (1968). Simple models or simple processes? Some research on clinical judgments. *American Psychologist, 23*(7), 483–496. Goldberg also had a major role in realizing Fiske's vision of a framework like the Big Five personality factors.

[67] Dawes, R. M. (1979). The robust beauty of improper linear models in decision making. *American Psychologist, 34*(7), 571–582.

[68] As a do-it-yourself example, draw a curve and then draw the line that fits it best.

[69] More formally, that would be a model with signed (plus or minus) unit (equal) weights on standardized measures of how a case rated on a predictor.

of those models would do. For theoretical purposes, though, it is impossible to know which tells the truest story. In such cases, interpreting the weights can be an exercise in futility.[70]

The third piece to the puzzle is that people, including experts, have limited insight into the factors shaping their judgments. One critical limit is not realizing how inconsistent they can be, even when trying hard to make nuanced predictions. As a result, models that reliably apply simple rules can outperform humans who unreliably apply complex ones.

Thus, the disciplinary conjunction at ORI led decision scientists to abandon regression models as a source of insight into how people think. They concluded that those models could not distinguish among accounts of decision-making processes.[71] However, that conclusion does not undermine the practical value of models that structure researchers' work by specifying generally useful predictors (e.g., perceived costs, benefits, social norms, self-efficacy), thereby reducing the chances of missing important factors.[72]

Conclusions

Following a strategy common to management science, decision science frames its research in terms of a normative standard for how things should be done. Typically, that ideal is the Bayesian model of inference, for judgment, coupled with the expected utility model, incorporating Bayesian inferences, for choice. That strategy provides a common framework for analytical and descriptive research in diverse domains. The success of interventions is a measure of how well researchers understand the decision and the decision maker.

Decision science arose from one set of disciplinary collaborations, between analytical and behavioral researchers. Further collaborations have been essential to its development. Engagement with cognitive psychology helped it to escape the task monoculture of ball-and-urn-type experiments. Engagement with clinical psychology helped it to move past regression models. Chapter 4 describes engagements that can help bring order to the proliferation of biases that occupy much of the field.

---

[70] One of Paul Hoffman's best-known papers argued for the practical value of "paramorphic" models of judgment, which matched input–output relations without claiming to capture the underlying processes, as needed by theoretically motivated models. Hoffman, P. J. (1960). The paramorphic representation of clinical judgment. *Psychological Bulletin*, 57(2), 116–131.
[71] Leamer, E. (1983). Let's take the con out of econometrics. *American Economic Review*, 72(1), 31–43.
[72] A friend, working for the Veterans Administration, once told me that his boss knew and accepted the result, and used to divert money from expert assessments with little value, to clinical treatment. He relied on inexpensive statistical prediction to guide case management, paid my friend to write up that prediction as though a person had done it, billed for the expert assessment, and invested the savings in client services.

Chapter 4
Questions of Competence

Disciplined Empathy

Like medical science, decision science relies on pathology to reveal processes hidden by functioning systems. Physical health reflects balancing processes whose complexity defies simple understanding.[1] Diseases reveal the limits to those adaptive processes. Good decisions reflect complex combinations of wisdom, instruction, mimicry, constraints, and trial and error. Poor decisions reveal their limits. Poor health and poor decisions may also suggest interventions, with informative results, even when unsuccessful.

However, accentuating the negative comes at a price: seeing people as the sum of their failings, while neglecting their strengths. That biased perspective can be bad for science, by obscuring those strengths. It can be bad for society, by depicting people as incompetent, undermining their right to manage their own affairs. In boundedly rational disciplines, researchers define the performance standard, whether that be for good health or good decisions. That standard reflects the discipline's bounds, which the people being judged are presumed to accept. In medicine, disability advocates, among others, have challenged how "health" is defined and measured. Analogous questions can be asked about "decision-making competence."

That competence affects how people fare in the world—as do beliefs about it. Individuals who overestimate their competence can unwittingly get into trouble, by overextending their reach. Individuals who underestimate their competence can unwittingly miss opportunities, by needlessly fearing to tread. Individuals whose competence is underestimated by others can be denied opportunities. Individuals whose competence is overestimated by others can be denied protections. Thus, the stories that researchers tell about people's competence matter, in terms of how those people see themselves and how others see them.

Those stories also affect researchers' welfare, in ways that can conflict with the welfare of the people whose stories they tell. Presuming to judge

---

[1] The weekly Obesity and Energetics Offerings show that daunting complexity in nutrition research. https://www.obesityandenergetics.org (accessed August 15, 2024).

Bounded Disciplines and Unbounded Problems. Baruch Fischhoff, Oxford University Press. © Baruch Fischhoff (2025).
DOI: 10.1093/9780191997266.003.0004

someone's competence is an assertion of authority. Those judgments can be used to support programs that may or may not serve their interests. Claims of incompetence may be invoked to justify interventions carried out "for their own good" (e.g., public service ads, nudges). Claims of competence may be invoked to remove protections (e.g., truth-in-advertising standards, workplace safety regulations). The former may favor research on biases, the latter research on heuristics.

Avoiding a Rush to Judgment

Medical scientists must balance wellness and sickness in how they conduct, interpret, and apply research. So, too, must decision scientists balance competence and incompetence. To my mind, our default should be doing all that we can do to empower people in making autonomous choices, while not abandoning them in situations beyond their coping ability. Those situations can arise when people lack the intellect, knowledge, motivation, freedom, material, or psychological resources needed to make sound choices.[2] Given the heterogeneity of people and situations, there is no scientifically or socially responsible simple answer to the question, "How good are people at decision making?" It depends on the decision and the decision maker.

Analytical decision science can identify classes of decisions that are more and less demanding. For example, decisions with discrete options are often relatively insensitive to how outcomes are weighed, as long as good ones can balance bad ones.[3] The critical thing is to include the relevant outcomes (or markers correlated with them). Similarly, theoretical analysis of decisions with continuous options (e.g., invest $X, study Y hours, exercise Z minutes) have found that they are often relatively insensitive to the exact value chosen.[4] Other decisions, though, are less forgiving, as seen in the horror stories in popular accounts of decision science research.[5]

Descriptive decision science pursues a form of structured empathy, designed to capture decision makers' perspectives in terms comparable to normative analyses. The consulting practice of *decision analysis* does that

---

[2] Fischhoff, B., & Barnato, A. E. (2019). Value awareness: A goal for end-of-life decision making. *Medical Decision Making: Policy and Practice*, 4(1).
[3] The limiting case being Ben Franklin's prudential algebra, comparing the number of reasons for and against an option. Chapter 3.
[4] von Winterfeldt, D., & Edwards, W. (1986). *Decision analysis and behavioral research*. Cambridge University Press.
[5] As captured in, arguably, the breakthrough title in this genre: Ariely, D. (2008). *Predictably irrational*. Harper Collins.

through sustained interactions with individual clients.[6] Researchers, though, must create those descriptions for classes of individuals, typically with limited opportunities for the interactions needed to understand them. Their disciplines may even discourage such interactions, fearing *reactive measurement*, whereby the research process changes the people it studies. Instead, researchers study tasks that they construe as being like ones that people face in their lives.

Prescriptive (intervention) research tests whether researchers have learned enough about decisions and decision makers to improve decision-making processes. The hope is that, over time, better processes will produce better outcomes. The immediate goal, though, is better processes. Indeed, decision science recognizes that overemphasizing tactical gains, from securing better specific outcomes, can undermine strategic gains, from learning how to make better decisions.[7] Focusing on process rather than outcomes distinguishes decision science interventions from the *consequentialist* nudges and boosts of behavioral economics.[8]

All scientists face the professional challenge of balancing disciplinary demands for studies simple enough for theory building with people's need for help with complex problems. Scientists also face the ethical challenge of summarizing their disciplinary knowledge in ways that convey its bounds. Decision scientists bear the special duty to balance heuristics and biases (strengths and weaknesses) when making statements about decision-making competence. In popular accounts, bias is overwhelmingly the story. Indeed, heuristics are often lumped in with them, in phrases like "people are subject to heuristics and biases." My experience is that outsiders (e.g., reporters) often have difficulty hearing a good word about decision makers or working it into their narrative.

The Discipline of Decision Science

When fully implemented, the internal discipline of decision science protects against misguided claims of competence. Elaborating on the brief descriptions above, that discipline entails:

Normative analysis: Use the best available analytical methods to identify the information most relevant to specific decisions. These analyses winnow the

---

[6] Raiffa, H. (1968). *Decision analysis: Introductory lectures on choices under uncertainty.* Addison-Wesley Howard.
[7] Einhorn, H. J. (1986). Accepting error to make less error. *Journal of Personality and Social Psychology, 50*(3), 387–395.
[8] Johnson, E. J. (2021). *The elements of choice.* Riverhead Books.

information that it might be nice to know down to the sometimes tiny subset that decision makers need to know. They may lead subject matter experts to create information that their discipline would not naturally consider. They may find that a discipline's "basic facts" have no practical value, however central they are to its members.[9]

Descriptive research: Use the best available empirical methods to determine how well decision makers have already mastered that critical information. Tests of that mastery may range from recall to active problem solving. Perhaps the most robust result in social psychology is that people overestimate how well they understand other people, and other people understand them.[10] The greater the differences in their backgrounds, the greater the bias.[11] As a result, scientists may have particularly poor intuitions about other people's perspectives, making empirical assessment essential.

Prescriptive interventions: Use the best available practical methods for improving decision making. Those interventions may involve closing the gap between what people know and what they need to know. They may involve providing perspectives that people might want to consider. They may involve reducing time, social, and emotional pressure, so that people can better process the information. They may involve changing the decision, so that people have better options.

The decision science arc is intrinsically iterative. Descriptive research may reveal concerns that are important to people, but were omitted in the analyses. Interventions may reveal a need to better understand the decision or the decision makers, or pose the question of how people have acquired mastery. The iteration stops when a satisficing solution is reached—good enough for practical purposes or as good as it is going to get, given the limits to the science and its practice.

Structured Empathy

The foundation of the decision science process is normative analysis. It establishes the performance standard for what people need to know, and for the success of interventions intended to help them. It is a form of disciplined empathy, identifying the information most relevant for decision makers, given their objectives. Decision trees are a common form of analysis;

---

[9] At a curricular level, the equivalent choice is between courses that prepare students for the next course in a sequence (e.g., economics, statistics) and courses that emphasize practical mastery.
[10] Nickerson, R. A. (1999). How we know—and sometimes misjudge—what others know: Imputing our own knowledge to others. *Psychological Bulletin*, 125(6), 737–759.
[11] Tullis, J. G., & Feder, B. (2022). The "curse of knowledge" when predicting others' knowledge. *Memory and Cognition*, 51(5), 1214–1234.

however, any approach in the management science toolkit could be useful. The following brief descriptions will give a feeling for the process. Each was part of a project that developed an analytical approach to a special case of a general class of problem.

Medical malpractice suits can hinge on whether patients were properly informed about risks.[12] However, there are often so many possible risks that full information would exceed patients' cognitive capacity. As a way to set priorities, Jon Merz created a form of analysis that simulated the impact of learning about each risk on the choices of a simulated population of patients for whom a treatment would otherwise be attractive. Using carotid endarterectomy as an example, he found that only three risks would matter to many patients: dying, stroke, and facial paralysis.[13] He argued that providing that information made competent decision making possible.[14]

Manufacturers bear a duty to inform consumers about proper use. Here, too, priorities are needed, lest useful information be buried in plain sight amidst useless information. Donna Riley created a form of analysis that estimated the impact of following different instructions on the risk from toxic chemicals.[15] Using methylene chloride-based paint stripper as an example, she showed that only two instructions mattered: open a window and have a fan blow outward. She also found that those instructions were not readily available, or sometimes available at all, on many such products.[16]

When food and drink products become contaminated, those responsible for them must spread the word quickly enough for consumers to make competent usage decisions. Liz Casman and colleagues developed an analytical approach that estimated the impact of improving different aspects of alert systems. These included how long it took to suspect a problem, confirm it, authorize warnings, and disseminate them, as well as how effectively the warnings reached consumers and prompted action.[17] Using cryptosporidium

---

[12] Less often, it seems, about the expected benefits and associated uncertainties.
[13] Merz, J., Fischhoff, B., Mazur, D. J., & Fischbeck, P. S. (1993). Decision-analytic approach to developing standards of disclosure for medical informed consent. *Journal of Toxics and Liability*, 15(1), 191–215.
[14] The analysis assumed that patients were rational decision makers. That assumption made the analysis possible and separated out the ethical questions involved with surrogacy.
[15] Riley, D. M., Fischhoff, B., Small, M., & Fischbeck, P. (2001). Evaluating the effectiveness of risk-reduction strategies for consumer chemical products. *Risk Analysis*, 21(2), 357–369.
[16] The context for the project was a regulatory decision about whether warning labels could allow safe use of the chemical.
[17] Casman, E., Fischhoff, B., Palmgren, C., Small, M., & Wu, F. (2002). Integrated risk model of a drinking-water-borne cryptosporidiosis outbreak. *Risk Analysis*, 20(4), 493–509.

infiltration to municipal water supplies as an example, she found that the process was too slow for even the best "boil water" notice to reduce risks. The analysis implied that where contamination risks exist, vulnerable people needed another water source.[18]

"Literacy" Tests

These analyses of specific information needs stand in stark contrast to the various "literacy" tests that use general questions to evaluate people's competence to make decisions about finance, health, climate, science, or many other things. These tests score people based on their knowledge of a small set of items from the vast set of facts in a domain. For example, the US National Science Foundation has long tested science literacy with questions like whether the earth revolves around the sun and whether the center of the earth is hot.[19]

It is an empirical question whether knowing these facts predicts knowing the facts relevant to specific science-related decisions. It is also an empirical question whether the 20 percent of people who answer the first question wrong are scientifically illiterate (or Ptolemaists) or struggle with actual literacy (e.g., confuse which is going around which). The first empirical question is hard to answer, given the vast array of science-related decisions and associated facts. The second empirical question is easier to answer, using methods described in Chapter 5. Absent answers, it is unclear what such literacy says about competence. The best answers might be found with financial literacy tests, which focus on specific, common decisions (e.g., involving interest rates).

The first answer might be derived analytically, by identifying items that are markers for knowledge of other items, even if not important in themselves. For example, they might capture knowledge not taught in school, suggesting that individuals read broadly in the area; or they might reflect errors associated with known sources of misinformation.[20] The answer might be derived theoretically by identifying foundational knowledge without which other knowledge cannot be understood or applied. Science education research

---

[18] In this case, the most vulnerable people were individuals with AIDS, who should routinely use bottled water or home purifiers.
[19] Drummond, C., & Fischhoff, B. (2017). Individuals with greater science literacy and education have more polarized beliefs on controversial science topics. *Proceedings of the National Academy of Sciences*, 114(36), 9587–9592.
[20] Adaptive testing, with item response theory, might select the most efficient set of items within a set thought to represent a domain.

seeks such dependencies. Chapter 5 discusses mental model tests of domain mastery.

These tests of substantive knowledge are distinct from tests of skill mastery. The best developed tests may be those for numeracy, which have shown both reliability and predictive validity. Ellen Peters's *Innumeracy in the Wild* is an excellent introduction.[21] It also makes the case for a test of perceived numeracy, noting the importance of situations where people do not realize what abilities they have, or lack. Caitlin Drummond, as part of her dissertation research, developed a test of scientific reasoning skills, whose items reflected skills taught in methodology texts, translated into vignette tests (e.g., potential confounds without randomization).[22] The next section describes the development and evaluation of an individual differences measure of decision-making competence, showing what such measures entail as well as some of the disciplinary barriers that they face.

Individual Differences

Individual differences in decision-making competence would be of theoretical interest, especially if they could be linked to life experiences and were distinct from other competencies. They would have practical value if they revealed places where additional decision support was needed, or opportunities to strengthen that competency were required. Despite its essential interest in how people perform specific tasks, decision science has historically paid perhaps surprisingly little attention to how well they perform in general. The primary reason has been its focus on understanding the processes that determine task performance, which it reveals by varying task features.[23] As a result, the field has lacked standardized tests like those for verbal and nonverbal intelligence.

However, that experience in the lab does create a large inventory of tasks with well-understood properties. In his dissertation research, Andrew Parker drew on that inventory to create a battery of well-understood tasks, each representing a basic decision-making skill.[24] He selected and evaluated them according to the standards of a neighboring discipline: psychometrics, as

---

[21] Peters, E. (2021). *Innumeracy in the wild*. Oxford University Press.

[22] Drummond, C., & Fischhoff, B. (2017). Development and validation of the Scientific Reasoning Scale. *Journal of Behavioral Decision Making, 30*(1), 26–38.

[23] A secondary reason, addressed in Chapter 6, is the difficulty experienced by psychologists seeking individual differences in personality. That difficulty includes attempts to measure one feature potentially central to decision making: individual differences in propensity for risk-taking.

[24] One missing skill was decision structuring, which does not lend itself to standard administration and scoring.

described in Box 4.1. The resulting test has two versions: Youth-Decision Making Competence (Y-DMC) and Adult-Decision Making Competence (A-DMC).[25]

Box 4.1 Psychometric Tests for an Individual Difference Measure of Decision-Making Competence (DMC)

Theoretically defined item sampling. Tasks addressed each decision science skill except decision structuring, a lightly studied topic with no tasks suitable for a standardized test.

Method variance. Tasks posed questions and elicited answers in different ways, so that a response preference would not be mistaken for a performance difference.

Reliability. People who perform better when they take the test once also perform better when they take it again.

Shared variance. People who score more highly on one measure in the battery tend to score higher on others, indicating a common skill.

Predicted antecedents. People with higher DMC scores were also less likely to have home conditions that might not model and reinforce that skill (e.g., father with substance abuse problems).

Predicted consequences. People with higher DMC scores were also less likely to report poorly considered behaviors (e.g., multiple sexual partners, acting out).

Distinguishing variance. People with higher DMC scores also had higher scores on verbal and nonverbal IQ tests. Although they, too, were related to the antecedents and consequences, DMC score had its own additional relationship to them.

Longitudinal stability. People with higher scores at age 18–19 (Y-DMC) also had higher scores at age 30 (A-DMC).

Behavioral measures are evaluated in terms of *reliability, internal validity*, and *construct validity*. The DMC measures were reliable in the sense of people receiving similar scores when they took them twice, with short time intervals (two weeks) for one test (Y-DMC) and with long time intervals (eleven years) using two versions of the test (Y-DMC and A-DMC). Experimentalists' long experience refining these tasks contributed to that reliability, as did their creation of an inventory from which to choose examples suited to standardized administration for diverse samples. The tasks showed internal validity

---

[25] Parker, A., & Fischhoff, B. (2005). Decision-making competence: External validity through an individual-differences approach. *Journal of Behavioral Decision Making, 18*(1), 1–27; Bruine de Bruin, W., Parker, A., & Fischhoff, B. (2007). Individual differences in adult decision-making competence (A-DMC). *Journal of Personality and Social Psychology, 92*(5), 938–956.

in the sense of being correlated with one another, suggesting that there was a common skill, expressed in how resistant people were to framing effects and how consistent their risk beliefs were.

Construct validity entails finding predicted patterns of correlation (and noncorrelation) with other measures. In this case, they were mostly measures developed by other disciplines and selected in consultation with experts in those disciplines.[26] For example, we expected and found modest correlations with measures of verbal and nonverbal intelligence,[27] believing them to tap some shared skills (including, perhaps, test-taking ability), but not to be so similar as to be highly correlated. We expected and found that DMC scores were correlated with plausible antecedents of decision-making competence (e.g., being fortunate enough to have parents without substance abuse problems and to live in a safe neighborhood). We also expected and found correlations with plausible consequences of decision-making competence (e.g., not having oppositional defiance disorder or multiple early sex partners).[28]

Successful construct validity tests increase confidence in all the measures and assumptions involved. Failures raise the question of which are to blame. For example, other studies have found weak correlations between DMC scores and self-ratings on traits like being a rational thinker or optimizer.[29] Whether these results reduce faith in DMC scores depends on whether one believes that the relationship should exist (e.g., competent decision makers try to maximize) and how much faith one has in the other measures (e.g., can people tell how rational they are? will they report honestly?)[30]

DMC is a relative measure. Whether people with high or low scores are sufficiently competent to make sound decisions, in an absolute sense, is a separate question. Box 4.2 contrasts the rates of self-reported poor decision outcomes for people with high and low DMC scores, among people for whom each outcome is possible (e.g., people without credit cards cannot have more

---

[26] Our primary consultant was Ralph Tarter, who heroically led the University of Pittsburgh's Center for Education and Drug Abuse Research (CEDAR) over its quarter century of activity, and generously added our questions to the CEDAR suite, which also provided many of the correlates mentioned in Box 4.1. The terms in Box 4.1 are informal variants of those found in the technical publications.

[27] Formally called crystallized and fluid intelligence, respectively.

[28] These correlations largely remained after controlling for verbal and nonverbal intelligence, indicating that they play other roles in these processes.

[29] Chapter 6 picks up the individual differences thread, including Huber's conclusion that researchers should stop looking for evidence regarding individual differences in decision style in using management information systems. Given the many futile attempts, if anything was eventually found, the effects would be too small to matter. Huber, G.P. (1983). Cognitive style as a basis for MIS and DSS designs: Much ado about nothing? *Management Science, 29*, 567-579.

[30] Ironically, although the development of Y-DMC applied psychometric methods, the available sample (N=120) was below the size demanded by individual difference journals. Our paper was eventually accepted by a decision science journal, which welcomed a study examining the external validity of common laboratory tasks.

than $5,000 in credit card debt).[31] In all but two cases, the rate is higher for people with lower DMC scores.[32] Looking at the most extreme example (and assuming the validity of these self-reports), if one believes that cheating on a romantic partner suggests poor decision making, then the difference between the groups (7.2 percent vs. 32.9 percent) supports the validity of the DMC scale. Whether either rate is unacceptably high is a separate question.

Box 4.2 Prevalence of Poor Decision Outcomes (DOI) for People with High and Low Decision-Making Competence (A-DMC) Scores

DOI outcome	% in Low A-DMC	% in High A-DMC	Difference
Had more than $5,000 in credit card debt	30.1	43.6	−13.5*
Gotten lost or gone the wrong way for more than ten minutes while driving	60.5	70.6	−10.1*
Had a mortgage or loan foreclosed	12.9	2.9	10.0**
Been in a jail cell overnight for any reason	13.1	2.9	10.2***
Paid a rent or mortgage payment at least two weeks too late	31.6	19.4	12.2*
Been kicked out of a bar, restaurant, or hotel by someone who works there	15.7	3.0	12.7***
Had a condom break, tear, or slip off	39.1	25.7	13.4+
Had an unplanned pregnancy (or got someone pregnant, unplanned)	24.5	9.9	14.6**

Continued

---

[31] Parker, A. M., Bruine de Bruin, W., & Fischhoff, B. (2015). Negative decision outcomes are more common among people with lower decision-making competence: An item-level analysis of the Decision Outcome Inventory (DOI). *Frontiers in Psychology*, 6, Article 363. https://doi.org/10.3389/fpsyg.2015.00363

[32] Additional analyses look at the roles of sex and socioeconomic status.

Continued

DOI outcome	Prevalence of DOI outcome		
	% in Low A-DMC	% in High A-DMC	Difference
Had to spend at least $500 to fix a car you had owned for less than half a year	41.6	26.8	14.8*
Been suspended from school for at least one day for any reason	24.4	7.9	16.5**
Been divorced	26.2	9.3	16.9**
Had your ID replaced because you lost it	32.6	15.6	17.0***
Been kicked out of an apartment or rental property before the lease ran out	23.6	3.4	20.2***
Quit a job after a week	23.2	2.6	20.6***
Had the key to your home replaced because you lost it	35.0	13.2	21.8***
Had your electricity, cable, gas, or water shut off because you didn't pay on time	27.9	4.6	23.3***
Cheated on your romantic partner of one year by having sex with someone else	34.9	7.2	27.7***
Mean percentage of outcomes	32.3%	24.8%	7.5%***

Difference in prevalence tested using chi-square test of independence for individual outcomes and using two-sample t-test for mean percentage; $^+p < 0.10$; $^*p < 0.05$; $^{**}p < 0.01$; $^{***}p < 0.001$. The final six items had no conditioning event.

Source: Parker, A. M., Bruine de Bruin, W., & Fischhoff, B. (2015). Negative decision outcomes are more common among people with lower decision-making competence: An item-level analysis of the Decision Outcome Inventory (DOI). *Frontiers in Psychology, 6*, Article 363. https://doi.org/10.3389/fpsyg.2015.00363

Merchants of Bias?

Decision science is known to some as the science of human frailty, documenting the myriad ways in which decisions can go astray. Chapter 3 asked whether that strategy has been good for the science: perhaps spreading scientific resources over so many biases that none are understood well, perhaps missing the analytical framework needed to observe their commonalities and distinctions, perhaps increasing the risk of nonreproducibility if the premium on demonstrations of bias is too high.

Whatever story scientists see, they mostly tell it to their peers, emphasizing what is new and skipping what goes without saying. In pathology-focused sciences, those messages are primarily tales of woe. They are the stories that they tell their students and the stories requested by outsiders, often framed as "What's wrong with people?" The downbeat drumbeat can be depressing and disempowering, encouraging people to doubt their own competence. It can, conversely, be empowering for people who benefit from depicting others as incompetent, such as the officials who promote the "myth of panic" in order to assert their authority to control people in emergencies.[33]

Neglecting disciplinary boundaries leads to overgeneralizing results. There is no meaningful simple answer to the question of "How competent are people as decision makers?" It depends on the people and the decisions. Some people are more competent than others, as measured by tests like DMC or as reflected in better performance on specific tasks, where there is almost always some variability in responses. Some decisions are easy enough for even poor decision makers, making lackluster efforts; some are too hard for even the most skilled and hardworking. Responsible extrapolation from any experimental result requires careful matching between the conditions where it was observed, as the focus of attention, and any other setting where many other things may be going on. That matching requires experts in disciplines familiar with the subject matter (and the facts that could be known) and in disciplines familiar with the setting (and the opportunities for intervention).

Decision scientists should have no incentive to see people as generally competent or incompetent. Indeed, without variability in performance, scientists lack clues as to its drivers.[34] However, there can be professional incentives to tell a simple story rather than a complex one, acknowledging that "it depends" and that it requires structured empathy analyses to determine how. Trade books and TED talks require simple stories.

Worryingly, biases have been an epicenter of psychology's reproducibility crisis. In the landmark Open Science study, two-thirds of the fifty selected social psychology studies failed to replicate their published results, often

---

[33] Wessely, S. (2005). Don't panic! Short and long term psychological reactions to the new terrorism. *Journal of Mental Health*, *14*(1), 1–6.

[34] For example, research on overconfidence stalled until researchers found ways to probe the hard–easy effect observed in early studies. Lichtenstein, S. & Fischhoff, B. (1977). Do those who know more also know more about how much they know? The calibration of probability judgments. *Organizational Behavior and Human Performance*, *20*(2), 159–183.

featuring biases.[35] The wisdom of psychology's tradecraft has prompted a revolution in safeguards. They include raising the profile of long-standing practices like power analyses,[36] meta-analyses,[37] and data sharing.[38] They include innovations like multisite replications of individual studies and data analyses. Although these reforms are largely within the discipline's bounds, they may support interdisciplinary collaboration by restoring faith lost due to the crisis.[39] On the other hand, they may stifle collaboration, if its less predictable results are discounted as "exploratory" relative to strict replications.

Scientists Are People, Too

Conceivably, scientists who study biases are immune to them when interpreting results from studies or decisions in the world around them. However, studies of *debiasing* find that knowing about biases alone has little effect. It might even make matters worse if that knowledge induces an unwarranted feeling of immunity. That may be the experience of some readers who read or watch popular bias-focused accounts.[40]

More successful debiasing interventions have involved restructuring how people perform tasks, encouraging them, in effect, to reason more like the scientific ideal: explicitly consider a wide range of alternative explanations and evidence. Although scientists are trained in such thinking, they are also constrained in its application, by the bounds of their discipline. For decision scientists, that may mean focusing on readily quantified factors (e.g., money, risk), neglecting potentially more important ones (e.g., stress, self-image); restricting themselves to a fixed set of options, neglecting opportunities to create better ones, or implementing clumsy interventions, lacking skills found in other disciples (e.g., design, user testing).

---

[35] Along with one-third of the fifty selected cognitive psychology studies: Open Science Collaboration (2015). Estimating the reproducibility of psychological science. *Science, 349*(6251), Article aac4716.

[36] Cohen, J. (1962). The statistical power of abnormal-social psychological research. *Journal of Abnormal and Social Psychology, 65*(3), 145–153; Cohen, J. (1992). A power primer. *Psychological Bulletin, 112*(1), 155–159.

[37] Rosenthal, R. (1991). *Meta-analysis for social research*. Sage Publications.

[38] Invented in psychology. Hardwicke, T. E., & Vazire, S. (2024). Transparency Is Now the Default at Psychological Science. *Psychological Science, 35*(7), 708–711. https://doi.org/10.1177/09567976231221573.

[39] A separate story is attribution to malfeasance or sloppy thinking (as the biases would suggest).

[40] Milkman, K. L., Chugh, D., & Bazerman, M. H. (2009). How can decision making be improved? *Perspectives on Psychological Science, 4*(4), 379–383.

Decision science requires interdisciplinary collaboration that can avoid such neglect. Experts in analysis need to work with experts in behavior in order to characterize decisions in terms relevant to decision makers' current and possible goals, options, and information. Experts in behavior need to work with experts in interventions in order to identify the opportunities and circumscribe the barriers to improvement. Experts in intervention need to work with experts in analysis to assess the costs and benefits of any changes.

Conclusions

Presuming to judge others' competence poses an ethical burden, lest they be given more or less credit than they deserve, with more or less authority than the evidence warrants. Decision science provides safeguards, in the transparency of its normative analyses, the vigor of its discourse over empirical results, and the acid test of its interventions' effectiveness. However, procedures that are transparent to members of a discipline may be opaque to outsiders. The structured empathy of normative analysis increases the chances of getting things right, by defining the problem that researchers are solving and the collaborations needed to solve it.

Bringing together the disciplines needed to address complex decisions can be challenging. Needed experts may be in short supply. Their professional worlds may reward them for specialization rather than collaboration. Completing the decision science arc of normative, descriptive, and prescriptive research requires time and resources, as does implementing novel solutions. Chapters 5 and 6 show, in greater detail, what the work entails and the payoff from that attention to detail. Chapters 7 to 10 propose a strategy for overcoming institutional barriers, which management science can lead.

Chapter 5
Slow Science (Beliefs)

In their article "Systems of (non-)diversity," Medin, Ojalehto, Marin, and Bang lament the "lack of diversity in study populations, research methodology and the researchers themselves ... in social, educational, and behavioral research." After detailing the behavioral processes that are missed and misrepresented as a result of these blinders, the authors call for *slow scholarship*, "informed by a holistic engagement with work ... [capable] of enabling novel perspectives."[1] They add that its success depends on "a definition of scholarly work that includes care, community building, and advocacy ... that requires longer timescales than the standard publishing race would admit."

This chapter and the next ask how far decision science can go toward achieving these goals within its disciplinary bounds, for two central topics: assessing beliefs (Chapter 5) and assessing preferences (Chapter 6). Chapter 7 proposes a strategy for realizing the potential of science that respects the wisdom held within disciplinary bounds, while seeking the shared wisdom from transcending them. Decision science plays a facilitative role in that strategy by providing platforms that enable disciplines to collaborate with one another and with decision makers in ways that respect their goals.

Any discipline is limited to the skills and perspectives mastered in its apprenticeship programs. Graduates can rightfully cringe at outsiders' blind spots without recognizing their own. Decision science provides some protection against such insularity, when it fulfills its commitment to the normative-descriptive-prescriptive arc. Its normative analyses reduce the risk of ambiguous questions. Its descriptive research reduces the risk of misunderstanding decision makers' perspectives. Its normative interventions reduce the risk of irrelevance. Nonetheless, the research is constrained to the perspectives of those who have sought and received the training. In the spirit of slow scholarship, one way for a closed social or behavioral science community to transcend its bounds is by engaging the people it studies. Indeed, that engagement is essential to reducing the risks of ambiguity, misunderstanding, and irrelevance.

---

[1] Medin, D., Ojalehto, B., Marin, A., & Berg, M. (2017). Systems of (non-)diversity. *Nature Human Behavior 1*(5), Article 0088, p. 3.

What Are We Asking? The Face Validity of Questions

It is a truism of behavioral research that people respond to the world that they perceive, and that their relationship to the world that they inhabit depends on their life experiences. Those experiences include their education, culture, faith, travel, family, peers, biological development, genetics, and epigenetics. As a result of that diversity, understanding perceptions is the starting point for research. That is true whether people are responding to standard experimental tasks or personal real-life ones. *Face validity* is psychology's term for the extent to which research participants interpret tasks in the same way that researchers interpret them.

Given the diversity of personal experiences, researchers cannot presume to know how people perceive situations without asking them. Documenting failures to understand others' perspectives is a—perhaps the—focus of cognitive social psychology. One corollary is the "common knowledge effect," whereby people overestimate how much goes without saying, because they assume that other people already know it.[2] Another is the "false consensus effect," whereby people overestimate how far their goals are shared, because they cannot imagine how other people's values might differ from their own.[3]

As a result, asking how people interpret tasks is an essential empirical question in any behavioral research. With research tasks, questions must be revised until they are clear enough that participants understand them as intended. With real-life tasks, the question must be asked until researchers understand how people view their world. In both cases, there may be gaps between the tasks that interest researchers, in pursuing their research, and the tasks that interest people, in pursuing their lives.

Misunderstood tasks are bad for research. They are also bad for participants, leading to research that fails to serve their needs and misrepresents their competence.[4] The simple slow science response to this threat is to pretest questions, by asking a few people from the target population to say whatever comes into their minds as they work their way through draft material, making it clear that it is the material that is being tested, not them. Such *think aloud protocols*[5] can reveal things that were clear to the authors, but

---

[2] Nickerson, R. A. (1999). How we know—and sometimes misjudge—what others know: Imputing our own knowledge to others. *Psychological Bulletin*, 125(6), 737–759.
[3] Dawes, R. M. (1987). Statistical criteria for establishing a truly false consensus effect. *Journal of Experimental Social Psychology*, 25(1), 1–17.
[4] See Chapter 4.
[5] Ericsson, K. A., Simon, H. A. (1992). *Protocol analysis*. MIT Press.

not to the readers; things that were clear to the readers, who interpreted them differently than the authors intended; things whose tone readers found problematic; and missing things, whose content did not go without saying. Anyone who has been befuddled by a poorly worded survey question must wonder whether such testing was done and how their answers will be interpreted.[6]

Even with the most rigorous pretesting, the vagaries of language and the heterogeneity of personal experiences will leave some variability in how people interpret tasks. *Manipulation checks* ask people how they interpreted questions that they just answered. For example, we once asked college students how they interpreted this question from a major national survey: "How likely do you think that a person would get AIDS or the AIDS virus from sharing plates, forks, or glasses with someone who has AIDS?"[7] For someone who believed (erroneously) that such transmission was possible, the answer should depend on the intensity and frequency of the sharing. Most respondents thought that it meant eating out of the same bowl; they disagreed about how often.[8] Where there happened to be consensus (as with intensity), researchers would still have to guess what it was. Where there was no consensus (as with frequency), researchers would have to guess which version of the question each person was answering. Without manipulation checks, researchers would not know.

Frequency and intensity are just two dimensions defining these events. Box 5.1 shows a coding scheme developed to accommodate the defining factors that a diverse group of teens raised, when asked to think aloud while answering the question in its title.[9] The richness of these issues reflects the richness of these teens' thinking about that one topic. Thoughtful teens answering the question could give different answers depending on how they resolved the ambiguities in its definition.

---

[6] In principle, I believe that people who dish it out, in terms of asking questions, should be able to take it, in terms of answering them. In practice, though, I can't answer most surveys, needing more clarity than their questions provide and not wanting to be misinterpreted. An occasional exception arises with questions that telegraph the researchers' attempt, which I may be tempted to foil or reinforce. Drummond, C., & Fischhoff, B. (2017). Individuals with greater science literacy and education have more polarized beliefs on controversial science topics. *Proceedings of the National Academy of Sciences*, *114*(36), 9587–9592.

[7] Linville, P. W., Fischer, G. W., & Fischhoff, B. (1993). AIDS risk perceptions and decision biases. In J. B. Pryor & G. D. Reeder (Eds.), *The social psychology of HIV infection* (pp. 5–38). Erlbaum (republished 2015).

[8] Another question from the same national survey asked about "having sex with someone who has AIDS." There students agree both about the implicit intensity (vaginal sex without a condom) and about the implicit frequency (once).

[9] Box 5.1 is drawn from Marilyn Jacobs Quadrel's 1990 dissertation, Department of Social and Decision Sciences, Carnegie Mellon University. After being rejected by several journals, we abandoned the attempt to publish an article summarizing her multimethod study. Perhaps there was something wrong with the work. However, I think the main problem was that the journals did not see value in such slow science.

Box 5.1 Issues Raised by Teens when Interpreting "What is the probability that a person will have an accident while drinking and driving?"

Framework element	Risk factor categories	Example variables, drinking and driving question

Behavior	Dose
	  Amount
	  Potency
	  Method
		Amount of alcohol consumed

Other behaviors	Risk buffers Risk amplifiers Time-related Place-related	Amount of food eaten Other drugs consumed Night or day; day of the week Where alcohol was consumed
Actor	Physical Cognitive Social-psychological Material Spiritual Skill Character Age Gender Genetic history Status Luck Motivation Self other	Tolerance to alcohol Awareness of effects of alcohol Mood Wealth Faith Driving skill Responsible; mature

Context	Social
	General, cultural
	  Family
	    Peers, others
	Environmental
		Drinking norms
		Family approval
		Peer approval
		Road conditions

Risk outcome	Social reactions
	Personal effects
	  Physical
	  Psychological
	  Cognitive-physiological
	  Cognitive-psychological
	  Material
	  Accidents
	  Lifestyle
	  Complex
	Effects on others
	Behaviors
	Severity, type when measured
		Get in trouble
		Injury
		Worry, guilt
		Kill brain cells
		Can't think
		Lose car, lose license
		Get in a wreck while high
		Become a bum
		Get high
		Hurt your friends, family
		Use more, do heavier drugs

Source: Fischhoff, B. (1996). The real world: What good is it? *Organizational Behavior and Human Decision Processes*, 65(3), 232–248.

People facing ambiguous questions, in research as in life, have three options:[10]

(a) Use their own natural definition, giving a well-considered answer, but forcing the researcher to guess what the implied question was.
(b) Try to guess what the researcher had in mind, interpolating the missing details and, again, forcing the researcher to guess what the implied question was.
(c) Give a gist response to a gist question, assuming that the researcher won't read too much into the answer.[11]

Unless researchers can guess what respondents have guessed, they will misinterpret their answers. Unless they realize that they are guessing, researchers will have unwarranted confidence in their interpretation, whether they guess correctly or not.

The interpretative richness seen in Box 5.1 poses a challenge for researchers. They can reduce ambiguity by providing all relevant details. However, that means forcing respondents to master those details. That task will be harder, the more details there are and the greater the distance between the worlds of the researcher and the respondent. A classic article in psychology proposed that people can master seven, plus or minus two, details, unless they have learned to chunk them into higher order units.[12] Experimentalists complicate learning by constantly varying task details. People describing actual decisions must undo chunks created over a lifetime, with the kind of probing reflected in Box 5.1.

The richness in Box 5.1 also provides a window into how people make sense of their world. What features do they discern? How do they encode them? What do they miss? How similar are the salient features for different events? Which people notice (and overlook) which features? Better understanding of these *construal* processes could simplify life for researchers with precise questions, by identifying features that they must provide and that they can ignore. There is no way to know without asking. Such slow science requires resources. However, it can also save resources, by reducing the noise from ambiguous questions. It saves even more resources when that noise is mistaken for a signal, leading researchers in pointless directions.

In this slow science view, asking people to interpret structured tasks is not only a means to the end of better data collection, but also a means to

---

[10] Fischhoff, B., Welch, N., & Frederick, S. (1999). Construal processes in preference elicitation. *Journal of Risk and Uncertainty, 19*(1–3), 139–164.
[11] Reyna, V. F. (2012). A new intuitionism: Meaning, memory, and development in fuzzy-trace theory. *Judgment and Decision Making, 7*(3), 1–45.
[12] Miller, G. A. (1956). The magical number seven, plus or minus two: Some limits on our capacity for processing information. *Psychological Review, 63*(2), 81–97.

the end of deeper engagement with them. That engagement is, in turn, an end in itself, fulfilling one part of the social contract between science and society. Another part of that contract is studying issues that matter to people, and not just researchers, especially when society funds the research. The answers in Box 5.1 emerged from the simple engagement of semi-structured interviews. Each issue in it suggests a variable that might support, and benefit from, further research (e.g., the role of spirituality in drinking and driving).

Slow science when developing measures may prompt collaboration with other disciplines. For example, categorization research can identify natural concepts. Psychophysical research can avoid number-related artifacts. Developmental research can reveal age-appropriate phrasings.

What Are They Telling Us? The Face Validity of Answers

Analogous issues affect the face validity of the answers to questions. The AIDS-related survey (cited earlier) compounded the problems created by its ambiguous questions by offering answers with well-documented ambiguity. *Verbal quantifiers* (e.g., likely, large, some) can be interpreted differently by different people in a given setting, and differently by the same person in different settings.[13] A classic example, described by Sherman Kent, a founder of US intelligence analysis after World War II, involves a National Intelligence Estimate stating, "Although it is impossible to determine which course the Kremlin is likely to adopt, we believe that the extent of Satellite military and propaganda preparations indicates that an attack on Yugoslavia in 1951 should be considered a serious possibility."[14] Kent asked the analysts who signed the consensus document what probability each had in mind. The distribution of numerical answers was relatively flat and broad. There was no report on how President Truman interpreted the probability—or how that interpretation affected his decision making.[15]

For some research purposes, such ambiguity may be irrelevant. As long as people use verbal quantifiers consistently, a researcher studying the effects of emotion might only need to know whether they are more likely to say that a disaster is "possible" when feeling sad than when feeling angry.[16] Ambiguity

---

[13] Fillenbaum, S., & Rapoport, A. (1971). *Structures in the subjective lexicon*. Academic Press.
[14] Kent, S. (1964). Words of estimative probability. *Studies in Intelligence, 8*(4), 49–65.
[15] Lanir and Kahneman report that senior policy makers liked intelligence analyses structured in decision analytic terms, including conditional probabilities (what happens if X happens), but reported that they ignored the numbers. There was no way to tell if they paid attention to the gist of the numbers. Lanir, Z., & Kahneman, D. (2006). An experiment in decision analysis in Israel 1975. *Studies in Intelligence, 50*(4).
[16] Lerner, J. S., Small, D. A., & Fischhoff, B. (2003). Effects of fear and anger on perceived risks of terrorism: A national field experiment. *Psychological Science, 14*(2), 144–150.

68 Bounded Disciplines and Unbounded Problems

matters, though, when decisions are sensitive to whether "likely" means 40 percent or 70 percent. That practical concern has prompted a steady stream of basic research looking at how people encode, remember, and use numerical and verbal expressions of uncertainty. The research varies factors such as subject matter, payoffs, and elicitation method.

Figure 5.1 shows results from one study that asked people to give an upper and lower bound for the numerical probability corresponding to various verbal quantifiers. All agreed that the highest possible value of "almost certain" was about 1.0. However, the lowest possible value could be anywhere from about 0.65 to 0.85. For some reason, there was much less disagreement about the numerical equivalent of "almost impossible." There is less asymmetry in the interpretation of "likely" and "unlikely."[17] "Possible" could mean just

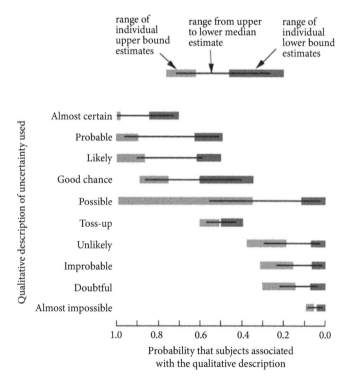

Figure 5.1 Ranges of numerical probabilities for verbal quantifiers

Source: Wallsten, T. S., Budescu, D.V., Rapoport, A., Zwick, R., & Forsyth, B. (1986). Measuring the vague meaning of probability terms. *Journal of Experimental Psychology: General*, 115(4), 348–365.

---

[17] The probability weighting curve central to prospect theory has seemingly related asymmetry, as did that found by Zur Shapira when he asked people to express their confidence using a dynamometer handgrip. Shapira, Z. (1975). Measuring subjective probabilities by the magnitude estimation method. *Organizational Behavior and Human Performance*, 14(3), 314–320.

about anything.[18] "Toss-up" seems to be consensually defined—although, as I will discuss shortly, the numbers might not mean what they seem.

Ambiguous answers can undermine research asking unambiguous questions. A central topic for labor economists is how young people estimate the return on investment in decisions like whether to stay in school or delay family formation. Our colleague Charles Manski faced pressure to remove related questions from a major national survey because teens' decisions were only weakly related to their answers to questions like "What is the chance that you will be working more than 20 hours a week a year from now, if you are no longer in school?" Although the question was precise, the answer options were verbal quantifiers, adding noise that could bury any signal in teens' responses.

A chance encounter led to an interdisciplinary collaboration that benefited our field and his. In a concurrent project, we were studying adolescent decision making per se.[19] Our studies often asked for numerical probabilities. They had found, for example, that, contrary to common folk wisdom, when asked for probabilities of bad things happening to them, adolescents do not have a unique sense of invulnerability. Rather, teens are much like adults, underestimating their risks from seemingly controllable events (e.g., auto accidents), but not uncontrollable ones (e.g., explosions, terrorist attacks).[20]

We offered to see whether teens could provide numerical probabilities for questions that economists could use in their models of human capital formation. Our collaboration was successful enough to become part of the expectations module of the 1997 National Longitudinal Survey of Youth. That success was seen in the construct validity[21] of teens' responses. Their probabilities correlated in predicted ways with their responses to other survey questions (e.g., young women who reported being sexually active gave higher probabilities of getting pregnant). Their accuracy was also consistent with studies of their beliefs (e.g., young women underestimate that probability).

The collaboration also prompted basic research in decision science. In keeping with slow science, we began with formative interviews, hearing teens think aloud as they answered draft questions. Wändi Bruine de Bruin, who led the interviews, observed that when teens said "fifty" they sometimes meant a number and sometimes "fifty-fifty"—a number-like answer, but not a probability. That observation led her to study when people experience such

---

[18] Much of Kent's essay is about problems with "possible." His bottom line is that it should only be used to attract attention to a problem and never have a modifier, like "distinctly possible."
[19] Fischhoff, B. (1996). The real world: What good is it? *Organizational Behavior and Human Decision Processes, 65*(3), 232–248.
[20] Quadrel, M. J., Fischhoff, B., & Davis, W. (1993). Adolescent (in)vulnerability. *American Psychologist, 48*(2), 102–116.
[21] See Chapter 3.

epistemic uncertainty, how they express it, and how to account for it in survey research. For example, it appears to be more common with negative events that people can't or won't think about (e.g., dying). It is less common among the Dutch, for whom "fifty-fifty" is not a common expression.[22]

Attuned to look for "fifty blips" in distributions of probability judgments, we discovered them in widely publicized studies whose authors claimed that people exaggerated the risks of breast cancer and lung cancer from smoking.[23] Treating the blips as numeric (50 percent), rather than as verbal (fifty-fifty), inflated the means of generally low probabilities. That meant accusing women of being overly alarmed about breast cancer and defending the smoking industry against the charge that people underestimate the risks of smoking. Were those claims believed, poor measurement could lead to poor policy. The simplest protection is to engage people in the research process, rather than assume that they can answer any question that is put to them.

Given the limits to how well any task will work with heterogeneous participants, all studies carry the implicit caveat, "Among people who interpreted our task as we intended, we observed [X behavior]. We cannot tell how other people would have behaved." However, such disclaimers are hand-waving without hypotheses about what the different interpretations might be and what difference they might have made. Manipulation checks can help. For example, teens who gave "fifty" as their probability of dying in the next year were more likely to report living in dangerous neighborhoods, suggesting that they meant "fifty-fifty."[24] An "I'd rather not answer" option might have improved the study by meeting some teens' need not to give a probability.

How Much Do People Think about the World?

The "causes of death" study[25] used to illustrate decision science research in Chapter 3 addressed the face validity of its questions by using familiar causes and units (annual fatalities). It addressed the face validity of its answers by providing anchors (the number of deaths from electrocution or motor vehicle accidents) to give people a ballpark feeling for what kind of numbers to use. We evaluated our success by construct validity: how consistent judgments were when elicited in different ways.[26]

---

[22] Fischhoff, B., & Bruine de Bruin, W. (1999). Fifty/fifty = 50%? *Journal of Behavioral Decision Making*, 12(2), 149–163.
[23] Fischhoff & Bruine de Bruin, Fifty/fifty = 50%?
[24] Fischhoff, B., Bruine de Bruin, W., Parker, A. M., Millstein, S. G., & Halpern-Felsher, B. L. (2010). Adolescents' perceived risk of dying. *Journal of Adolescent Health*, 46(3), 265–269.
[25] Lichtenstein, S., Slovic, P., Fischhoff, B., Layman, M., & Combs, B. (1978). Judged frequency of lethal events. *Journal of Experimental Psychology: Human Learning and Memory*, 4(6), 551–578.
[26] One of the construct validity assumptions was that people had consistent beliefs, if we could only tap them.

The intricacies of that study are echoed in the vast literature of risk perception studies,[27] the even vaster literatures on quantitative estimates of other quantities,[28] and the vaster still literatures on other *propositional knowledge*, in the sense of questions whose answers could be looked up. Getting the details of these studies right requires expertise in the substance and the form of the questions. Anyone who has grappled with an ambiguous survey or test question will know that failure is an option.

At times, people need more than just the knowledge required to predict a decision outcome. They also need to understand the underlying processes. For example, someone who knows why the AIDS virus cannot be transmitted through food (and not just that the probability is 0) should be more confident in that knowledge, less likely to misremember whether they had heard "cannot" or "can," better able to defend that belief, and more adept at deducing whether "food" includes "drink."

Cognitive psychology has a long tradition of studying how people create and use *mental models* corresponding to formal models of diverse phenomena. In the earliest studies, the formal models were maps and the mental models were inferred from watching laboratory animals navigate mazes. A "cognitive revolution" sought evidence that animals had mental representations of their environment, and were not just responding to stimulus–response contingencies as behavioralists claimed (e.g., when rats explored new pathways, despite having experienced ones with consistent rewards).

Studies with humans have looked at how they understand mapped worlds when they encounter them in different ways.[29] How do they extract point-by-point directions from overview maps? (Often, not very well.) How do they change course when following point-by-point directions, without an overview map? (Typically, worse.) How do they extrapolate from topographical maps to physical terrain? (Typically, even worse.) How well can they draw maps of their experienced environment? (Typically, worse, still.) How do they translate prepositional knowledge into graphical representations? (It depends on how well the description maps onto their mental one.)[30]

In other large research literatures, the formal models include syllogisms, the circulatory system, physical systems, macroeconomics, and geometry.[31] Like much science, these lines of research often focus on faults for insight

---

[27] Breakwell, G. M. (2019). *The psychology of risk*. Cambridge University Press.

[28] How deep is the ocean? How far is it from Reno to Las Vegas? What is the case-fatality rate among people who contract COVID-19? How many emperors has China had?

[29] Thorndyke, P. W. (1981). Distance estimations from cognitive maps. *Cognitive Psychology, 13*(4), 526–550.

[30] One common example of misrepresentation is the known warmth of Italy leading people to overestimate how far south it is (Rome is further north than New York). Another is knowing that Georgia is a coastal state leading people to overestimate how far east it is (Atlanta is further west than Detroit).

[31] Gentner, D., & Stevens, A. L. (1983). *Mental models*. Lawrence Erlbaum.

into processes where correct answers are overdetermined, and for places to help.[32] One such finding is that people tend to believe that balls rolling over a table edge fall straight down, rather than along a parabola.[33] Another such finding is that undergraduate degrees in economics do not improve intuitive inferences about the economy.[34] A third is that teaching heuristics can improve mathematical problem solving.[35] Sometimes, the studies identify general mental models (e.g., the circulatory system is plumbing, with the heart as pump). Sometimes, they identify fragmentary ones (e.g., unconnected ideas about how the economy works, producing inconsistent inferences about the effects of monetary and fiscal policies).

For decision science studies of mental models, the formal model is not a mechanistic one, like the circulatory system, but a probabilistic one. Figure 5.2 shows such a model, at two levels of detail, predicting the effects of climate change on malaria. In this *influence diagram*, each box is a factor predicting the risk; each arrow is a relationship between factors.[36] When there is no arrow, there is no direct relationship (e.g., between climate change and host populations), although there might be an indirect one (e.g., through changes in land use and land cover).

Such formal models are *computable*, in the sense that one could "run the numbers" if they were available.[37] In the example, that would mean knowing the conditions for malaria (e.g., temperature and humidity, means and variation), public and private health capabilities (e.g., geographical distribution, resources, affordability), and the other factors well enough to predict malaria risk. Influence diagrams and *Bayesian belief networks* are two related formalisms for representing such knowledge, with computational options when numerical estimates are available.[38]

For behavioral research, though, a computable model typically suffices. It provides a template for studying how people circumscribe the universe of factors predicting a decision-relevant outcome. Computability ensures that the elements are clearly enough defined that researchers can tell whether people have understood questions about them, ensuring face validity for behavioral research. Requiring computability, and not computation, avoids

---

[32] See Chapters 3 and 4.
[33] Chi, M. T., Feltovich, P. J., & Glaser, R. (1981). Categorization and representation of physics problems by experts and novices. *Cognitive Science*, 5(2), 121–152.
[34] Voss, J. F., Blais, J., Means, M. L., Green, T. R., & Ahwesh, E. (1986). Informal reasoning and subject matter expertise in the solving of economics problems by naïve and novice individuals. *Cognition and Instruction*, 3(3), 269–302.
[35] Polya, G. (1945). *How to solve it*. Princeton University Press.
[36] A variable is included in a diagram if knowing its value influences predictions of another variable. There need not be a causal influence.
[37] Fischhoff, B., Bruine de Bruin, W., Guvenc, U., Caruso, D., & Brilliant, L. (2006). Analyzing disaster risks and plans: An avian flu example. *Journal of Risk and Uncertainty*, 33(1), 133–151.
[38] Such formal models are a foundational element for the change strategy proposed in Chapter 7.

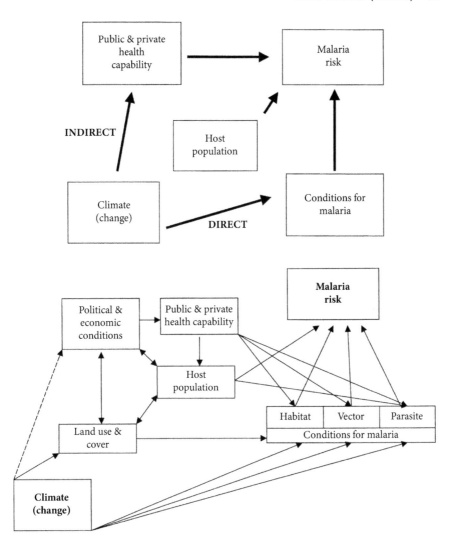

Figure 5.2 Formal models of the impact of climate change on malaria risk

Source: Fischhoff, B., Fischhoff, I., Casman, E., & Dowlatabadi, H. (2002). Integrated assessment of malaria risk. In E. Casman & H. Dowlatabadi (Eds.), *Contextual determinants of malaria* (pp. 331–348). Resources for the Future.

preferencing readily quantified factors (e.g., money). It allows experts to consider topics where they wished that they had numbers.[39] It avoids tests of mental arithmetic, asking nonexperts to intuit the results of calculations, in situations where experts would not trust their own intuitions.

Mental models research addresses face validity by beginning with open-ended interviews, structured around the formal model. These interviews first ask people about the domain in general ("tell me what you have heard about

---

[39] The next section discusses one way to get missing numbers.

the risk of malaria"), then proceed to more specific questions ("How do you think health systems affect malaria risk?"), and increasingly specific ones ("How do you think climate change affects malaria risk?"). The opening questions are meant to avoid missing factors in lay mental models that experts have neglected. The final questions are meant to avoid missing factors that got lost in the flow of the interview. Interviewers ask people to elaborate on whatever they say, to be sure that they have been understood and maintain a collaborative relationship.

After transcription, the interviews are coded into the formal model. The clarity of its elements typically allows *reliable* coding, in the sense that coders agree on which model element corresponds to each interview statement, as well as when none do. Where there is a mismatch between the world of the experts (in the model) and the world of the interview, provisional elements are added. Further research can determine whether these are factors that experts have missed or factors that people have imagined.

Whereas previous mental model studies looked at domains defined by experts, these studies look at domains jointly defined by experts and decision makers. Thus, rather than using a formal model that captures disciplinary knowledge (e.g., syllogisms, macroeconomics), these studies use formal models compiled from multiple disciplines.

Many qualitative researchers use methodologies like *grounded theory*, whereby transcripts are analyzed in terms of *emergent properties*, as discerned by researchers immersed in them.[40] In contrast, the mental model approach uses a predetermined coding template, the computable expert model. That strategy sacrifices some richness, in return for more reliable coding and a focus on decision-relevant factors in terms that experts can understand and inform. The coding preserves participants' words, allowing locally emergent properties regarding how people talk about specific issues.[41]

What Do Experts Believe?

Slow science also applies to characterizing the expert knowledge that nonexperts might want, or be expected, to know. Every discipline has its conventions for summarizing its state of knowledge. For efficient communication within a discipline, those summaries naturally omit boundary details that are common knowledge. As a result, they omit limits that people outside the

---

[40] Glaser, B. G. (2001). *The grounded theory perspective I: Conceptualization contrasted with description.* Sociology Press.
[41] As rich as they are, grounded theory studies lack the richness of ethnography, which interprets words in the context of individual and group behavior, cultural and religious artifacts, etc. Thus, they represent a compromise of one sort, just as mental models research represents a compromise of another, from the standardization of structured experiments.

discipline need to know. These limits may also fade from disciplinary consciousness, becoming *normalized pathologies*—limitations that are no longer considered.

Box 5.2 shows a general scheme for characterizing a discipline's state of knowledge, in decision-relevant terms.[42] NUSAP (Numeral Unit Spread Assessment Pedigree) is a vector representation that captures, in turn, a discipline's notational norms (N, U), procedural conventions (S, A), and maturity (P). These are elaborated in terms of the discipline's standards for collecting and analyzing evidence, and institutional norms for evaluating their rigor and value. Higher grades are aspirational, reflecting a discipline's self-discipline, rather than inherent properties of its phenomena.

Box 5.2 NUSAP Characterization of the Pedigree of Statistical Evidence

Grade	Definitions & standards	Data-collection & analysis	Institutional culture	Review
4	Negotiation	Task-force	Dialogue	External
3	Science	Direct survey	Accommodation	Independent
2	Convenience	Indirect survey	Obedience	Regular
1	Symbolism	Educated guess	Evasion	Occasional
0	Inertia	Fiat	No contact	None
0	Unknown	Unknown	Unknown	Unknown

Source: Funtowicz, S. O., & Ravetz, J. R. (1990). *Uncertainty and quality in science for policy*. Kluwer.

Psychology's vigorous response to the reproducibility crisis[43] can be seen as one discipline's reflection on its Pedigree (P). With respect to Definitions and Standards, researchers are increasingly expected to preregister their analyses (science), rather than exploring data and reporting only the most interesting (or confirmatory) results (convenience). That practice reduces the temptation to leave uninteresting results in the "file drawer," thereby increasing the risk that published results are statistically significant by chance. With respect to Data-collection and Analysis, multisite replications (task-force) are increasingly common. With respect to Institutional culture, there are more frank discussions of practices (dialogue), including bullying of and by

---

[42] Funtowicz, S. O., & Ravetz, J. R. (1990). *Uncertainty and quality in science for policy*. Kluwer. For additional applications see van der Sluijs, J. P., Cray, M., Funtowicz, S., Kloprogge, P., Ravetz, J. R., & Risbey, J. (2005). Combining quantitative and qualitative measures of uncertainty in model-based environmental assessment: The NUSAP system. *Risk Analysis*, 25(2), 481–492.

[43] Open Science Collaboration (2015). Estimating the reproducibility of psychological science. *Science*, 349(6251), Article aac4716.

researchers whose work has been criticized. With respect to Review, systematic meta-analyses of all studies are increasingly common (external), rather than summarizing the evidence that authors find most relevant (occasional).

Meta-analysis emerged from the realization that tallying studies with and without an effect gives equal weight to good and bad ones.[44] A straightforward first step is to weight studies by their sample size.[45] A more demanding second step is to weight studies by the quality of their evidence (as well as its quantity). In medicine, the CONSORT (Consolidated Standards of Reporting Trials) criteria provide consensual rules for characterizing study design and results in comparable terms that capture the quality of the evidence.[46] Steps 1–4 in Box 5.3 apply these criteria to characterizing medical clinical trials. Step 5 applies the Assessment element of NUSAP.

Box 5.3 A Protocol of Summarizing Scientific Uncertainty, Illustrated with Medical Clinical Trials

Step 1	Identify key outcomes for decision makers (e.g., stroke) and how to measure them (e.g., annual probability)
Step 2	Summarize variability
Step 3	Summarize internal validity
Selection bias	Do the initial groups differ from randomly assigned ones? Were the groups drawn from same population, over the same time periods, and with the same inclusion and exclusion criteria?
Attrition bias	Do the final groups differ from the initial ones? Did the groups differ as a result of participants dropping out (e.g., because the treatment did not seem to be working or their lives were too disorderly to continue) or being excluded from analyses (e.g., for incomplete data or seemingly anomalous responses)?
Administration	Was the study conducted as intended? Were instructions followed in administering the treatment and analyzing the results?
Performance bias	Does the manipulation have unintended effects? Were participants affected by knowing that they were in the study (or in a study), perhaps trying to satisfy researchers' (real or perceived) expectations?

---

[44] Historically, it started in psychology, then migrated to medicine.

[45] A recent review of prejudice reduction studies found that larger samples tended to have smaller effects, suggesting that smaller studies tended to reflect chance results. Paluck, E. L., Porat, R., Clark, S. S., & Green, D. P. (2021). Prejudice reduction: Progress and challenges. *Annual Review of Psychology*, 72, 533–560.

[46] Butcher, N. J., Monsour, A., Mew, E. J., Chan, A. W., Moher, D., Mayo-Wilson, E., Terwee, C. B., Chee-A-Tow, A., Baba, A., Gavin, F., Grimshaw, J. M., Kelly, L. E., Saeed, L., Thabane, L., Askie, L., Smith, M., Farid-Kapadia, M., Williamson, P. R., Szatmari, P., ... Offringa, M. (2022). Guidelines for reporting outcomes in trial reports: The CONSORT-Outcomes 2022 extension. *JAMA*, 328(22), 2252–2264.

Step 4	Summarize external validity
Population bias	Do treatment groups differ from the general population? Might they be relatively sensitive to positive effects or to unintended side effects?
Intervention bias	Are treatments administered differently in different conditions? Might they be applied less consistently, intensively, or obviously?
Control group bias	Do untreated groups differ in other ways? Might they receive more (or less) of other treatments with more (or less) supervision?
Scenario bias	Do other conditions differ from those of the study? Might other factors diminish (or enhance) the treatment's effect? Might the world have changed?
Step 5	Summarize the strength of the basic science
Directness	How well do a field's measures capture key outcomes? The strongest sciences measure outcomes directly rather than relying on proxy measures (e.g., biomarkers that appear related to health states)
Empirical basis	How strong are the best available estimates? The strongest sciences base their theories on large, well-controlled experiments rather than on data sets that are small or collected under variable conditions (e.g., dose–response relationships derived from epidemiological data)
Methodological rigor	How strong are the best methods? The strongest sciences have methods with well-understood strengths and weaknesses, and extensive experience in their application
Validation	How well are theoretical results confirmed? The strongest sciences have foundations (theories, hypotheses, relationships) that are strongly confirmed by evidence from multiple independent sources
Step 6	Summarize uncertainty (e.g., 95 percent credible interval) Statements of the form, "Considering the variability of the evidence (Step 2) and my assessments of the internal validity of the studies that collected it (Step 3), their relevance to the decision-making domain (Step 4), and the strength of the underlying science (Step 5), I am 95 percent certain that the true value of the critical outcome (Step 1) is between Y and Z."

Steps 3 and 4 are based on CONSORT criteria for evaluating medical clinical trials. Step 5 is based on the NUSAP criteria for evaluating the strength of sciences.

Source: Fischhoff, B., & Davis, A. L. (2014). Communicating scientific uncertainty. *Proceedings of the National Academy of Sciences, 111*(Suppl. 4), 13664–13671.

These procedures characterize research within the bounds of a discipline's universe of discourse; formal models, as in Box 5.3, circumscribe those bounds. They do not say what to do about factors that lie outside them, including factors that nonexperts raise in mental model interviews. When experts acknowledge the potential relevance of those factors, *expert elicitation* offers a way to address them.[47] As exemplified in Box 5.3, it asks experts for their professional judgment regarding the impact of those factors, expressed as probability distributions over valued outcomes.

As described in Chapter 2, these extended interviews include practice exercises, familiarizing experts with the response mode, to increase its face validity. Because the actual state of the world is not known, these judgments cannot be evaluated in terms of accuracy. In philosophy of science terms, rather than looking at the *correspondence* between these judgments and the world, elicitors evaluate them by their *coherence*, or internal consistency, a form of construct validity. If experts express the same opinion however a question is posed, then they are held to have coherent mental models.[48]

As an example, in Fall 2005, as a highly uncertain threat of avian flu (H5N1) loomed, we asked a group of public health experts to complete a survey designed to characterize the distribution of opinions prior to a meeting. The first survey question asked, "What is the probability that H5N1 or a similar virus will become an efficient human-to-human transmitter (capable of being propagated through at least two epidemiological generations of affected humans) sometime during the next three years?" The twenty-third, and last, question asked how long it would be before that event had a 10 percent, 50 percent, and 90 percent chance of happening. The two judgments were, by and large, internally consistent. The many intervening questions, with numerical answers, were meant to reduce the chance that experts would infer the second answer from the first.[49]

The median probability judgment for efficient human-to-human transmission was 10 percent. Three years later, that had not happened. Giving a low probability to a nonevent suggests that these judgments were accurate as well as consistent. However, determining how well experts can assess probabilities requires enough predictions to assess their *calibration*—that is, whether XX percent of events assigned a probability of XX percent occur. Meteorologists' probability of precipitation forecasts are well calibrated. It rains about 10 percent of the time that they assign a 10 percent probability.[50] They have excellent conditions for learning: large amounts of prompt, unambiguous feedback, with incentives for candor (e.g., avoiding "umbrella

---

[47] Morgan, M. G., Fischhoff, B., Bostrom, A., & Atman, C. (2001). *Risk communication: A mental models approach.* Cambridge University Press.
[48] Bruine de Bruin, W., Fischhoff, B., Brilliant, L., & Caruso, D. (2006). Expert judgments of pandemic influenza. *Global Public Health, 1*(2), 178–193.
[49] Another consistency check involved answers to three questions: the expected number of people infected, the expected number of deaths, and the expected case-fatality rate. Here, too, the answers were relatively consistent, with the latter answer being alarmingly high (15 percent).
[50] Murphy, A. H., & Winkler, R. L. (1977). Can weather forecasters formulate reliable probability forecasts of precipitation and temperature? *National Weather Digest, 2*(2), 2–9.

bias," overstating the probability of rain so that people are not caught without one). Not all experts are so lucky, including those making fateful long-range predictions, as with climate change. Using their judgments wisely requires the fuller picture of slow science like that in Boxes 5.1, and Figures 5.1 and 5.2.

Conclusions

Many disciplines rely on evidence subject to statistical analysis. To that end, they must standardize their measurement. Over time, details lost in that process can be lost to the discipline. Slow science can provide a bulwark against such creeping insularity. As illustrated here with the study of beliefs, slow science values the path to standardization as well as its goals. By observing how conventional measures evolve, it can situate them in the universe of possible measures. By juxtaposing the worlds of experts and nonexperts, it can reveal their respective conventions. By delineating disciplinary boundaries, it can bound claims for existing results and identify terrain for future exploration. Creating a roadmap in that terrain depends on researchers' insight.

Chapter 6
Slow Science (Preferences)

Asking people what matters to them is a staple of management science. Those questions may test theoretical constructs or address practical problems. In common with much other behavioral research, studies typically assume that "if we've got questions, they've got answers." And, as with beliefs (Chapter 5), a rush to get those answers can lead to poor ones, while missing valuable scenery along the way. As with beliefs, slow science for preferences can produce better questions and answers. Realistically, people cannot know what they want for every choice that life or researchers send their way.

Ostensibly Simple Tasks

Clyde Coombs,[1] one of the founders of decision science, addressed these bounds with his landmark book, *A Theory of Data*.[2] He argued that, for any set of options, people might know which three options are best or worst. They might know which are acceptable or unacceptable. They might be able to rank some, all, or none of the options. Coombs showed how to extract values from answers to simple comparison questions, with the one strong assumption that how much people value an option depends on how close it is to their ideal.[3]

Coombs's elegant exposition shows how to test the assumption of single-peaked preference functions. It also shows the price paid with any structured elicitation method. Here, one price is having to make many paired comparisons. The more judgments people make, the less time and energy is available for each one. People with well-articulated preferences may be able to speed through such tasks. People without preferences might devise a formulaic response strategy, just to get through the task, thereby appearing to have preferences when they have none.[4]

---

[1] Tversky, A. (1992). *Clyde Hamilton Coombs (1912–1988)*. National Academy of Sciences. https://www.nasonline.org/wp-content/uploads/2024/06/coombs-clyde-h.pdf.

[2] Coombs, C. H. (1964). *A theory of data*. Wiley.

[3] An archetypal example was preferences for shades of gray, reflecting how close they were to the ideal gray.

[4] The exercise would be an example of *reactive measurement* if their actual preferences came to follow their expressed ones, as discussed later in the chapter.

People can often find some way to answer just about any question that is put to them.[5] Within the self-contained world of a structured procedure, it is hard to tell if they are expressing deeply held preferences or ones that they improvised in order to seem informed, help the researcher, or get through the task. As with studying beliefs, a discipline can pursue slow science and develop tasks in collaboration with the people being studied. As with beliefs, that investment may reveal new research directions, as well as improve understanding of familiar ones. As elsewhere, the illustrations that follow are from decision science, in cases where applications spurred disciplinary bonding.

Unlike research on beliefs, which considers both accuracy (correspondence) and consistency (coherence),[6] for preferences, decision science considers only the latter. In keeping with other fields grounded in rational actor models (e.g., economics), it treats people as sovereign to their preferences. If they know what they want, then valid measurement should reveal consistent preferences, however questions are posed and answers are expressed. If not, then valid measurement should reveal inconsistency.[7]

As with beliefs, the primary test of preference measurement is face validity. Do tasks mean the same thing to the scientists studying them and the people performing them? Without that shared understanding, one cannot tell whether consistency reflects successful measurement of coherent preferences or superficial responses, improvised to complete a task. Nor can one tell whether inconsistent preferences mean that people do not know what they want, or that the researchers failed to ask appropriate questions.[8] As with beliefs, measurement and theory inform one another. The next sections illustrate that linked growth, prompted by decisions that straddled disciplines.

What Are We Asking: The Face Validity of Questions

Defining Risks

The top sections of Box 6.1 show factors affecting the probability of traffic accidents. The bottom section shows possible measures of their severity. People's willingness to take those risks would depend on how large they seem—a question of beliefs—and how bad they seem—a question of preferences.

---

[5] The exceptions can be revealing, as in the examples discussed later in the chapter.
[6] See Chapter 5.
[7] From standardization of wording to standardization of meaning. Gobo, G., & Mauceri, S. (2014). *Constructing survey data: An interactional approach*. SAGE Publications.
[8] For example, people may have different time–money trade-offs for large and small items. Perhaps they are wasting time by not shopping around for savings on large one-time purchases, hence not acting on their preferences. Perhaps they have more confidence in their ability to shop efficiently for groceries.

Those preferences would be reflected in decisions like buying a safer car, wearing a seatbelt, forgoing a trip, or handing the keys to someone else. In order to ask people about those preferences, researchers need to specify which risks they have in mind. Without those details, people will not know which preferences to give and researchers will not know which were given. As with beliefs, casual respondents may provide gist responses to what they see as gist questions. Thoughtful respondents may infer missing details. The former responses might predict how much attention people pay to the issue. The latter might predict what happens when they do pay attention.

Providing these details is an essential burden for researchers studying driving (or drinking and driving). It can be an overwhelming burden for researchers studying multiple risks, each with its own details. In a seminal article on risk management, Starr argued that society sought consistent trade-offs between risks and benefits, which it defined similarly in all domains.[9] He posited that society defines "risk" as "fatalities per person/hour of exposure" and benefit as "average annual benefit per person involved (dollars)." He argued, further, that US society had achieved such consistency that current trade-offs reflected society's preferences. As depicted in Figure 6.1, that means a *revealed preference* for accepting risks proportionate to the cube of the benefits, while accepting an order of magnitude lower risks for involuntary than for voluntary sources of risk.

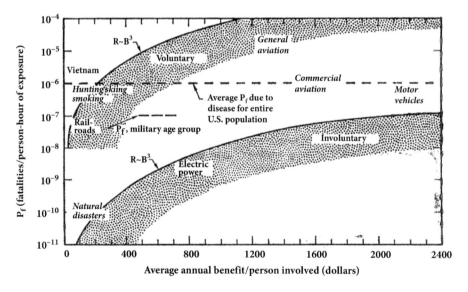

Figure 6.1 Comparing estimates of aggregate risks and benefits for select activities and technologies

Source: Starr, C. (1969). Social benefit vs. technological risk. *Science, 165*(3899), 1232–1238.

---

[9] Starr, C. (1969). Social benefit vs. technological risk. *Science, 165*(3899), 1232–1238.

The double standard for voluntariness was meant to be controversial, reflecting what Starr saw as a misguided societal preference, forgoing benefits of involuntary technologies by demanding too much risk reduction. His measures of risk and benefit were, however, not meant to be as controversial as they turned out to be, as they followed conventions of the disciplines from which he drew them. All three controversies illustrate the challenges and opportunities in creating the shared definitions needed for assessing preferences.[10]

With respect to benefits, economists have long debated how to aggregate them over time and over people. Starr chose one common convention: mean direct expenditures per person involved. However, some economists follow other conventions. The picture might look different if people's preferences were assumed to reflect the distribution of benefits over people or over time, and if risks were plotted as a function of those measures of benefit.

With respect to risks, too, there are different disciplinary conventions. Starr followed one convention in considering just fatalities, as though people's preferences ignore morbidity, well-being, and realizing human potential. He measured fatalities in lives lost, as though people do not consider life-years lost, which give extra weight to risks to younger people who have more years to lose (e.g., accidents vs. chronic diseases). He did not follow healthcare analysts' convention of considering the quality of lives, or life-years, lost, assuming that people do not discount losses to people with disabilities.

If one assumes that political and market processes give people the trade-offs that they prefer, then the measures that produce the most orderly relationship are, arguably, the ones that people consider.[11] That would not be the case if one believes that markets and politics are rigged, such that some activities and technologies get away with much more risk than others with the same benefits.

William Lowrance joined the controversy over a double standard for voluntariness by examining the ethical implications of that principle.[12] He did the same for other possible principles, such as how new the risks are, how well they are known (to science and to those exposed), how many people are affected in an incident, and how immediately negative consequences occur. Other authors proposed many other principles. If people got their preferred trade-offs, then the clearest picture would reveal which one was most important.

The proliferation of principles made it impractical to study them all. Fortunately, many of them are correlated. Voluntary risks tend to be controllable

---

[10] This passage uses Starr's "Social benefit vs. technological risk" (Figure 6.1) to illuminate the need for clear, consensual definitions in preference studies. It is not a critique of that article, which states its assumptions and explains why they were made, creating a platform for alternative ones.
[11] Also assuming the accuracy of their perceptions.
[12] Lowrance, W.W. (1973). *Of acceptable risk: Science and the determinants of safety*. William Kaufmann.

and to affect few people when things go bad. Old risks tend to be better known to science and to those exposed. Thus, considering voluntary risks more acceptable also means finding controllable risks more acceptable. As part of a study asking whether people's expressed preferences matched those that Figure 6.1 claimed to reveal, we had people rate thirty *hazards* (sources of risk) on nine principles. Factor analysis found two dimensions underlying the nine principles, as shown in Figure 6.2. One reflected, roughly, how well it was known, the other how much dread it evoked.[13] Given these correlations, if Starr's figure does reveal American society's preferences, there is no way of knowing whether voluntariness, controllability, or any other correlated principle drives the double standard.[14]

Starr's bold proposal gradually engaged other disciplines, beginning a slow science process that created the field of risk analysis. The Society for Risk Analysis (SRA), founded in 1981, is unusual in having both researcher and practitioner members, from diverse disciplines and application areas.[15] As a decision science, shared (and debated) analyses form the platform for its work. The Society has been a home for empirical studies on revealed and expressed preferences elaborating topics like those in Figures 6.1 and 6.2. It has also been a home for theoretical and ethical discussions over what society's preferences should be, informed by moral philosophy (e.g., Lowrance) as well as economics (conditions for growth, innovation), political science (regulatory processes), and sociology (information sharing).

The gradual accretion of perspectives is a natural process for a self-critical field. The United Nations Human Development Index is an example of a slow science approach to consolidating such healthily unmanaged growth. Its creators have sought insight from diverse disciplines in defining measures that could inform decision makers with diverse preferences, while being practical enough to apply in a wide range of settings. Recognizing that diversity of preferences, it offers calculations of national averages, equity-adjusted national averages, and gender-adjusted national averages, explicating each measure's rationale and implications.[16]

---

[13] Fischhoff, B., Slovic, P., Lichtenstein, S., Read, S., & Combs, B. (1978). How safe is safe enough? A study of attitudes towards technological risks and benefits. *Policy Sciences*, 9(2), 127–152.

[14] Other parts of that study found that people did not believe that US society produced the risk–benefit trade-offs that they wanted. Forty years later, that result was substantially replicated in: Glassman-Fox, K. T., & Weber, E. U. (2016). What makes risk acceptable? Revisiting the 1978 psychological dimensions of perceptions of technological risks. *Journal of Mathematical Psychology*, 75, 157–169. The risk-space part of the study has been replicated many times, using different hazards, elicitation procedures, principles, and statistical techniques. To a first approximation, the same two factors emerge.

[15] It has also found its size limited by groups leaving to become groups within their home discipline, enriching that discipline, while losing touch with the intellectually diverse SRA community.

[16] Much as with the committee on equitable allocation of vaccine.

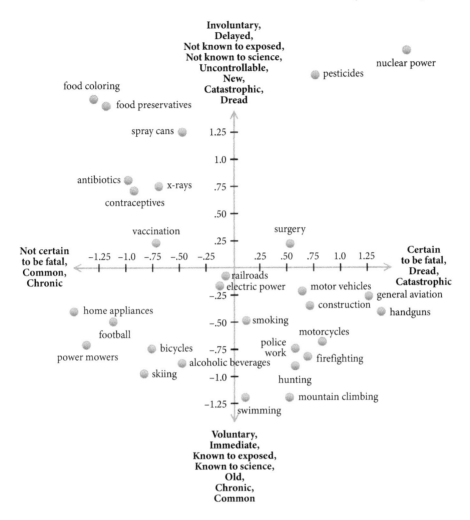

Figure 6.2 A two-factor space defined by qualitative aspects of risks
Source: Fischhoff, B., & Kadvany, J. (2011). *Risk: A very short introduction*. Oxford University Press.

Defining Benefits

Revealed preference analyses are a natural starting point when observations of actual behavior are available, if analysts can confidently deduce what they mean. Expressed (or stated) preference studies are needed when interpretable observations are absent. The need for clear, shared definitions of benefits is seen in *contingent valuation* studies, which try to monetize non-market goods, to give them standing in a world that runs on money.[17] The thousands of such studies ask people questions like, "How much would you

---

[17] As real as they might be for the individuals experiencing them, such effects are often called "intangible" by economists, reflecting the clarity of the disciplinary boundaries of economics. Mitchell, R.C., &

be willing to pay to preserve clear skies over the Grand Canyon?" or "How much would you need to feel compensated for the damage done by the Exxon Valdez spill?" Government officials forced to use cost–benefit analysis need answers to the first question to justify the costs of reducing atmospheric haze. Courts needed answers to the second question in order to include the *existence value* of a more pristine Prince William Sound in the damage settlement.

Such studies often have thoughtful displays of the good being evaluated (e.g., pictures of the Grand Canyon with degrees of haze). Conveying the rest of the preference question is another matter. People are asked to imagine a "contingent" market in which they could secure the (intangible) good. However, markets are complex social institutions. If people are to take the question as literally as researchers will take their answer, they need many, typically missing, details. Who guarantees the hypothetical contract, delivering the good and securing the payment? What else will they be expected to pay for, if clean air and water are funded this way? Who else is being asked to contribute? Are people answering for themselves or their household? If the latter, how should they weigh any perceived differences of opinion?

In slow science mode, researchers have a duty to ensure that people are expressing the preferences that they want to elicit. Fulfilling that duty also provides an opportunity to learn what issues are on people's minds, how they think about them, and what issues they might welcome considering, if presented clearly and respectfully. For example, what guarantees do they assume implicitly, and need to hear explicitly, when evaluating unfamiliar transactions, as posed by researchers, firms, government entities, or unknown others? What features of public goods (e.g., clean air) determine the legitimacy of securing them through private payments? What features do people notice in a description? Which features do they miss, but wish that they had noticed?

A long-standing puzzle in stated preference studies is *scope insensitivity*: people's seeming willingness to pay the same amount of money for very different amounts of a good. In a seminal study, Kahneman and Knetsch found that people were willing to pay the same amount to preserve fishing in one, five, or all the lakes in Ontario.[18] How one interprets that result depends on how one believes people interpreted the question. At one extreme, they might have given a gist response to a gist question, asking about a vaguely described

---

Carson, R.T. (1989). *Using Surveys to Value Public Goods: The Contingent Valuation Method* (1st ed.). RFF Press.

[18] Kahneman, D., & Knetsch, J. L. (1992). Valuing public goods: The purchase of moral satisfaction. *Journal of Environmental Economics and Management*, 22(1), 57–70.

transaction. In that frame of mind, they might have barely thought about the fish, the lakes, or Ontario, much less the quantities. At the other extreme, people might have felt entrusted with providing public input on an important environmental policy. In that frame of mind, they might have diligently tried to fill in the missing details. That inferential process would lead to similar values for the three scopes (one, five, or all the lakes) if people reasoned that, "If they're asking me about one lake, they must be asking other people about the other lakes. I'll state the amount that I am willing, and able, to spend on protecting Ontario fishing." They might go on to think, "I wonder if this is my share of all environmental protection, and other people are being asked about boreal forests. In that case, I am willing, and able, to pay much more for the lake(s)."

For a time in the 1980s and 1990s, Lita Furby and I were enlisted in evaluating and designing contingent valuation studies, beginning with one on the value of clear air.[19] In a slow science spirit, which I learned from Lita, we began with open-ended interviews, asking people to think aloud as they worked their way through contingent valuation surveys. The result was the framework for specifying transactions given in Box 6.1. It includes task features that we heard in the interviews or found in at least one survey, whose researchers felt that it needed saying. Although the interviews focused on preferences for atmospheric visibility, we included features that people might want to know about the good, the payment, and the social context of any proposed transaction, before signing a study's implicit contract. The "social context" takes seriously the "contingent market" metaphor, recognizing that transactions involve relationships among the parties, enforcement mechanisms, social norms, externalities, and potential precedents, among other things.

The framework could be used formatively to draft surveys and structure pretest interviews. It could be used descriptively to compare preferences elicited by studies that specify features differently—or omit them. That knowledge can help researchers in communicating their tasks and in conducting manipulation checks and construct validity tests of their success. It can also reveal how people orient themselves in the complex world where the fate of non-market goods is decided.

Lita and I argued that transactions are incompletely specified without those details, whose omission might itself send a message (e.g., "never mind any precedent setting"). For a while, the Environmental Protection Agency

---

[19] The invitations included ones from the Environmental Protection Agency, which needed the numbers for regulatory analyses; the Department of Justice, which needed them for the Exxon Valdez damage assessment; and the Electric Power Research Institute, whose member firms had to implement regulatory requirements and pay damage assessments.

distributed our framework as optional guidance for designing contingent valuation studies. For researchers trying to monetize non-market goods, such a framework can be a mixed blessing. On the one hand, it can make estimates more defensible, by improving their completeness and comparability. On the other hand, it can increase the set of features that must be communicated and defended. Manipulation checks can reveal problems, by showing heterogeneous interpretations, or solutions, when interpretations are systematically related to preferences, reflecting construct validity.[20]

The article that first explicated the framework has been fairly widely cited (GS=376),[21] as have two related general statements of its philosophy (GS=653,857).[22] It is hard to assess its impact on practice, when applications are proprietary or reported in the gray literature of technical reports. It is my sense that the period, in the 1980s and 1990s, when environmental economists actively engaged psychologists, our work enhanced their methods. Research guidelines now address issues that worry psychologists,[23] despite (or perhaps because of) the contentious interactions at the time.[24] For reasons pondered below, economists' concerns have had less influence on psychological preference studies, where well-specified transactions regarding real-world goods are rare.

What Are They Telling Us? The Face Validity of Answers

The value measure component in Box 6.1 lists issues that thoughtful respondents might want to consider. For example, they might be willing and able to pay more in time or in money. If money, the payment vehicle might affect how much they can spend (sales tax vs. income tax), how much it seems right to spend (entry fee vs. annual donation), and whether they are willing to spend at all ("voluntary, yes; taxes, no"). Preferences on each measure may be affected by different transient states (e.g., energy level, time pressure, cash flow).

---

[20] Box 6.1 comes from an article applying the framework to studies where incoherent preferences could be traced to people seeing differences between tasks that researchers saw as the same.

[21] Fischhoff, B., & Furby, L. (1988). Measuring values: A conceptual framework for interpreting transactions with special reference to contingent valuation of visibility. *Journal of Risk and Uncertainty*, 1(2), 147–184.

[22] Fischhoff, B., Slovic, P., & Lichtenstein, S. (1980). Knowing what you want: Measuring labile values. In T. Wallsten (Ed.), *Cognitive processes in choice and decision behavior* (pp. 117–141). Erlbaum; B. Fischhoff (1991). Value elicitation: Is there anything in there? *American Psychologist*, 46(8), 835–847.

[23] Hoyoa, D. (2010). The state of the art of environmental evaluation with discrete choice experiments. *Ecological Economics*, 69(8), 1595–1603.

[24] As part of the Department of Justice's team in the Exxon Valdez damage settlement suit, I was called "the enemy" for doubting the estimates, while also believing that they understated the *intangible* (i.e., nonmonetized) damage.

Box 6.1 Features Defining the Good, Value Measure, and Social Context of Transactions

The good
 (e.g., visibility)
  Substantive definition
   Attribute(s)
    Haze intensity
    Visual range
    Plume (color)
    Light extinction
   Context
    Natural or built
    Judged uniqueness
    Associated activities (e.g., hiking, viewing, playing)
    Significance (e.g., religious, cultural, historical)
   Source of change
    Predominantly natural (e.g., vegetation, forest fires, dust storms, humidity)
    Predominantly human (e.g., power plant, other factories, field burning, slash burning, motor vehicles)
  Formal definition
   Reference and target levels
    Magnitude and direction of change
    Statistical summary
    Representation (mode, richness, organization)
   Extent of change
    Geographical
    Temporal (existence, direct enjoyment)
    Timing of change
    Certainty of provision

The value measure
 (e.g., money, time, discomfort, effort)
  Substantive definition
   Attribute(s)
    Leisure, work (for time)
    Physical, emotional (for discomfort)

   Context
    Electric bill, sales tax, income tax, park entry fee, environmental fund (for money)
    When convenient, when demanded (for time)
    When rested, when exhausted (for effort)
   Constituency
  Formal definition
   Reference and target levels
    Magnitude and direction of change
    Statistical summary
    Elicitation (response mode, response format, cues, feedback)
   Extent
   Frequency
   Duration
   Timing of payment
   Certainty of payment

The social context
  Other people involved
   Provider of the good
   Others present
  Resolution mechanism
   Determining parties
   Iterations
   Constraints
  Other stakes
   Externalities
   Precedents
   Legitimacy of process

Source: Fischhoff, B., & Furby, L. (1988). Measuring values: A conceptual framework for interpreting transactions with special reference to contingent valuation of visibility. *Journal of Risk and Uncertainty*, 1(2), 147–184.

People with fully articulated preferences might need to guess at missing features. People who are not sure what they want might look for cues in the features that are provided. Some studies use "bidding games," asking questions like, "Would you pay $1, $2, $3, …?" until people say "no," and then asking if they would pay $0.50 less. People might reasonably infer that the expected answer is in the single-digit dollar range. They might make other inferences if the opening bid were $10, with similar increments. The signaling properties of numerical anchors have long been studied by psychophysicists for artificial tasks and used by marketers for real ones.[25]

One strategy for avoiding numerical artifacts is to elicit ordinal judgments, like those explicated by Coombs. To that end, *discrete choice* methods ask people to compare options described in terms of a set (or vector) of common features.[26] These methods found their way from psychology, through marketing, to environmental economics. An early application to moose hunting in west central Alberta had as its attributes: moose population, hunter congestion, hunter access, forestry activity, road quality, and distance to site.[27] Each attribute had either two or four levels. People expressed preferences for sixteen pairs of options, selected to represent the much larger universe of possibilities. Analytical methods derived implicit trade-offs among the attributes. Some studies add a monetary attribute (e.g., hunting license fees) as a way to monetize other attributes.[28]

Discrete choice methods are used extensively in healthcare policy analysis. Treatment decisions may pose difficult tradeoffs among outcomes. For example, a cancer treatment may offer some chance of increased life expectancy, greater life quality, and reduced worry, in return for some certainty of short-term suffering and some probability of long-term side effects. Healthcare policies often seek public guidance on these tradeoffs, when recommending procedures and allocating resources.

Figure 6.3 shows a discrete choice task from a pioneering study.[29] At the time, lung cancer patients were more likely to be alive in the short run with radiation therapy, but more likely to be alive in the long run with surgery. The two survival curves crossed at about two years (at about 35 percent). The convention was to recommend surgery, implying that each year was equally valuable. The authors argued, though, that some patients might value the near years more (e.g., to vest in a pension plan or see a first grandchild).[30]

Fearing perhaps that people could not, or would not, tell them which treatment scenario they preferred, if asked directly, the authors opted for the

---

[25] See Chapter 3. Poulton, E. C. (1989). *Bias in quantifying judgments*. Lawrence Erlbaum; Poulton, E. C. (1994). *Behavioral decision making*. Lawrence Erlbaum.
[26] Carson, R. T., & Mikołaj Czajkowski, M. (2014). The discrete choice experiment approach to environmental contingent valuation. In S. Hess & A. Daly (Eds.), *Handbook of choice modelling* (pp. 202–235). Edward Elgar.
[27] Boxall, P. C., Adamowicz, W. L., Swait, J., Williams, M., & Louviere, J. (1996). A comparison of stated preference methods for environmental valuation. *Ecological Economics, 18*(3), 243–253.
[28] See preference reversal studies in Chapter 1.
[29] McNeil, B. J., Weichselbaum, M. D., & Pauker, S. G. (1978). Fallacy of the five-year survival rate in lung cancer. *New England Journal of Medicine, 299*(25), 1397–1401.
[30] Research and clinical experience found similar quality of life with both treatments.

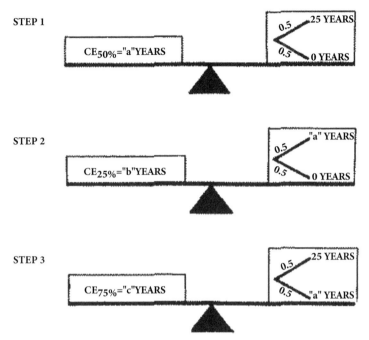

Determination of certainty equivalents (time in years) corresponding to three utility values: 25%, 50%, and 75%. In each step, the patient was asked to assess the survival time in years for which the patient was indifferent (as represented in the balance between that time, for certain, on the left and the 50:50 gamble on the right. Patients whose certain survival times were less than the expected value of the gamble on the right were called "risk averse"; those whose certain survival times were equal to the gamble's expected value were called "risk neutral"; patients whose certain survival times greater than the gamble's expected value were called "risk seeking."

Figure 6.3 Certainty equivalent trade-offs for assessing health utility functions
Source: McNeil, B. J., Weichselbaum, M. D., & Pauker, S. G. (1978). Fallacy of the five-year survival rate in lung cancer. *New England Journal of Medicine, 299*(25), 1397–1401.

indirect question in Figure 6.4, imported from applied decision science.[31] Each of these *standard gambles* asks for the number of guaranteed life-years that is the *certainty equivalent* of a gamble with equal chances of dying immediately or living a fixed number of years. These preferences are used to create a *utility curve*, showing the relative value (utility) for each length of life. Combining individual patients' utility curves with their survival probabilities made it possible to calculate the expected utility of each treatment. Reinforcing the authors' motivating concern, lung cancer patients' utility curves varied, such that surgery had higher expected utility for some, radiation for others.

---

[31] Keeney, R. L., & Raiffa, H. (1976). *Decisions with multiple objectives: Preferences and value tradeoffs.* Cambridge University Press; Raiffa, H. (1968). *Decision analysis.* Addison-Wesley.

The elegance of the standard gamble, grounded in basic decision science, gives it scientific credibility. Its simplicity addresses pressure for shared decision making, combining individual patients' values with physicians' knowledge to identify treatment preferences. It has become a foundation for a vast array of patient decision aids. A recent review of 209 studies included aids for cardiovascular, cancer, mental health, and joint replacement surgery treatment decisions, among others.[32] It found that aids increased patients' knowledge and feeling of having an active role in decision making, with no effect on decision regret or physician consultation time. It also found that the interventions probably increased "informed value-congruent choices." As decision aid development has become a discipline, it has adopted its own conventions, including ones that might not find a home in decision science, such as using correlations between attitudes and behaviors as congruence criteria.[33]

Standard gambles are also used to assess public preferences, as inputs to healthcare resource allocation (or rationing) decisions. These studies might ask representative samples of people questions like whether they would prefer a 20 percent chance of the worst possible pain, "so severe that you could think of nothing else" or or a 100 percent chance of pain that was sometimes "distressing to you." One large study asking such questions derived a utility function that was relatively flat for low levels of pain and relatively steep for high levels, indicating that people were relatively insensitive to changes in low levels of pain and highly sensitive to changes in high levels.[34] Healthcare analysts combine these utilities with probabilities distributions of expected treatment outcomes (e.g., pain levels) to identify public policy preferences.

If We Have Questions, Do They Have Answers?

The goal of these studies is to capture preferences in terms precise enough to inform specific public or private decisions. The result has been tasks that pose trade-offs that are unfamiliar, however familiar their substance (pain,

---

[32] Stacey, D., Lewis, K. B., Smith, M., Carley, M., Volk, R., Douglas, E. E., Pacheco-Brousseau, L., Finderup, J., Gunderson, J., Barry, M. J., Bennett, C. L., Bravo, P., Steffensen, K., Gogovor, A., Graham, I. D., Kelly, S. E., Légaré, F., Sondergaard, H., Thomson, R., ... Trevena, L. (2024). Decision aids for people facing health treatment or screening decisions. *Cochrane Database of Systematic Reviews*, 1, Article CD001431, https://www.cochranelibrary.com/cdsr/doi/10.1002/14651858.CD001431.pub6/full (accessed August 16, 2024).

[33] Stacey et al., Decision aids for people facing health treatment.

[34] Dewitt, B., Fischhoff, B., Davis, A. L., Broomell, S. B., Roberts, M., Hanmer, J. (2019). Exclusion criteria as measurements II: Effects on utility curves. *Medical Decision Making*, 39(6), 704–716.

pollution). They might involve seemingly concrete settings (contingent valuation) or clearly abstract ones (discrete choice). Importance rating scales would require much less effort, but would also be much less informative. Indeed, from a decision science perspective, general importance ratings are meaningless. Money is important, but not when everything costs the same or sacred values are at stake.

As much as researchers might want these preferences, there is no guarantee that people can provide them. People who join studies often feel compelled to complete them. They have made a commitment. They don't want to disappoint the researcher. They don't want to feel or seem like they don't know or care about the topic. Classic studies found that people may give opinions on nonexistent issues. Saying "fifty" in the sense of "fifty-fifty" is an example of seeming compliance.[35]

Indeed, a striking result in contingent valuation and discrete choice studies is how often people give no answer or a seemingly meaningless or confused one. A review of contingent valuation studies found "protest response" rates of 2 percent to 43 percent, depending on how questions were posed.[36] A review of healthcare discrete choice studies found similar rates of responses that were disqualified because they failed "exclusion criteria," such as giving the same value to all health states, assigning greater utility to "dead" than to any living state, or finishing too quickly.[37]

As a result, after working hard to recruit representative samples, researchers may end up with unrepresentative ones after rejecting protest and excluded responses.[38] There are procedures for estimating the effect of exclusions on population utility functions.[39] However, these procedures do not correct for other, less obviously inappropriate preferences that might be lurking in a data set. Researchers' diligence in reporting these problems reflects the importance that they attach to the estimates. Nonetheless, their analyses do need the numbers, without which public preferences may be neglected.

---

[35] Bruine de Bruin, W., Fischhoff, B., Halpern-Felsher, B., & Millstein, S. (2000). Verbal and numerical expressions of probability: "It's a fifty-fifty chance." *Organizational Behavior and Human Decision Processes, 81*(1), 115–131.

[36] Meyerhoff J., & Liebe, U. (2010). Determinants of protest responses in environmental valuation: A meta-study. *Ecological Economics, 70*(2), 366–374.

[37] Engel, L., Bansback, N., Bryan, S., Doyle-Waters, M. M., Whitehurst, D. G. T. (2016). Exclusion criteria in national health state valuation studies: A systematic review. *Medical Decision Making, 36*(7), 798–810. Empirically, some of these violations tend to co-occur. For example, people who rate death as at least as good as full health also tend to say that they didn't understand the task. Eliminating people who fail one of these tests effectively eliminates people who fail the other.

[38] Unless they are distributed equally across population groups.

[39] Dewitt et al., Exclusion criteria as measurements II.

Might They Have Answers, If We Slowed Down?

Discrete choice studies are attractive because their utility functions can be used consistently and efficiently in many analyses. Those benefits may outweigh the threat to data quality posed by task difficulty. But that trade-off is less justified when the stakes rise on getting individual decisions right. The US Preventive Services Task Force periodically revises breast cancer screening guidelines in light of current evidence. After its previous revisions had evoked controversy, the Task Force sought input from women. Asked to design a discrete choice survey, we argued that the questions would be too hard for many women and were not needed. We proposed just asking women to choose among the four screening options (every one, two, or three years, or never), informed by estimates of three critical outcomes:[40] the rates of breast cancer deaths, false alarms, and unnecessary treatment (for cancers that might never have advanced). With a multidisciplinary slow science process, we created a survey with construct validity, such that women understood the risks and themselves well enough to provide coherent preferences.

In order to promote that understanding, the survey suggested possible perspectives. Decision analysts routinely do that for their clients, hoping to help them triangulate on the ones that suit them best. In this slow science view, preferences are viewed as *constructed* rather than reported, as though they were there for the asking, whatever question researchers present. When successful, no new perspective prompts people to think, "I wish that I had thought of that," indicating that the construction process is complete.

Such interactions are uncommon, even anathema, in much behavioral research. Its conventions proscribe helping people, lest researchers somehow influence the preferences that people form and share. Fear of such *reactive measurement* favors fast science, which assumes the face validity of questions and answers, hoping to observe natural responses to researchers' often unnatural tasks. Manipulation and construct validity checks, which show how well researchers' best efforts have fared, are also uncommon.

Decision science's apprenticeship includes lessons in the sometimes subtle cues that can inadvertently bias responses (e.g., context effects, nonverbal communication). It also includes practice in pretesting and revising draft instruments. The return on that investment includes being able to work with smaller samples, because measurement precision increases statistical power. At some point, though, researchers must stand back and let people grapple with their tasks.

---

[40] As identified by previous research.

They should be willing to take "no answer" for an answer. That can happen when people cannot make sense of a task, cannot sort out their feelings, or do not want to say anything. Medical decisions, for example, can pose more momentous choices than people can handle, however well they understand them (e.g., end-of-life decisions for themselves or a loved one). They may be of two minds, which they cannot reconcile.[41] They may struggle to bear full responsibility. Their heart and mind may disagree. They may not feel empowered to make the choice, even if asked.

It takes slow science to reveal and welcome such issues and then to live with the untidy preferences that may follow. The normative analyses of decision science can structure that search, focus it on decision-relevant issues, and determine satisficing results. One reward for embracing that complexity is reducing the risk of misinterpretations that are bad for science and for the people whose preferences are described. Another reward is developing more systematic accounts of where fast science tasks fall in the space of possible tasks (as in Box 6.1). A third is identifying novel fast science tasks for understanding that space (Figure 6.2). A fourth is improving the statistical power of those tasks through more precise measurement. A fifth is improving their representativeness by reducing protest and excluded responses. These benefits are less tangible than are those of fast science studies with statistical analyses of structured responses. Chapter 7 considers how to value them.

Conclusions

Preferences are central to social and behavioral science. The normative analyses of decision science set standards for defining the questions and answers. Its empirical methods provide ways of making them as clear and tractable as possible, and ways to evaluate their success. Untested assumptions about how people interpret the questions and answers in preference tasks can reduce the quality of research and interventions. The result can be stated preferences tasks that are too demanding, observed behaviors with too many possible interpretations to reveal preferences, and confusing gist responses with contractual ones. As with eliciting beliefs (Chapter 5), slow science can improve science and practice, while illuminating the richness of the human experience.

---

[41] Fischhoff, B., & Barnato, A. E. (2019). Value awareness: A new goal for end-of-life decision making. *MDM Policy & Practice*, 4(1). doi:10.1177/2381468318817523; Haward, M. F., Lorenz, J. M., Janvier, A. et al. (2023). Antenatal consultation and deliberation: Adapting to parental preferences. *Journal of Perinatology*, 43(7), 895–902.

Chapter 7
A Strategy for Bonding Bounded Disciplines

In Herbert Simon's framing, there are two approaches to dealing with complexity: bounded rationality and satisficing.[1] Each approach depends on heuristics for its success. Scientific disciplines pursue bounded rationality, constraining themselves to a focal set of issues, pushing those bounds only as needed. A discipline's wisdom lies in its heuristics for operating within those constraints, acquired through apprenticeship and refined through collaboration and peer review. These heuristics guide the selection of problems, the design of studies, and the evaluation of evidence.

The alternative approach, satisficing, embraces complexity, looking anywhere for solutions that are good enough. Satisficing heuristics show where to look and when to stop, given the demands of the task and the expected yield of further search. Humanities disciplines satisfice by creating coherent holistic accounts. Their heuristics guide defining problems, circumscribing evidence, and evaluating accounts. Practical professions satisfice by selecting templates for applied problems, assembling relevant expertise, and deciding when solutions are good enough to deploy (e.g., computer programs, product designs, bridge inspection protocols).[2]

Novel problems require disciplines skilled in both approaches. Satisficing disciplines are needed to scope the space of potentially relevant goals, constraints, and options. Boundedly rational disciplines are needed to understand those elements in enough depth to expand, winnow, and refine those spaces. Satisficing disciplines are needed to manage the process, integrating the contributions of the boundedly rational disciplines. That may entail having those disciplines dig deeper, examining new issues within their bounds, and work together, creating bonds that transcend their bounds.

---

[1] Portions of this chapter are adapted from Fischhoff, B. (2019). Evaluating science communication. *Proceedings of the National Academy of Sciences*, 116(16), 7670–7675. See Chapter 1 for more on the two approaches.

[2] This characterization, like Simon's distinction, is a heuristic one. It captures some general features, while breaking down in ways that reveal the communities' need for one another.

Bounded Disciplines and Unbounded Problems. Baruch Fischhoff, Oxford University Press. © Baruch Fischhoff (2025).
DOI: 10.1093/9780191997266.003.0007

This chapter proposes a management science strategy for this joint mission. It is a *theory of change*[3] for bonding bounded disciplinary sciences in ways that advance those sciences by collaborating on complex problems. The strategy respects the heuristic wisdom of the sciences, and their limits. Its elements reflect disciplinary sciences. Its value depends on its satisficing usefulness. How well does it explain past experiences and anticipate future ones? Both its elements and their integration are drawn from management sciences. Thus, the strategy offers a vision of management science as central to the future of the sciences and their role in society. The next section discusses the challenges to bonding bounded disciplines, followed by my proposal for addressing them.

Barriers to Bonding Bounded Disciplines

Scientists' bounded rationality entails ignoring issues that they cannot treat systematically, hoping to reach strong conclusions within their discipline's self-imposed constraints. Scientists from different disciplines struggle to collaborate because they bound problems differently. Experimental researchers may be uncomfortable with unruly field observations. Field researchers may question the artificial conditions of experiments. Both may puzzle over computational models, while computational modelers may have little patience for the simplification of experiments or the qualitative evidence of field research. Scientists who study individuals may not know what to do with the context provided by those who study groups or cultures, who may in turn shake their heads at being ignored. Each discipline owes its success to tacit knowledge of how to work within its bounds.[4] Those bounds can be so incommensurable that scientists from different disciplines may be unable to agree about how to disagree.[5]

Practitioners' satisficing entails paying attention to anything that might be relevant and accepting imperfect solutions. Practitioners of different persuasions struggle to collaborate because they have different skills and norms. Among communication practitioners, for example, those skills might include designing visual materials, crafting text, attracting media attention, convening stakeholders, and branding programs. Those norms might

---

[3] Taplin, D. H., & Clark, H. (2012). *Theory of change basics.* ActKnowledge, http://www.theoryofchange.org/ (accessed August 20, 2024). Despite the name, these are not theories, in the sense of being refutable.
[4] Polanyi, M. (1966). *The tacit dimension.* Doubleday.
[5] Kahneman, D., & Klein, G. (2009). Conditions for intuitive expertise: A failure to disagree. *American Psychologist*, 64(6), 515–526.

include how relevant they find social science evidence, whether they subscribe to a design philosophy, and their professional code of ethics. Their design constructs may be so different that they effectively speak different languages.[6]

When the worlds of theory and practice fail to connect, each is the worse for it. Scientists can overestimate how far their results generalize and offer practitioners unsupported advice or summaries. Practitioners can absorb fragments of science, unable to assess its value. Scientists can unwittingly let their values color their research or expositions. Practitioners can selectively pursue and accept convenient scientific truths. Conversely, the two worlds support one another when they connect, with practitioners helping scientists to situate their work outside its natural bounds, and scientists helping practitioners to do their work.[7]

A Strategy for Bonding Bounded Disciplines

Disciplinary sciences address complexity by answering these three challenges:

Staffing: Are people with the needed expertise involved?
Internal consultation: Are those experts communicating effectively with one another?
External consultation: Are those experts communicating effectively with other stakeholders?

The proposed strategy for achieving these objectives is captured in three kinds of graphic representation, drawn from management science: influence diagrams, social network diagrams, and communication process diagrams. Each is meant to meet Jill Larkin and Herbert Simon's criteria for being worth a thousand words:[8] facilitating *search* (finding relevant elements), *recognition* (seeing those elements in context), and *inference* (extracting lessons). Each is also meant to meet Eric Ashby's criterion of *requisite variety*, allowing

---

[6] Alexander, C., Ishikawa, S., & Silverstein, M. (1977). *A pattern language*. Oxford University Press.
[7] Dietz, T. (2013). Bringing values and deliberation to science communication. *Proceedings of the National Academy of Sciences, 110*(Suppl. 3), 14081–14087; Scheufele, D. A. (2013). Communicating science in social settings. *Proceedings of the National Academy of Sciences, 110*(Suppl. 3), 14040–14047; Scheufele, D. A. (2014). Science communication as political communication. *Proceedings of the National Academy Sciences, 111*(Suppl. 4), 13585–13592.
[8] Larkin, J. H., & Simon, H. A. (1987). Why a diagram is (sometimes) worth ten thousand words. *Cognitive Science, 11*(1), 65–100.

solutions whose complexity matches that of the problems that they address.[9] Each is a simplified version of sophisticated analyses found in the research literature. Each is meant to require no special training, just clear thinking. Each is meant to degrade gracefully, in diverse settings and diverse hands. Each is meant to provide a platform for shared work, bringing collaborators together in a *community of practice*.

The risk criteria for equitable allocation of COVID-19 vaccine pursued this strategy.[10] The four criteria captured the gist of the ethical principles guiding national policy. They were simple enough that anyone, expert or nonexpert, could understand and evaluate that policy. But they were specific enough to accommodate health statistics. They were transparent enough to reveal their limitations and guide sensitivity analyses. They created a community of practice for the committee. They were also general enough that state, tribal, local, and territorial health officials[11] could apply them to their circumstances and explain them to their constituencies. Despite the political chaos surrounding the pandemic, the criteria broadly framed the ensuing program.[12] The committee rejected more complex allocation schemes as satisficing less fully (e.g., weighting and summing the criteria, rather than leaving them in vector form).

The mental model approach to risk communication reflects the strategy as well.[13] The formal model simplifies a complex domain, providing a platform for experts to pool their knowledge. Its computability requirement ensures common terminology, without privileging quantitative factors. Its outcomes focus experts on decision makers' concerns. The model provides a standard for evaluating decision makers' understanding. It has created communities of practice for many complex decisions (e.g., reproduction, climate change, breast cancer), and has identified recurrent topics for basic research (e.g., uncertainty, cumulative risk, time frames).

Conversely, climate scientists failed to create a community of practice whose staffing and internal communications included social and behavioral scientists.[14] Expecting the science to speak for itself, they neglected external consultation with decision makers or messages tailored to their needs.[15]

---

[9] Ashby, W.R. (1956). *An introduction to cybernetics*. Chapman & Hall.
[10] See Chapter 2.
[11] This is the accepted order of jurisdictions in this context.
[12] Apparently, it was the first proposal that recognized the authority of Native Americans and Alaska Natives to govern their own such allocation.
[13] See Figure 7.2.
[14] Chapter 2.
[15] Sadly, that has not changed much.

Indeed, their disciplinary incentives favored investments in ever more elaborate, and insular, analyses (e.g., ocean currents, geochemistry, biochemistry, heat transfers, albedo, glaciology).

In order to produce knowledge worth sharing, science needs disciplinary expertise as diverse as the issues facing the people it hopes to serve. It needs ways to coordinate that expertise, bringing together scientists who live in different worlds and speak different languages. The challenge is both intellectual and organizational. Experts need common language for talking with one another and with their public(s). They also need settings and incentives for doing so, addressing the supply and demand for useful science. Decision science can, I believe, provide the common language. It needs the rest of management science for the organization.

Like the vaccine allocation criteria and the mental model approach, these proposals were adapted from more complex options in the hope that they would "degrade gracefully." That is, they would be interpreted similarly enough by people with different backgrounds to create communities of practice, while preserving the logic of their underlying analytical formulation. The goal is to have everyone talking about more or less the same things, relevant to their decisions, and in terms that use and direct scientists' expertise. The graphic representation is part of this strategy for bonding bounded disciplines, both with one another and with those they seek to serve.

Staffing: Are the Right People Involved?

An influence diagram, as introduced in Chapter 5, depicts the factors believed to predict outcomes valued by decision makers. By a like token, it depicts the expertise needed for those predictions. It also suggests the uncertainties and biases arising from omissions. Figure 7.1 shows an influence diagram for pharmacological interventions to control infectious disease, created in Fall 2005 for a possible H5N1 (avian flu) pandemic that did not materialize (at that time).[16] It is more detailed than the conceptual influence diagrams created for malaria and climate change (see Figure 5.2).

The rectangle has the decision options (*vaccines* and *antiviral strategies*). The grayed ovals have valued outcomes. Two outcomes are affected directly by the decision: *morbidity* and *health care costs* from the programs. The other outcomes are affected indirectly: *health care costs* from morbidity, *mortality*,

---

[16] As I write, in Spring 2024, the threat is back.

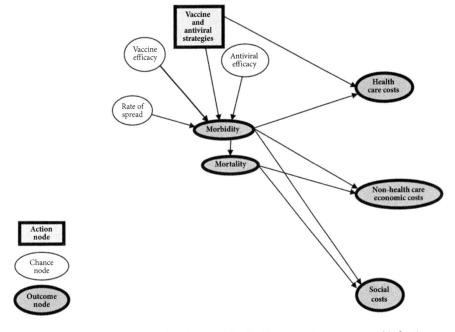

Figure 7.1 Influence diagram for pharmacological interventions to control infectious disease
Source: Fischhoff, B., Bruine de Bruin, W., Guvenc, U., Caruso, D., & Brilliant, L. (2006). Analyzing disaster risks and plans: An avian flu example. *Journal of Risk and Uncertainty, 33*(1), 133–151.

non-health care economic costs, and *social costs* (from morbidity and mortality). The clear ovals reflect uncertainties at the time of the decision: *vaccine efficacy*, *antiviral efficacy*, and *rate of spread* of the disease.

Each node or link requires different expertise. Unless the team includes, for example, scientists who know about the social cost of mortality, those benefits of successful interventions may be neglected or wrongly estimated. In many settings, that is the fate of outcomes that are not readily monetized.[17] An influence diagram offers a ready guide to staffing a project, and a ready way to audit its completeness and anticipate its blind spots. Deeper audits can examine the resources available for the links and nodes, and who is at the table to direct them. A quantitative *value-of-information analysis* can inform the allocation of resources, identifying best bets in data collection by estimating the expected effect of resolving an uncertainty on decision making. However, even the gist may tell a lot (e.g., is anyone monitoring nursing homes or evaluating different antiviral dosing regimens?)

[17] See Chapter 5.

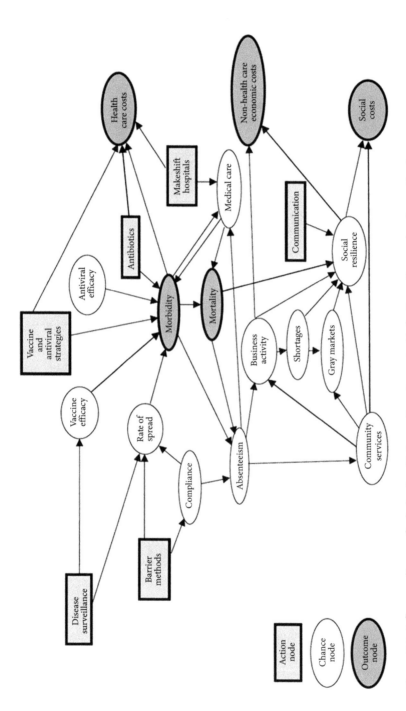

Figure 7.2 Influence diagram for behavioral interventions to control infectious disease: barrier methods

Source: Fischhoff, B., Bruine de Bruin, W., Guvenc, U., Caruso, D., & Brilliant, L. (2006). Analyzing disaster risks and plans: An avian flu example. *Journal of Risk and Uncertainty, 33*(1), 133–151.

Figure 7.2 has an influence diagram for one class of behavioral interventions, with the same five valued outcome nodes (grayed ovals). That class involves *barrier methods*, such as quarantine, self-isolation, masks, and social distancing in public places. Their deployment depends on decisions made about *disease surveillance* (a box). Their effectiveness depends on people's *compliance* with an intervention (e.g., do they stay home when they think they might be sick?). Greater compliance should reduce the rate of spread. It could also both increase absenteeism (by keeping people at home) and decrease it (by reducing morbidity), with cascading effects on *business activity*, *shortages*, *medical care*, *community services*, and *gray markets*, filling gaps in legal ones.[18] These events are inputs to *social resilience*, reflecting how well and how equitably needs are met. In that light, the social costs include whether society is strengthened or weakened by its response. *Communication* will play a role here.

Figure 7.3 elaborates on the roles of *compliance* and *communication*. Drawing on those research literatures, it has three *intermediate nodes*: *comprehension*, *feasibility*, and *trust*. Do people understand what they are being asked to do? Can they do it, given their resources and constraints? Do they have faith in the people (or organizations) asking them to do it? The figure includes "upstream" actions that authorities might have decided to do in preparation: *household subsidies*, *prior communication*, *prior education*, and *community services*. The figure includes their major influence paths.

Influence diagrams are an easy formalism to master.[19] All that it requires is clear thinking and vigorous discussion in order to ensure that the variables and links are *computable*.[20] Once created, such qualitative formal models can serve parties with different needs. Scientists can see where their boundedly rational evidence fits into the big picture. Practitioners can look for satisficing solutions, addressing the overall problem. Decision makers can readily check that their concerns have been addressed. Anyone can check that a community of practice covers its domain. Having clearly defined variables and relationships helps ensure that all parties are talking about the same things. Realizing this potential requires the relevant people to be involved and talking to one another—the next two elements in creating a community of practice to support those discussions.

---

[18] The figure was drawn in 2005, when there was much different technology for remote working than was available in 2020. Had the H5N1 pandemic materialized, the story could have been very different than with COVID-19.

[19] A simple step-by-step guide can be found in Table 2 of Fischhoff, B., Bruine de Bruin, W., Guvenc, U., Caruso, D., & Brilliant, L. (2006). Analyzing disaster risks and plans: An avian flu example. *Journal of Risk and Uncertainty*, 33(1), 133–151.

[20] As described in Chapter 5: one could "run the numbers" and predict the outcomes, if one had the necessary inputs, without requiring that to happen, so as not to privilege readily (or consensually) quantified factors.

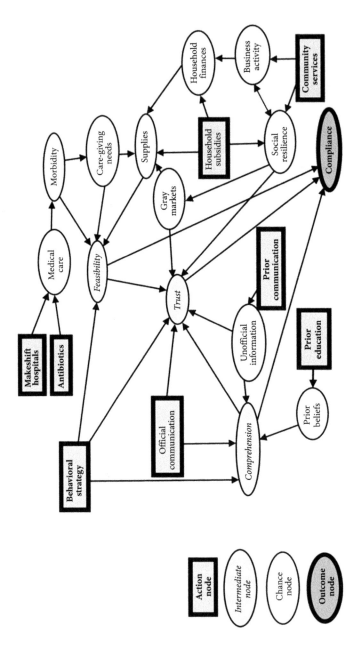

Figure 7.3 Influence diagram for the roles of compliance and communication in behavioral interventions to control infectious disease

Source: Fischhoff, B., Bruine de Bruin, W., Guvenc, U., Caruso, D., & Brilliant, L. (2006). Analyzing disaster risks and plans: An avian flu example. *Journal of Risk and Uncertainty*, 33(1), 133–151.

Internal Consultation: Are Those People Talking to One Another?

By situating expertise in a broader picture, an influence diagram also highlights its boundary conditions. In Figure 7.3, for example, there are scientists who study the comprehensibility and feasibility of behavioral strategies, including the role of trust in compliance. The influence diagram suggests possible boundary conditions on their results. Do feasibility studies consider the effects of morbidity, care-giving needs, or the availability of supplies? Do comprehension studies consider the effects of prior communication through unofficial sources (e.g., social media) on how people interpret new messages, or the effect of prior education (e.g., science classes) on their mental models for interpreting those messages?

Awareness of such concerns can prompt a discipline to probe its boundaries. For example, psychology has gradually awakened to its heavy reliance on readily available research participants, often characterized as "WEIRD": Western Educated in Industrialized Rich Democracies. With infectious disease, until those practices are addressed, they weaken the relevance of its research, and researchers, for people with limited resources, care-giving needs, or access to gray markets.

Behavioral researchers might be tempted to rely on their intuitions for imagining the effects of morbidity, care-giving needs, and supplies on the feasibility of strategies. But they are likely to learn faster by collaborating with experts in those topics, who could, in turn, expand their boundaries by thinking about their variables in these new contexts. For example, how do eldercare and childcare responsibilities affect the feasibility of mask wearing or voluntary isolation?

A community of practice brings those people together on a project, legitimating their different disciplines' expertise. A *community of discourse* is needed to get them talking and working on their boundary issues, giving them a seat at the table when projects are developed, executed, and interpreted. Network analysis is an accessible way of characterizing groups in those terms.[21] Figures 7.4 and 7.5 illustrate the kind of network analysis that can be used to create and audit communities of discourse.[22] They come from a study of six interdisciplinary centers funded by the US National

---

[21] Carley, K., & Prietula, M. J. (1994). *Computational organization theory.* Lawrence Erlbaum; Moreno, J. L. (1951). *Sociometry, experimental method and the science of society.* Beacon House.
[22] Hybrid Vigor Institute (2003). *A multi-method analysis of the social and technical conditions for interdisciplinary collaboration.* Hybrid Vigor Institute.

Center 2 researchers on average have 15 close and collegial relationships. There are two disciplinary-based clusters and a small "core" of central researchers. The larger of the two clusters and the "core" are both dominated by the center's "majority" disciplines (engineering and public policy, decision sciences, and risk analysis/assessment).

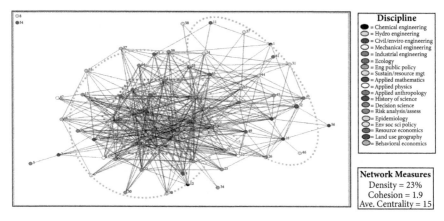

CENTER 2 CRN-T: **shows** all "close and collegial" connections by DISCIPLINE/FIELD based on responses to: *"Please indicate the strength of your relationship with other center affiliates."*

Figure 7.4 Network diagram showing close and collegial connections between disciplines in Center 2

Source: Hybrid Vigor Institute (2003). *A multi-method analysis of the social and technical conditions for interdisciplinary collaboration.* Hybrid Vigor Institute.

Science Foundation program on Biocomplexity in the Environment.[23] They show which disciplines are represented and which are talking to one another.

Each diagram tells a different story, partially summarized in its top caption. In both, researchers report fifteen "close and collegial" relationships. In Center 2, those relationships are within two relatively distinct clusters and with members of a coordinating cluster of management science disciplines. Center 4 has one overall cluster, with researchers at varying distances from its core. There are no social, behavioral, or management scientists, and just a smattering of non-engineering scientists.[24] Other analyses look at who interacts most, in terms of seniority (center directors? graduate students?), discipline (subject matter experts? methodologists?), and status (tenure track? adjunct?).

---

[23] I headed one of these centers at the time. Judging by the disciplines involved, I believe that it was Number 2, although they were not directly identified.

[24] For another center (not shown), the study concluded that "most ... interactions are concentrated in a small core of researchers ... Disciplines from the physical sciences dominate the core ... environmental scientists/social scientists dominate the periphery" (Hybrid Vigor Institute, *A multi-method analysis*, p. 57).

Center 4 researchers on average have 15 close and collegial relationships. There is one primary cluster and a small "core" of central researchers. The "core" and the cluster are both dominated by the center's "majority" disciplines from engineering sciences (civil/environmental engineering and chemical engineering) with a smaller representation of other engineering and physical science disciplines.

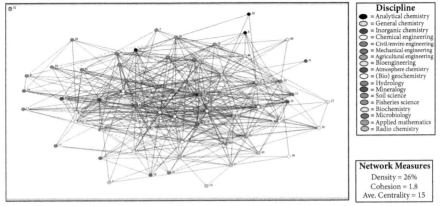

CENTER 4 CRN-T: diagram shows all "close" and "collegial" connections by DISCIPLINE/FIELD based on responses to: "Please indicate the strength of your relationship with other center affiliates."

Figure 7.5 Network diagram showing close and collegial connections between disciplines in Center 4
Source: Hybrid Vigor Institute (2003). *A multi-method analysis of the social and technical conditions for interdisciplinary collaboration*. Hybrid Vigor Institute.

The figures allow anyone to conduct simple network analyses. They might be submitted with proposals, used to structure working relations, or consulted when problems arise. Organizational scientists could draw on their vast research to inform (or study) those structures, looking at topics like how communications fall off with degrees of separation, when central hubs help and hinder, and how many close and collegial relationships people can realistically sustain. Might it be about fifteen, as in the analyses for Center 2 and Center 4?[25] If so, then Figure 7.4 shows an effective structure for working with large working groups coordinated by management scientists.

Direct connections between disciplines are needed because, as mentioned, people overestimate how well they understand one another—and that bias grows with the distance between them. Recognizing boundary conditions need not allow transcending them. Reading another discipline's publications will not reveal its unspoken and unwritten assumptions. People need to talk in order to reveal boundaries and find common ground.

Translating science into the decision-relevant form of an influence diagram requires consultation on three levels. One is summarizing the science

---

[25] I once heard that chickens can remember 150 pecking order relationships. Larger flocks have chaos.

at each node (e.g., what quantities of antivirals will be available) and link (e.g., how effectively vaccines will reduce morbidity). The second is estimating interactions (e.g., how morbidity and mortality will combine to affect social costs). The third is identifying contextual factors (sometimes called "index variables") that affect many model elements (e.g., whether the society is developed or developing). A project should have the "close and collegial" relations need to support these consultations.

External Consultation: Are Those People Talking with Stakeholders?

Proper staffing and internal consultation will come to naught unless they serve people's needs. That means working through their problems and providing useful solutions. An infectious disease control program that addressed the focal outcomes in the boxes in Figure 7.1 (morbidity; mortality; health care, economic and social costs) would fail if it neglected intermediary outcomes that are ends in themselves (e.g., trust, social resilience). It could also fail if it defined outcomes inappropriately (e.g., neglecting equity issues),[26] or if it delivered solutions that neglected practical realities. There is no way of knowing without talking to people.

Figure 7.6 gives a model for those communications. It is framed in terms of risk, but applies to any outcome, including reduced risks and expected costs. It posits sustained, two-way communication between experts and those they serve. In initial interactions (at the top), experts hear people's concerns and elicit comments on their preliminary thinking. Continuing interactions seek to keep the parties' visions from drifting apart, as they learn and reflect in their otherwise separate worlds. That contact can, for example, keep experts from unwittingly making changes that seem functionally equivalent to them but are radical changes for people affected by them.[27]

As with all communications, the *speech act* itself is part of the message. When and how the parties communicate affects nonexperts' actual and perceived right to hear and be heard. If the communication process affects trust in experts, it can affect outcomes as well, by reducing compliance with their proposals (as in Figure 7.3). Good process promotes good content, and vice versa. When experts fail to address nonexperts' information needs, they can create a vicious circle of decreasing trust and understanding. Conversely,

---

[26] See Chapter 6.
[27] Dietz, T., & Stern, P. (Eds.) (2008). *Public participation in environmental assessment and decision making.* National Academies Press.

A Strategy for Bonding Bounded Disciplines   109

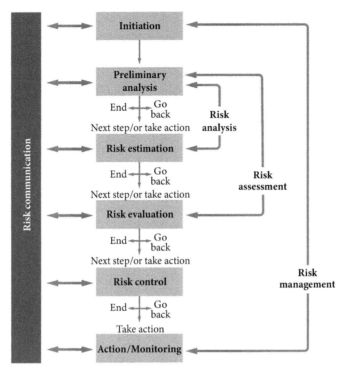

An analytical–deliberative process in which analysts and decision makers collaborate in managing risks. The process begins by defining the terms of the analysis (initiation), proceeds to preliminary analysis, identifying the issues meriting greatest attention, and continues through estimation of the magnitude of the risks, evaluation of their acceptability, and consideration of control mechanisms, improving the risk-cost-benefit trade-offs. Once an action has been selected, monitoring assesses how well the ensuing reality corresponds to the analytical conclusions. At all stages, analysts communicate with those potentially affected by the risks in question. Analogous processesss apply to cost and benefit analyses.

Figure 7.6 A model for ongoing two-way communication in project management.

Source: Fischhoff, B. (2015). The realities of risk–cost–benefit analysis. *Science, 350*(6260), 527. https://www.science.org/doi/10.1126/science.aaa6516 (adapted from Canadian Standards Association (1997). *Risk management: Guidelines for decision makers* (Q8550). CSA).

when they succeed, the resulting *community of consultation* is both a means to better solutions and an end in itself.

Communities of consultation also allow nonexperts to share their expertise, acquired by living with a problem that experts merely visit.[28] That knowledge may be personal (e.g., about medical conditions, bullying experiences)

---

[28] In this light, the term "nonexpert" can be interpreted as "people without formal credentials in the specific issue at hand." For decisions of any complexity, there may be no overall experts, credentialed in all aspects.

or collective. Anthropologists have long documented *indigenous technical knowledge*.[29] Organizational scientists, sociologists, and others have studied the tacit knowledge of work and community groups. They have also studied when consultation practices enhance information sharing and mutual respect, or erode it—as with box-checking formulaic interactions, with no obvious pathway to influence analysis or action.[30]

Figure 7.6 posits the benefit of continuing, proactive, two-way communication for hearing and respecting stakeholders' concerns. It is also a strategy for avoiding a vacuum that others might fill, perhaps with mis- or disinformation. One challenge in implementing the model is engaging people early enough to achieve its potential benefits, when a topic is far off their radar. A second challenge is keeping them engaged, when there are other decisions in their lives. A third is giving people outside the consultation the assurance that someone they trust to represent them is at the table, expressing their concerns. A fourth is having satisficing heuristics for determining when to revisit a process ("go back") or abandon it ("end"). Addressing these challenges offers opportunities to test, and refine, the science.

Conclusions

This chapter proposes a strategy for integrating the boundedly rational wisdom of the scientific disciplines needed to identify satisficing solutions to complex problems. It creates three interdependent communities: a community of practice, for ensuring the appropriate staffing; a community of discourse, for pooling their knowledge; and a community of collaboration, for ensuring its relevance to decision makers. The platforms for these communities are *computable* models—conceptually clear, so that people are talking about the same things, while compatible with quantitative analyses where warranted. That compromise allows nonexperts to address the gist of topics, while experts can bring their detailed knowledge to bear and take away observations for future research.

The models are simple versions of core methods in management science: influence diagrams, with the factors affecting valued outcomes; social networks, with the ties shaping expert collaboration; and process diagrams, with a template for productive public engagement. Applying these methods

---

[29] Agrawal, A. (1995). Dismantling the divide between indigenous and scientific knowledge. *Development and Change*, 26(3), 413–439.

[30] Inuit Circumpolar Council (2021). *Ethical and equitable engagement workshop series summary report*. Inuit Circumpolar Council; Dietz, T. (2023). *Decisions for sustainability*. Cambridge University Press.

to peer-review standards requires professional training and patience for the necessarily somewhat adversarial processes of science. Here, though, they are vehicles for cooperation, facilitating shared understanding. Their application requires nothing more than the clear thinking of influence diagrams and the analogous connect-the-people processes in Figures 7.4 and 7.5. Experts could "run the numbers" to calculate expected outcomes of influence diagrams and network metrics like density and cohesion. However, that could mean forcing nonexpert others to take those results on faith. A jointly developed and applied computable model may be the sweet spot in creating a shared picture of a shared problem.

Chapter 8
A Vision for Management Science

Schools of engineering are comprised of disciplinary departments (e.g., mechanical, civil and environmental, chemical). Their members pursue boundedly rational issues in their specialties (e.g., corrosion, sensors, optimization), meeting the standards of excellence for each basic science. They come together for applied projects requiring coordinated contributions from multiple disciplines. Members bring the wisdom of their entire discipline, as well as their own specialized knowledge.[1] Each project extends the participating disciplines by testing their boundaries, revealing new topics, and exposing them to other disciplines, each with its own results, methods, and puzzles.

Such collaboration comes naturally for engineering faculty. Many have had project-based work experience. Many are expected to make themselves useful in complex projects, as well as publish in disciplinary journals. Many have freedom to complete those tasks asynchronously: work the problem first; write the papers later. Many have freedom to work on problems that test no single theory clearly, but reveal something about each theory involved.

These professional collaborations create communities of practice and discourse, for recruiting and pooling knowledge (Chapter 7). Many follow established practices, drawing members from disciplines with customary roles. Pressure to change those practices can come from within, when projects fail on their own terms (e.g., bridges collapse, computer systems crash, pharmaceuticals have unanticipated side effects) and new skills seem to be needed. Pressure can also come from without, when other members of the community of discourse bring new issues to the fore.

Management Science as General Contractor

In responding to these pressures, engineering sciences may be limited by their established practices. Their analytical methods may not readily

---

[1] Sweden has a term of art—*science and proven experience*—that is the required standard of evidence for government policies.

Bounded Disciplines and Unbounded Problems. Baruch Fischhoff, Oxford University Press. © Baruch Fischhoff (2025).
DOI: 10.1093/9780191997266.003.0008

accommodate new forms of knowledge (e.g., human behavior). Their disciplines may lack the shared frame of reference needed for internal consultation. Their external consultation processes may not readily accommodate new members. As a result, engineering sciences can stall when they lack the requisite variety for complex problems. The struggles of autonomous vehicle developers may reflect such stalling.[2]

Management science can, I believe, provide the missing links by embracing the proposed strategy for bonding bounded disciplines. Seizing that opportunity requires management science to adopt an engineering science mode of operation: embrace the diversity of its disciplines, respect the paths to wisdom within their chosen boundaries, and convene them for complex projects, with structured roles. As an engineering science, management science would honor contributions that "work the problem" rather than promote a discipline or favored theory. It would trust and reward asynchronous discovery processes, whereby scientists first find ways to make themselves useful and then translate those practical experiences into boundedly rational disciplinary science.

In this view, management science serves as a general contractor, creating plans for addressing complex problems; identifying disciplinary subcontractors with specialized expertise; coordinating their labors; and maintaining two-way communication with decision makers throughout the process. With feet in the worlds of both basic research and applications, management science can fashion projects that serve both.

In this vision, computable models play a vital coordinating role. They help experts translate their disciplinary wisdom into terms relevant to decision makers: influence diagrams show the valued outcomes and sciences assembled to secure them; network diagrams show how the experts work together; interaction process diagrams show how decision makers are consulted. Their graphic form makes them accessible to nonexperts, and their underlying formalisms enable experts to express their knowledge. They promote the *slow science* that complex problems demand.[3]

I have had the good fortune to be involved in many such projects, with collaborations facilitated by qualitative formal models. Each has offered opportunities to contribute my disciplinary knowledge and expand it through

---

[2] Vanderbilt, T. (2017, October 3). *Autonomous cars: How safe is safe enough?* Car and Driver, https://www.caranddriver.com/features/a15080598/autonomous-cars-how-safe-is-safe-enough-feature/ (accessed August 23, 2024).

[3] Medin, D., Ojalehto, B., Marin, A., & Berg, M. (2017). Systems of (non-)diversity. *Nature Human Behavior*, *1*(5), Article 0088.

the slow scholarship required to accommodate diverse perspectives. Each has involved consultation with nonexperts, as needed to identify problems and evaluate solutions. Each has raised issues studied by other management sciences, sometimes with the good fortune to engage them.

These experiences suggest three challenges to management science becoming the engineering science for complex decisions: (a) creating the intellectual commons, able to accommodate diverse forms of knowledge; (b) creating communities of practice, discourse, and consultation, with the sustained personal relations needed for mutual trust and understanding; and (c) creating institutional incentives, allowing management scientists to fulfill these roles. This chapter describes these challenges and potential solutions. They reflect my best understanding of the issues, recognizing that workers in other management sciences know much more than I do and welcoming their revisions.

Creating an Intellectual Commons

The success of any decision-related model depends on how well people can translate their beliefs and values into its terms—and how faithfully it communicates those perspectives to others. Chapters 5 and 6 addressed some of the many threats to those translations. Improving communication between people and models has long been a major topic for decision science. That research has produced translation methods for experts, who feel professionally bound to learn the language of analysis, and for nonexperts, who want analysis to come to them.

Methods for Assessing Experts' Beliefs

Figure 2.3 showed an early application of *expert elicitation*, an increasingly common method for enabling experts to express themselves in model-friendly terms.[4] The method provides a way to level the playing field for different kinds of knowledge. Rather than neglecting topics without ambitious data sets or relying on flawed or only indirectly relevant ones, it provides a disciplined way of quantifying any beliefs regarding the topic of immediate

---

[4] Morgan, M. G. (2017). *Theory and practice of policy analysis.* Cambridge University Press; O'Hagan, A., Buck, C. E., Daneshkhah, A., Eiser, J. R., Garthwaite, P. H., Jenkinson, D. J., Oakley, J. E., & Rakow, T. (2006). *Uncertain judgements: Eliciting experts' probabilities.* Wiley.

interest. For example, it could give standing to research on operator behavior in engineering analyses of new technologies.[5]

Figure 8.1 shows responses to four questions from the 2005 expert elicitation on H5N1 (avian flu), described briefly in Chapter 5. The survey addressed an acute need for quantitative risk estimates, at a time when there were no directly relevant observations. It reflects the beliefs of two groups of experts: the medical experts came from public health; the nonmedical experts came from technologies that might keep the world going in a pandemic.[6] The distributions of medical experts' judgments reflect the degree of scientific consensus on each issue. It was weak for the probability of transmission (a); strong, but depressing, for lethality (b) and preparedness (c), (d). The similarity of the two distributions indicates how well medical experts had communicated their beliefs to nonmedical experts, who would need to act on them. Generally speaking, the nonmedical experts saw greater risks than the medical experts had tried to convey.[7]

Methods for Assessing Nonexperts' Beliefs

Much of the research discussed in Chapter 5 was, in effect, expert elicitation with nonexperts, asking for their beliefs with the same attention to clarity in questions and answers as in research with experts. That research includes both quantitative beliefs (e.g., probabilities) and qualitative ones (e.g., mental models). It can be used to compare expert and nonexpert beliefs (as in Figure 8.1) or to elicit beliefs where nonexperts have unique knowledge. Mental model interviews capture some of the richness of people's perspectives, addressing issues relevant to them and preserving their language in transcripts. Pooling these beliefs creates an intellectual commons.[8]

---

[5] While also encouraging those scientists to reflect on the practical significance of their results. In my experience, engineers are often willing to talk to anyone who might be helpful, as long as they talk fast and in terms that they can use. Fischhoff, B. (2015). The realities of risk-cost-benefit analysis. *Science*, 350(6260), 527.

[6] As happened fifteen years later with COVID-19, with much better technology than the dial-up Internet of 2005.

[7] Our interpretation was that, in the absence of explicit numeric predictions, the nonmedical experts interpreted medical experts' alarm as implying a high probability of transmission. However, with an expected fatality rate of 10 percent, even a low probability of transmission would be cause for great alarm. The meeting was a precursor to the movie *Contagion*.

[8] This approach to qualitative research differs from that of grounded theory, in not trying to capture nonexperts' perspectives in their full richness, only those elements that are relevant to understanding or expanding the expert model.

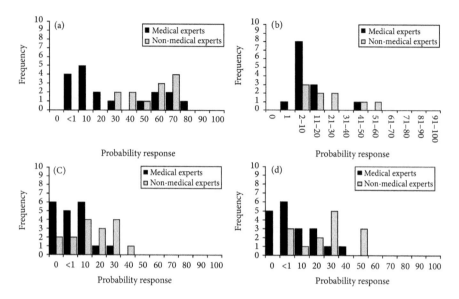

Figure 8.1 Expert elicitation for H5N1 (avian flu) in 2005
Response distributions for the probability that (a) H5N1 or a similar virus will become an efficient human-to-human transmitter in the next three years; (b) someone who is infected will die, the case-fatality rate; (c) we will have sufficient quantities of effective vaccines at that time, and (d) we will have sufficient quantities of effective antiviral pharmaceuticals at that time.
Figure (b) represents categories of open-ended responses, whereas the other figures represent responses on a probability scale.
Source: Bruine de Bruin, W., Fischhoff, B., Brilliant, L., & Caruso, D. (2006). Expert judgments of pandemic influenza. *Global Public Health*, 1(2), 178–193.

Creating Communities

Even the most in-depth expert elicitations and mental model interviews are mediated communications. A researcher extracts beliefs and shares them in aggregate form. Focused on what people think, the research does not try to capture how they think. Nor does it try to create the personal ties needed to build trust between experts and nonexperts. Both can be critical for understanding, by bringing together people with very different ways of thinking and acting. Management science has methods for helping people to understand one another and interact productively. When successful, these methods result in fewer, but better conflicts—by avoiding ones arising from needless misunderstandings and antagonisms.

Methods for Creating Shared Ways of Thinking

Analytical models, the platform for shared understanding, are not a common way of thinking for many people, including many experts. They are, however, easy enough to explain. Just walk people through the nodes and links, expressed in meaningful terms. Some of the connections will be obvious, putting familiar topics in a logical order. Some will need some explaining. For example, the model of behavioral interventions for pandemic protection[9] includes the nonlinear relationship between compliance and health effects. People may need help in seeing how small increases in risk (e.g., not using face masks) mount up through repeated exposures.[10]

Being able to follow such an exposition is not the same as having active mastery of the model. One strategy is to use metaphors that degrade gracefully to convey a system's properties (e.g., think of the heart as a pump, viruses as voracious parasites, the economy as balancing supply and demand). Where metaphors work, they provide a shared way of thinking for nonexperts and experts, who may use them in the classroom or talks. A central topic in formal and informal science education research is when metaphors, like other heuristics, break down.[11]

By definition, complex decisions involve more than one system. Even when there are effective intuitive metaphors for each system, mentally simulating their interactions is a daunting task. Experts who study complex problems use models because they do not trust their own, or one another's intuitions, and need to "run the numbers." Computable models offer transparent definitions of variables, inputs, and relationships. Computing the models offers auditable calculations and the option of performing different ones—for people with access, resources, and skills.

Although many people have some familiarity with experiments, few (including many experimental scientists) are familiar with models. As a result, they must accept on faith what these black-box operations say about economic policies, climate change, or herd immunity. The current pushback against machine-learning algorithms reflects limits to that faith, with models promoted as detecting patterns that no human can see. The modelers themselves are only gradually discovering, for example, the biases latent in their training sets, training coders, algorithms, and computing systems.

One possible way to secure warranted trust is to make model-based thinking more intuitive. Science museums offer hands-on exhibits, allowing visitors to get a feel for systems by manipulating inputs and observing outputs. Medical researchers offer decisions aids, providing expected utility calculations for patients who can describe their condition and preferences in those terms. Environmental analysts offer model simulations that people can manipulate to inform their intuitions, for topics as varied as setting air quality

---

[9] See Figure 7.2.
[10] Slovic, P., Fischhoff, B., & Lichtenstein, S. (1978). Accident probabilities and seat-belt usage: A psychological perspective. *Accident Analysis and Prevention, 10*(4), 281–285.
[11] Gentner, D., & Stevens, A. L. (1983). *Mental models.* Lawrence Erlbaum Associates.

standards,[12] anticipating sea-level rise,[13] and restoring electrical power after mass outages.[14]

A foundational approach to improving understanding is training in model-based thinking per se. There are several imaginative curricula for teaching decision-making skills, grounded in decision science research.[15] Although they address the need for critical thinking that educators often prize, it is hard to get them into packed school curricula, especially when these skills are not directly reflected in the standardized tests that dominate much education.[16] Universities have greater latitude in their offerings. For fifteen years, I headed a Decision Science major that seemed to serve students well. It has unique courses in the three prongs of decision science: analysis, description, and intervention. Students also take introductory courses in the constituent disciplines: statistics, economics, cognitive psychology, and empirical research methods. Their elective courses often include a capstone project course with engineering students. As easy as it would be to mount such a major, it remains a rarity.

Another option is in-service training. I chaired a NASEM committee asked to bring decision science into intelligence analysis, sponsored by the Office of the Director of National Intelligence (the coordinating body for the seventeen US federal agencies). Our report recommended that all analysts achieve conceptual mastery of how each discipline in Box 8.1 approaches problems.[17] We argued that *fluency* in these ways of thinking would enable analysts to discuss issues in those terms and seek experts' help when *technical proficiency* was needed.[18] The report envisioned courses that focused on such mastery, rather than preparation for the next course in a sequence. These disciplines are all branches of management science, whose professional school graduates provide absorptive capacity for these ways of thinking in their workplaces.[19]

---

[12] von Winterfeldt, D. (2013). Bridging the gap between science and decision making. *Proceedings of the National Academy of Sciences, 110*(Suppl. 3), 14055–14061.

[13] Wong-Parodi, G., & Strauss, B. (2013). Team science for science communication. *Proceedings of the National Academy of Sciences, 111*(Suppl. 4), 13658–13663.

[14] Baik, S., Davis, A. L., Park, J. W., Sirinterlikci, S., & Granger, M. G. (2020). Estimating what US residential consumers are willing to pay for resilience to large electrical outages of long duration. *Nature Energy, 5*(3), 250–258.

[15] Beyth-Marom, R., Dekel, S., Gombo, R., & Shaked, M. (1985). *An elementary approach to thinking under uncertainty*. Routledge; Gregory, R., & Moore, B. (2024). *Sorting it out: Supporting teenage decision making*. Cambridge University Press.

[16] Schachter, A. W. (2016). *No child left alone: Getting the government out of parenting*. Encounter Books.

[17] National Research Council (2011). *Intelligence analysis for tomorrow*. National Academy Press. A companion volume explained each discipline, in terms relevant to intelligence analysis. National Research Council (2011). *Intelligence analysis: Behavioral and social scientific foundations* (B. Fischhoff & C. Chauvin, Eds.). National Academy Press.

[18] The report has had some 25k downloads for each volume and almost no academic citations.

[19] Cohen, W. A., & Levinthal, D. A. (1990) Absorptive capacity: A new perspective on science and innovation. *Administrative Sciences Quarterly, 35*(1), 128–152.

Box 8.1 Management Science Disciplines Recommended for the Intelligence Community

Analytical Methods

- Operations research
- Game theory
- Signal detection theory
- Political theory
- Reasoning
- Judgment under uncertainty

Process Methods

- Communication with stakeholders
- Group processes
- Workforce development
- Accountability systems
- Organizational change

"For each method, mere familiarity will protect analysts from errors of judgments, while opening the door to future applications" (p. 26).

NASEM. (2011). *Intelligence analysis for tomorrow*. National Academies Press.

Methods for Creating Respectful Ways of Interacting

The curriculum in Box 8.1 includes both analytical and procedural management science disciplines. The latter recognize that any new way of thinking entails a social gamble as well as an intellectual one. Will other people go along? How well will they be trained? Will there be continuing support? Will the effort be rewarded and growing pains forgiven? Will it exacerbate or ameliorate intergroup rivalries and prejudices?

Our NASEM report translated general principles of management science research into the specific needs of intelligence agencies—and, by implication, to those of other organizations that require specialist units to collaborate on complex problems. The report on equitable allocation of COVID-19 vaccine did the same for the diverse constituencies interacting over public health issues. Each report had recommendations for creating the human connections needed to close gaps that fixed communications leave. Each adapts the general strategy of Chapter 7 to a specific class of applications.

These reports assume that mutual understanding does not happen the first time that people meet, however clearly information is shared. Experts who hope to be part of a conversation need to become part of the community hosting it. Sustained relationships demonstrate commitment to the problem and the people. They reveal how other people think, talk, and react. In the short run, they are inefficient: just talking, hanging out, and learning about one another. But the long-run return on that tangible investment is less tangible, improved collaboration, and, even less tangible, problems avoided. In the community of discourse with scientists, continuing interaction increases the permeability of disciplinary boundaries. In the community of consultation with nonexperts, it keeps their concerns in view—helping experts to get the right facts, as well as to get the facts right.

Good processes need good facilitation. Here, too, management science offers guidance.[20] Following it may require professionals skilled in creating communication channels, arranging meetings, recruiting participants, sending invitations (and reminders), minding legal constraints, anticipating cultural sensitivities, and gathering feedback. They may need a firm hand to keep normal social dynamics from recruiting, rewarding, and retaining people with shared backgrounds and blind spots, making them overly comfortable talking to one another, to the exclusion of others.

When successful, the consultation process creates a virtuous circle of sustained relationships. Decision makers believe that scientists might help them. Scientists believe that they might learn something from the engagement. The next section considers the incentives needed to make this happen.

Creating Incentives

Implementing the strategy for bonding bounded disciplines requires a leap of faith. Without it, scientists will not cross disciplinary boundaries to create an intellectual commons, collaborate with other disciplines to create communities of practice, or engage with stakeholders to create communities of consultation. Historically, such leaps have been impelled by a desire for public service, spurred by calamities like the Great Depression, World War II, and the nuclear arms race. That desire subordinates disciplinary norms to practical concerns, as scientists employ whatever methods and results from their discipline might be helpful. Advancing their own research programs is not an

---

[20] Rogelberg, S. G. (2109). *The surprising science of meetings: How you can lead your team to peak performance*. Oxford University Press.

immediate concern, although they may hope that the experience will benefit their research in the long run, through new observations and perspectives.

Boundary organizations support such ventures.[21] The Bureau of Applied Social Research arose from the turmoil in Vienna after World War I and continued through the rigors of the Great Depression and World War II at Columbia University, led by Paul Lazarsfeld and others. The American Soldier Project, MIT Research Center for Group Dynamics, and University of Michigan Institute for Social Research, among others, arose similarly, with leaders like Kurt Lewin, Rensis Likert, Leslie Kish, and others. Kenneth Craik, Donald Broadbent, and Alan Baddeley were among those who led the Medical Research Council Applied Psychology Unit (MRC/APU) to service in many areas, also with roots in World War II (e.g., development of the Cambridge cockpit, which reduced training time and accidents). Oleg Larichev created a decision science unit as part of the (USSR) All-Union Institute for System Studies. Decision Research, where I once worked with Paul Slovic and Sarah Lichtenstein, sustained itself by working on applied topics, to supplement the limited support available for basic research.

Today's crises appear to have increased many scientists' willingness to take that leap, motivated by environmental collapse, authoritarian populism, existential threats, or other calamities. Whether the result is similarly transformative will depend on their intellectual abilities and the opportunities to pursue them. It is my strong sense that scientists' demand for positions straddling the worlds of basic research and application is much greater than the supply in academic institutions. Keeping on the tenure track in most departments requires a steady stream of publications in a limited set of disciplinary journals, calibrated to the department's status aspirations. There may be no penalties for stakeholder engagement.[22] However, that time comes out of publication time.[23]

Young scientists hoping for tenure in such institutions have little choice but to set engagement aside until they have secured that prize. Once tenured, they might use their newfound freedom for collaborative projects, or they may stick with what has brought them success. Seeing the incentive structure of academia, talented graduate students may get rigorous disciplinary training,

---

[21] Santos, F., & Eisenhardt, K. M. (2005). Organizational boundaries and theories of organization. *Organization Science, 16*(5), 491–508; Gieryn, T. F. (1983). Boundary-work and the demarcation of science from non-science: Strains and interests in professional interests of scientists. *American Sociological Review, 48*(6), 781–795.

[22] As opposed to press releases and trade books promoting researchers' own labs and institutions.

[23] Medical researchers in wealthy countries can find support for bridging research on a prescribed set of applied problems. However, that set is narrow (albeit often vitally important), the opportunities for interdisciplinary collaboration limited, and the pressure for grant-writing withering.

then opt for an off-ramp so that they can apply it more meaningfully than within the bounded rationality of their discipline.

Institutions that hope to serve both science and society need incentive systems that equally value what the US National Science Foundation calls Intellectual Merit and Broader Impacts.[24] That is, they must have a place for scientists who both publish in top journals and provide valued service to society. The former requires staying abreast of their discipline, challenging its bounds with *applied basic* research, and expanding them with *basic applied* research.[25] The latter means suppressing their disciplinary ego in order to work together with other disciplines and nonexperts on shared concerns. Advocates of giving greater weight to Intellectual Merit have sought to estimate its contribution to Broader Impacts, in terms of how basic science increases productivity, trade, and innovation.[26] Disciplinary bonding posits the contribution of Broader Impacts to Intellectual Merit, by stimulating collaborations that breach disciplinary bounds.

Boundary Organizations for Bonding Bounded Disciplines

In order to offer those incentives to scientists, institutions need to respect the incentives that ensure their own survival. There are several models for such boundary organizations, committed to bonding bounded disciplines.

Event-driven organizations, like the American Soldier Project or the Deepwater Horizon Gulf Research Program,[27] focus on time-limited applications. They can attract basic researchers by supporting basic research that complements their applied mission, and allowing asynchronous publication of findings. To that end, they must convince their funders that diverting resources to basic research enhances the quality of the applications. They might also argue that they must fill gaps left by government funders driven by disciplinary priorities. Because they are time-limited, such organizations must enable scientists to continue enough basic research to retain their disciplinary standing, for when the work is over.

---

[24] https://new.nsf.gov/policies/pappg/24-1/ch-3-proposal-processing-review#a-merit-review-principles-and-criteria-af2 (accessed August 23, 2024).

[25] Baddeley, A. D. (1979). Applied cognitive and cognitive applied research. In L. G. Nilsson (Ed.), *Perspectives on memory research* (pp. 367–388). Erlbaum.

[26] Salter, A. J., & Martin, B. R. (2001). The economic benefits of publicly funded basic research. *Research Policy, 30*(3), 509–533.

[27] https://www.nationalacademies.org/gulf/gulf-research-program (accessed August 23, 2024).

A Vision for Management Science   123

Service-driven organizations, like national laboratories (e.g., MRC/APU), advocacy groups (e.g., the Urban League), think tanks (e.g., RAND), or industrial labs (e.g., Bell Labs), focus on enduring, rather than transient applications. They, too, can attract basic researchers by providing supplementary research resources. Maintaining their disciplinary standing by conducting such research will also help keep their scientists from losing touch with their disciplines and becoming captive of their clients. Those disciplinary ties can be strengthened by staff with joint appointments in academic departments, sabbaticals in academia for staff, temporary staff appointments for academics, and extended postdocs for scientists willing to gamble on creating novel research programs while they are still young and promising. Service-driven organizations must also protect researchers from any sense of compromising their scientific integrity for the cause.

Disciplinary departments can be boundary organizations if they reward collaboration and emphasize quality over quantity in basic research. A few excellent papers should be enough to demonstrate faculty members' intellectual prowess. Departments with that balance may have a competitive edge in attracting faculty and students eager for such engagement.[28] One source of inertia is slow staff turnover in disciplinary departments, with open slots often filled by people who can teach the same courses. A second source is the need to devise evaluative criteria for collaboration and for innovative research that cannot find a home in top disciplinary journals.[29]

Professional schools have the constituents of boundary organizations, conducting basic research while teaching applied classes. Embracing the bonding disciplines strategy would entail more deeply integrating their research and teaching, offering students a novel approach to creating practical solutions grounded in basic research. Decision science, which found its first academic home in business schools, can provide platforms for that integration. One challenge is to make the case to students for courses that are less immediately applied. A second is to better integrate real-world experience in the school's intellectual life, including that of adjunct faculty with practical day jobs.[30]

In each domain, academic disciplines are key gatekeepers. Institutional incentives for collaboration will mean little unless scientists' disciplines recognize their value. That would mean valuing satisficing applications

---

[28] Gibbs, K. D., & Griffin, K. A. (2013). What do I want to be with my PhD? The roles of personal values and structural dynamics in shaping the interests of recent biomedical science PhD graduates. *CBE—Life Sciences Education, 12*(4), 711–723.

[29] Heckman, J., & Moktan, S. (2020). Publishing and promoting in economics: The tyranny of the top five journals. *Journal of Economic Literature, 58*(2), 419–470.

[30] Littman, R. A. (1979). Social and intellectual origins of experimental psychology. In E. Hearst (Ed.), *The first century of experimental psychology* (vol. 5, Chapter 2). Psychonomic Society.

alongside boundedly rational disciplinary science. It would mean believing that collaborations will enrich disciplinary science. It would mean accepting the need to honor public service, as a way to earn public trust and ensure public support.[31]

Such changes will require intellectual and personal leadership, from scientists who can see the intellectual commons, create the needed communities, and ensure the institutional incentives. None of the historical examples cited in this chapter would have had as much impact, or perhaps have happened at all, without the people named. In some cases, leaders traded on their disciplinary reputations to secure resources, and breathing space, for boundary organizations. In other cases, they gambled their early careers on translating their passions into viable enterprises.[32]

Schools of management are natural homes for such sustained collaborations, if they pattern themselves on schools of engineering, with project-oriented working groups drawing members from disciplinary hubs. The hubs would need to be large enough to form socially viable groups, so that individuals are not isolated, with one person representing an entire discipline. The projects would need to have sustained internal and external interactions, so that members get to know one another and reflect together on approaches. Like the MRC/APU, such schools might require annual reports showing members' ability to publish in top journals and make themselves useful. Or, like Carnegie Mellon's Department of Engineering and Public Policy (EPP), they might have 50–50 joint appointments, with one department applying disciplinary standards and the other practical ones.[33]

The sustainability of such arrangements will depend on the school's initial commitment and long-term memory for it, lest unconventional programs be especially vulnerable during regime changes. Sustainability will also depend on leaders' ability to maintain the unstable equilibrium of any creative endeavor. The diagrams in Chapter 7 allow such an enterprise to be audited, in terms of the perspectives represented and the connections between them. As with any audit, insight and energy are needed to identify and address problems.

Schools of management also have advantages in creating the demand for such collaborations. People with problems often seek help from consultants rather than scientists, fearing that scientists cannot provide the client service

---

[31] Vazire, S. (2023). The next chapter for *Psychological Science*. *Psychological Science*, 35(7), https://doi.org/10.1177/09567976231221558

[32] Fenton, E. (2020). *Carnegie Mellon 1900–2000: A centennial history*. Carnegie Mellon University Press.

[33] In my experience, those are in effect 75 percent–75 percent appointments, willfully accepted by researchers passionate about both worlds.

and meet the time demands of the practical world. Many of those consultants are former management students. They have seen the science and can converse with those pursuing it. They could provide absorptive capacity for management science expertise, if it can organize itself to meet their needs.

Conclusions

Schools of engineering have a model for collaborative problem solving that respects disciplinary wisdom and the need to transcend it. They are the model for the proposed strategy for bonding bounded disciplines. However, they have limits that, I believe, schools of management can transcend.[34] Whereas engineering sciences focus on numerical analyses, management science theories implicitly embody computable models, starting with the issues, however quantifiable. Whereas engineering projects focus on technical issues, management science starts with behavior, situated in engineered settings. Whereas engineering analyses focus on "tangible" outcomes (costs, risks, and benefits), management sciences can embed those issues in their social context.[35] Whereas engineers typically interact with institutional clients, management scientists can engage more diverse communities.

Unlike most engineering schools, management sciences have expertise in anticipating and ameliorating the interpersonal and intergroup conflicts that can arise in any complex project. They have expertise in creating job descriptions, training programs, and performance evaluations that can recruit, reward, and retain valuable people. Within the management sciences, decision science offers behaviorally informed computable models that serve as platforms for sharing knowledge and concerns. Those analyses allow people to communicate with one another, while still speaking in terms close enough to their natural way of thinking for them to be, and to feel like, partners. Complex projects require a general contractor who can bring the parties together, cognizant of their skills and limitations. Schools of management science sometimes do that now, and could make it their centerpiece.

---

[34] From the perspective of someone with faculty positions, not in a school of management, but in policy-focused interdisciplinary departments in a college of engineering and a college of humanities and social science.

[35] Dutta, S., Armanios, D. E., & Dessai, J. D. (2021). Beyond spatial proximity: The impact of enhanced special connectedness from new bridges on entrepreneurship. *Organizational Science*, 33(4), 1620–1644.

Chapter 9
Change (in)Action

Science progresses through the bounded rationality of its disciplines. Isolating problems from the complexity of the world allows the attention to detail that comprises a discipline's wisdom. That relentless probing reveals complexity within those bounds that is lost in a broader, satisficing view. Disciplines fulfill their scientific potential advantage when they avoid research monocultures that explore only a subset of their domain. Instead, they practice slow science, employing varied methods and enlisting diverse perspectives. Disciplines fulfill their social potential by focusing their eye for detail on practical problems. Those engagements can, in turn, advance the science by revealing bounds that are hard to see from the inside, new phenomena to domesticate for their colleagues, and opportunities for cross-boundary collaborations.

The proposed bonding strategy seeks to realize this potential. It posits the need for three communities: a community of practice with proper staffing; a community of discourse, with proper internal communication; and a community of consultation, with proper external communication. Like any theory of change, it is not a theory but a framework. Its internal validity depends on the theoretical support for its elements. Its external validity depends on how useful it is for interpreting past experiences and for designing future ventures. Earlier chapters considered its internal validity, focused on its decision science elements. This chapter considers its external validity, focused on how well it accounts for decisions in the two domains considered in Chapter 2: COVID-19 and climate change.

Like other accounts that draw on my first-hand knowledge, they are incomplete and not entirely reliable. Some of their details are recorded nowhere except in my imperfect memory for imperfect observations. They are my best good faith attempts to reconstruct these encounters, trying to be fair with others and myself. Thus, they are better read as accounts of what can happen than of what did happen. The goal is to prepare for the future, not to settle scores with the past.

Both accounts ask what might have been done better. Sometimes, ready opportunities were not pursued, for some seemingly human reason—in which case intellectual leadership might have made a difference. Sometimes, the infrastructure for change appears to have been missing—in which case, institutional leadership was needed. Management science can empower both kinds of leadership.

COVID-19

Vaccines

The Committee on Equitable Allocation of COVID-19 Vaccine functioned within the National Academies' institutional infrastructure.[1] Founded by President Lincoln to provide scientific advice for the Union's Civil War effort,[2] the National Academy of Sciences (NAS) is an honorary body, electing 120 new members each year.[3] As basic science evolved, those being honored were decreasingly likely to have the experience (and perhaps inclination) to work on applied problems, while the demand for advice grew. The National Research Council (NRC) was formed to manage the workflow, with about 200 committees at any time, hoping for at least one member from NAS, National Academy of Engineering (NAE), or National Academy of Medicine (NAM), both formed much later and with greater recognition of their sciences' applications. Together, they form the National Academies of Sciences, Engineering, and Medicine (NASEM).[4]

NASEM has enormous experience and explicit protocols for creating the conditions for successful engagement. In terms of staffing, its committees have experts from diverse disciplinary and practical backgrounds, with opportunities for public comment on their composition.[5] In terms of internal consultation, committees that produce consensus reports must agree on shared text and recommendations, with the rarely used option of written dissents.[6] They have open sessions with invited speakers and opportunities for public input. However, their deliberations are confidential, to allow free discussion. Draft reports are reviewed anonymously by individuals who could have constituted a comparable committee. All comments

---

[1] This section reprises some material from Chapter 2, so that it will stand on its own.
[2] Its origin story includes one success, orienting the compasses on the Union's Monitor-class ironclads, and one failure, recommending that the US adopt the metric system.
[3] As well as about a dozen foreign members.
[4] I'm a member of both NAS and NAM and have served on about forty committees.
[5] https://www.gsa.gov/policy-regulations/policy/federal-advisory-committee-management/legislation-and-regulations/federal-advisory-committee-act (accessed August 23, 2024).
[6] There are also workshop reports, which are reviewed to ensure they reflect what was said, with no consensus recommendations, just ones attributed to individual speakers.

receive written responses, either making changes or defending the text. No one outside the committee and review process sees the text until it is completed, although agency sponsors may receive a briefing a day or two before official release. All completed reports are available online, free to download.[7]

NASEM committees rarely conduct formal analyses or empirical research. Rather, they synthesize expert opinion based on existing analyses and research. However, the vaccine committee needed to perform analyses applying its own risk criteria to public health statistics in order to derive allocation priorities. Those analyses had to be transparent enough to show how "equity" was defined and simple enough for public health officials to apply them to local conditions.[8] The principles, criteria, and statistics, along with the plans for implementing the resulting priorities, constituted the intellectual commons for the committee. In my assessment, it created the communities needed to realize the strategy for bonding bounded disciplines.

In terms of creating a community of practice, the committee's members brought overlapping backgrounds that enabled them to fulfill their interlocking roles. It had bioethicists who could identify relevant outcome- and procedure-focused principles. It had decision science members who could translate the outcome-focused ethical principles into risk criteria transparent enough to satisfy the procedure-focused ones. It had members familiar with public health statistics and experience in communicating with diverse audiences, as well as the international dimensions of disease spread and vaccine sharing.

In terms of creating a community of discourse, committee members' overlapping expertise (and some existing friendships) facilitated the discussions needed to derive the analytical scheme. And once in place, the committee's clear, flexible structure facilitated working through its complex details. Long online plenary sessions created personal relationships, aided by the chairs' superb moderation and the staff's excellent work between meetings and skill in recruiting members able to work together, given the right conditions. The committee's mission motivated members to contribute long hours of unpaid work, under great time pressure. Despite meeting entirely remotely because of the pandemic, the committee had the esprit de corps for an online post-release party.

---

[7] Barbara Kline-Pope, then head of communications for NASEM, convinced NRC leadership to make free access possible, in part by demonstrating that it had no effect on sales. People who wanted books still bought books. The websites for reports tally downloads (and other metrics), showing the influence that reports have. The vaccine report had about 20k downloads, from almost every country in the world, in the months immediately following its release on October 2, 2020, with a current Altmetric score of 1189.
[8] By public health authorities with resources partially provided by the federal government.

In terms of creating a community of dialogue, the committee's proposal was designed for transparency. Both the ethical principles and the criteria were simple expressions of complex constructs that, it was hoped, would degrade gracefully in actual use. Its external consultation included an open invitation for written comments on a draft of the proposed allocation criteria and inviting diverse voices to an online hearing.[9] Each speaker, whether from a major industry group or a small rural clinic, received the same five minutes.

To the best of my understanding, the committee's recommendations framed the allocation plans pursued by local public health authorities, all of which had some absorptive capacity for implementing vaccination plans. It reinforced their natural concern for health promotion, including the need for tailored messages and community partners.[10] There was, however, little response to its risk communication recommendation that a central body collect, analyze, and disseminate tested messages regarding vaccine safety and effectiveness. That failure reflected the agencies' lack of absorptive capacity, with no one responsible for "just the facts" communication. Arguably, it fed public distrust and made life easier for those intent on fomenting it.[11]

Face Masks

Episode 1. As a member of the NASEM COVID-19 Committee,[12] my first assignment[13] was to write a rapid response report with Richard Besser (another member of the committee) and two subject matter experts, on the effectiveness of homemade fabric face masks.[14] Our report was one of a dozen written, reviewed, and issued in seven to ten days, in March and early April 2020, compressing the usual one- to two-year timeline to meet the crisis. In some ways our task was easy, as there was virtually no research to review on a

---

[9] About 1,400 responses were received over a three-and-a-half-day period.
[10] Some committee members were already in the field, aligning community partners in anticipation of expected suspicions, especially among groups with historic mistreatment. As the vaccine programs progressed, some of those communities were less well represented among early adopters. After the vaccine proved safe and effective in general, they had some of the highest adoption rates.
[11] I had several invitations to write on this topic, in visible outlets, with no discernible effect. Fischhoff, B. (2020). Making decisions in a COVID-19 world. *JAMA, 324*(2), 139–140; Fischhoff, B. (2021, October 4). The COVID communication breakdown. Foreign Affairs, https://www.foreignaffairs.com/articles/united-states/2021-10-04/covid-communication-breakdown (accessed August 23, 2024).
[12] National Academies Standing Committee on Emerging Infectious Diseases and 21st Century Health Threats.
[13] Initially, the committee had no social, behavioral, or decision scientists. I was added, in part because I did a thorough rewrite of a rapid response report on crisis standards of care, which I was asked to review. NASEM. (2020). *Rapid Expert Consultation on Crisis Standards of Care for the COVID-19 Pandemic* (March 28, 2020). Washington, DC: The National Academies Press. https://doi.org/10.17226/25765.
[14] NASEM (2020, April 8). *Rapid expert consultation on the effectiveness of fabric face masks for the COVID-19 pandemic.* National Academies Press.

topic that had had little scientific and no commercial interest. Instead, we had to reason from first physical, biological, and social science principles about how effective homemade fabric face masks might be.

We concluded that there was good reason to believe they could contribute to layered defense. We also concluded that we knew nothing about whether using them would encourage other protective behavior, by becoming part of users' identity, or discourage it, by enabling users to check the self-protection box. Indeed, we cautioned against speculation about behavior in the absence of evidence. More people downloaded our report than any other from the committee. However, its title may have promised more than its text delivered, except for readers who valued a strong statement of ignorance.

In terms of creating a community of practice, we had (or had access to) expertise in most relevant topics in the universes circumscribed by the models of behavioral interventions for transmissible disease (see Chapter 7). In terms of creating a community of discourse, we had intensive online meetings and draft message exchanges, aided by familiarity with NASEM procedures and some personal acquaintances. There was no community of consultation with parties other than the reviewers. Our home institutions all supported our drop-everything-else participation. Our (appropriately) mumbled message may account for the lack of personal abuse following our report, even in that polarized time.

Episode 2. As the pandemic continued, so did efforts to assess the effectiveness of face masks, including large field trials in Denmark and Guinea. None found any effect. In November 2020, a Cochrane Collaboration meta-analysis, reviewing all studies, affirmed that conclusion.[15] However, although Cochrane is the world leader in meta-analyses, its protocols were created for medical clinical trials, not behavioral ones, where measuring the treatment dose can be much more difficult. In this case, it meant assessing how often and how well people wear face masks, and how wearing them affects their behavior and that of others around them. Recognizing the mismatch of methods, Cochrane leadership wrote an editorial cautioning against using its protocols for behavioral trials, arguing instead for analyses calculating expected effectiveness from estimates of factors like those in the models in Chapter 7 (Figures 7.2 and 7.3). I was recruited as a co-author to help tell that story.[16]

---

[15] Jefferson, T., Del Mar, C. B., Dooley, L., Ferroni, E., Al-Ansary, L. A., Bawazeer, G. A., van Driel, M. L., Jones, M. A., Thorning, S., Beller, E. M., Clark, J., Hoffman, T. C., Glasziou, P. P., & Conly, J. M. (2020). Physical interventions to interrupt or reduce the spread of respiratory viruses. *Cochrane Database of Systematic Reviews, 11*, Article CD006207, https://www.cochranelibrary.com/cdsr/doi/10.1002/14651858.CD006207.pub5/full (accessed August 23, 2024).

[16] Soares-Weiser, K., Lasserson, T., Jorgensen, K. J., Woloshin, S., Bero, L., Brown, B., & Fischhoff, B. (2020). Policy makers must act on incomplete evidence in responding to COVID-19 (Editorial). *Cochrane Database of Systematic Reviews*, (11), Article ED000149.

In January 2023, an expanded meta-analysis, including all additional studies, reached the same conclusion.[17] There was no direct evidence that face masks reduced users' COVID-19 risk. Taking a stronger position than Cochrane leadership could, two epidemiologists and I wrote an op-ed arguing that the measurement challenges were so great that field trials of face masks could not send a clear signal, hence should be discontinued. Not only could such trials provide no useful information, but they encouraged confusion between lack of evidence of effectiveness and evidence of lack of effectiveness.[18]

In terms of the bonding strategy, the research teams conducting the field trials either lacked expertise in compliance (Figure 7.4)—a flaw in their staffing—or did not incorporate it in their statistical analyses—a flaw in their internal consultation. Flawed external consultation might have limited their ability to communicate their ambiguous results faithfully. In terms of institutional support, Cochrane provides extraordinary training, templates, and guidance—but tailored to medical trials. Cochrane-like protocols might be helpful for auditing, combining, and communicating such processes.

Movie Studios

The pandemic created large, uncertain risks for any workplace that brought people into close contact. Movie studies were one of them. Governors of two of the three largest movie states (California and New York, but not Georgia) asked the industry to devise a reopening plan for their approval. They hoped to use the industry's expertise, while retaining state authority. Four union groups collaborated on a joint proposal, as a basis for negotiating with the studios and, subsequently, the two states. I was a consultant to one of those groups, the Directors Guild of America.

The resulting proposal included practices like removing shared facilities (e.g., makeup brushes, buffets) and severely restricting access to places with essential interactions (e.g., costumes, sets). The unions disagreed, though, on the frequency of COVID-19 testing, at a time when it was scarce, cumbersome, and costly. An epidemiologist estimated the risks with different testing

---

[17] Jefferson, T., Dooley, L., Ferroni, E., Al-Ansary, L. A., van Driel, M. L., Bawazeer, G. A., Jones, M. A., Hoffman, T. C., Clark, J., Beller, E. M., Glasziou, P. P., & Conly, J. M. (2023). Physical interventions to interrupt or reduce the spread of respiratory viruses. *Cochrane Database of Systematic Reviews*, 1, Article CD006207, https://www.cochranelibrary.com/cdsr/doi/10.1002/14651858.CD006207.pub6/full (accessed August 23, 2024).
[18] Fischhoff, B., Cetron, M., & Jetelina, K. (2023, May 2). *Do masks work? Randomized controlled trials are the worst way to answer the question*. STAT, https://www.statnews.com/2023/05/02/do-masks-work-rcts-randomized-controlled-trials/ (accessed August 23, 2024).

frequencies, as a function of prevalence and transmission rates in the surrounding community. The analysis identified a sweet spot: nightly testing for people in close proximity, weekly testing for everyone else. The unions adopted the report, *The Safe Way Forward*, including that recommendation.[19] After negotiations with studios and the states, production resumed in July 2020, and was largely disease-free.

What accounted for this largely unheralded success, in bonding strategy terms? For staffing, the states deferred to industry people who knew the realities of the work and recruited experts with COVID-related knowledge that they lacked. For internal discourse, the four union groups met and exchanged drafts regularly and intensively. When the qualitative discussions reached an impasse on testing, they commissioned a quantitative risk analysis. For external consultation, union members served as sounding boards for draft proposals, building on and strengthening long-standing relationships. It helped that an accomplished movie director drafted much of the report. I helped with explaining the risk analysis.

In one research project prompted by the experience, Victor Rodriguez tested nonexperts' understanding of the heatmap displays used to communicate risk analysis results. The displays showed two measures of risk (the probability of at least one COVID case during a shoot and the expected number of cases), as a function of two community risk factors (disease prevalence and transmission rate), for different testing protocols. Victor found that people's understanding was good enough for practical purposes.[20]

It is unfortunate that more states did not follow this model of deferring to workplace expertise, while leaving ultimate authority with government. Bernard Goldstein and I pitched the idea to Pennsylvania officials. We had the ear of one of two key state department secretaries, but the other was too frazzled with daily pressures to engage.

Climate Change

A tragic failure of the climate science community was assuming that the facts would speak for themselves, once they were known confidently enough for climate scientists to share them. The resulting vacuum let other parties speak in climate's name, framing the issues in ways that served their interests.

---

[19] DGA, SAG-AFTRA, IATSE, and Teamsters (2020). *The safe way forward* (Report no. 1), https://www.sagaftra.org/files/sa_documents/ProductionSafetyGuidelines_June2020EditedP.pdf (accessed August 23, 2024).

[20] Rodriguez, V. L., Fischhoff, B., & Davis, A. L. (2023). Risk heatmaps as visual displays: Opening movie studios after the COVID-19 shutdown. *Risk Analysis, 43*(7), 1356–1369.

Typically, those parties emphasized uncertainties, arguing for inaction until there was better evidence, demanding research that climate scientists were eager to produce.[21] Those scientists' sparse communications were often overly complicated, emphasizing intricacies that were precious to science, but not to the public. By the mid-1980s, the fateful gamble being taken with our collective future was clear enough to motivate strong action. That could have been the message extracted from the uncertainty.[22]

The solutions proposed for climate change often lacked detailed analyses of their costs and benefits to different parties. Without those analyses, climate activists were vulnerable to claims like: "one of the real tragedies that totally distorted the debate over climate change was that it got tied into the solution in a way that if you accepted the first you had to accept the second."[23] That belief would not justify attacking climate science per se. However, it does point to the lack of communications with balanced analyses of potential solutions. By now, the battle for belief in the reality of climate change has largely been won, except for people whose political identity commits them to radical skepticism or who see it as a convenient, if disingenuous, way to reject unwelcome solutions.

Yale Climate Change Communication's long-running Six Americas studies have found energy conservation behaviors to be most common among people who are most alarmed and people who are most skeptical about climate change—each acting for their own reasons.[24] *Risk communication* has become the term of art for providing information and trusting people to make their own decisions, including information about expected costs, risks, and benefits. It builds on the foundations created by *formal science education* (in schools), *informal science education* (in museums, scouts, 4-H, and the like), and *science communication* (about specific projects and scientists).

All are distinct from *persuasive* or *manipulative* communications, seeking to induce behaviors or attitudes. They are also incompatible. Any semblance of spin undermines the credibility of factual (risk) communications. Indeed, people who care deeply about climate change, or any other cause, hurt it when they cross that line. In the short run, mixing climate science and climate advocacy weakens individual messages. In the long run, the science

---

[21] Oreskes, N. & Conway, E. M. (2014). *Merchants of doubt*. Bloomsbury.
[22] Fischhoff, B. (2021). Making behavioral science integral to climate science and action. *Behavioural Public Policy*, 5(4) 439–453.
[23] Showstack, R. (2017, January 27). *Gingrich suggests ways to guide Trump on science and environment*. Eos, https://eos.org/articles/gingrich-suggests-ways-to-guide-trump-on-science-and-environment (accessed August 23, 2024).
[24] https://climatecommunication.yale.edu/about/projects/global-warmings-six-americas/ (accessed August 23, 2024).

disappears into the advocacy. Not letting the facts speak for themselves can be as problematic as expecting the facts to speak for themselves.

The next sections illustrate bonding strategies for (nonpersuasive) climate-related risk communication, with some of our more and less successful attempts to implement them. As elsewhere, my participant-observer view includes otherwise unrecorded activities, while being constrained by my powers of observation and memory.

Better Story Telling

The mental model methodology[25] arose from a feeling that, while most people had heard about climate change by the early 1990s, few had heard clear messages about its drivers and control options. Indeed, in formative reading and interviews, we often found confusion between climate change and ozone depletion. Our research was motivated by the belief that "Both the United States and the rest of the world are currently considering policy responses to the issue of climate change [that] would entail costs ... amounting to trillions of dollars. US society cannot have intelligent democratic debate on these choices unless lay mental models are better informed."[26] Our research led us to conclude that "fortunately, the clarifications needed to produce adequate public understanding appear to be well within the capabilities of modern risk communications."[27]

Figures 9.1 and 9.2 show two products of that research: ratings of the expected impacts of global warming (as we called it then) and strategies for addressing it, collected from convenience samples of nonexperts in 1992.[28] Some options were drawn from the technical literature; the others came from open-ended (mental models) interviews, in pretests—translated into terms that experts and nonexperts found clear, in pretests. These judgments suggest generally valid mental models, except for confusion with the ozone hole (e.g., increased skin cancer). I can only wonder, ruefully, whether pursuing communications built on such research, forty years ago, would have affected climate policy and climate change.

---

[25] See Chapter 5.
[26] Bostrom, A., Morgan, M. G., Fischhoff, B., & Read, D. (1994). What do people know about global climate change? Part 1. Mental models. *Risk Analysis*, 14(6), 959–970.
[27] Read, D., Bostrom, A., Morgan, M. G., Fischhoff, B., & Smuts, T. (1994). What do people know about global climate change? Part 2. Studies of educated laypeople. *Risk Analysis*, 14(6), 971–982, on p. 982.
[28] They were recruited at Pittsburgh's Point State Park July 4th celebrations or at a Leadership Council meeting of the Pittsburgh Chamber of Commerce. Responses were sufficiently similar that the two groups were combined.

Change (in)Action 135

Cause	Mean DA +2 to −2	Distribution T, ≈T, ?, ≈ F, F
Agricultural problems and starvation in many places	1.28	
Increase skin cancer	1.00	
Ecological disasters all over the world	0.97	
Shorter milder winters all over the world	0.95	
Cause sea level to rise	0.83	
More and larger storms all over the world	0.80	
Shortage of oxygen in the atmosphere	0.78	
Make the climate "steamier"	0.68	
Increase precipitation and humidity all over world	0.49	
Reduce photosynthesis	0.41	
War and large immigration problems	0.25	
The main cause of species extinction today	−0.35	

Figure 9.1 Expected impacts of global warming (1992)

Responses to closed-form questions about the effects of global warming, rank-ordered by mean degree of agreement (DA) with each statement on a scale from -2 to +2. The full distribution of responses is displayed in the right-hand column. T=True, ≈T=Probably true; ?=Don't know; ≈F=Probably false; F=False.

Source: Read, D., Bostrom, A., Morgan, M. G., Fischhoff, B., & Smuts, T. (1994). What do people know about global climate change? Part 2. Survey studies of educated laypeople. *Risk Analysis*, *14*(6), 971–982.

These studies implicitly followed, and indeed informed, the bonding strategy proposed here. Their staffing included climate experts, who could speak for themselves, and decision scientists who could help nonexperts speak in policy-relevant terms. The internal consultations included regular meetings and jointly authored papers. The term "mental model" resonated with behavioral, natural, and engineering scientists. The external consultations included open-ended interviews and structured surveys with members of diverse audiences, followed by articles, talks, and policy briefings—but not direct engagement in decision-making processes. The papers from the study were rarely cited for the ensuing fifteen years, followed by a surge beginning in 2009, thirty years after the abortive DOE-AAAS collaboration.[29]

---

[29] At the moment, they have about 900 and 450 citations respectively, per Google Scholar.

Cause	Mean BA +2 to −2	Distribution ⇓, ≈⇓, 0, ?, ≈ ⇑, ⇑
Using all known energy conservation measures	1.41	
Planting trees	1.29	
Stopping use of fossil fuels	1.16	
Stopping pollution from chemical plants	1.11	
Stopping use of aerosol spray cans in the US	1.09	
Making national parks out of remaining trop. rain forests	1.08	
Recycling most consumer goods	1.05	
Stopping release of coolant from refrigs and ACs.	1.03	
Ban chlorofluorocarbons	1.02	
Meet clean air act standards	1.02	
Convert to electric cars	0.98	
Reduce population growth	0.95	
Switching from styrofoam to paper cups	0.78	
Switching to florescent or other efficient lights	0.67	
High tax on all fossil fuels	0.67	
Switching from coal to natural gas	0.66	
Switching from fossil fuels to nuclear power	0.44	
Fertilize ocean to make algae grow faster	0.38	
Stop the space program	0.28	
Make more clouds high in the atmosphere	0.24	
Put dust in the stratosphere	−0.39	

Figure 9.2 Expected impact of climate change measures (1992)

Responses to closed-form questions about the likely impacts on global warming of various strategies, rank-ordered by mean Belief in Abatement (BA) rating, on scale from −2 (strong belief that strategy will aggravate climate change) to +2 (strong belief that strategy will abate climate change). The full distribution of responses is displayed in the right-hand column. ⇑=Will speed up climate change, ≈⇑=Probably will speed up climate change; [white bar]=No effect; ?=Don't know; ≈⇓= Probably will slow climate change; ⇓= Will slow climate change.

Source: Read, D., Bostrom, A., Morgan, M. G., Fischhoff, B., & Smuts, T. (1994). What do people know about global climate change? Part 2. Survey studies of educated laypeople. *Risk Analysis*, *14*(6), 971–982.

In terms of institutional support, our department at Carnegie Mellon (EPP) rewarded faculty who advanced basic science in the context of applied collaborations. It was an early home for *integrated assessments*, computational models of complex systems, including social factors.[30] However, like other engineering schools, it requires faculty to pay graduate students' tuition and stipend. Lacking those resources for these topics, we did little additional research.[31] During the 2000s, some climate scientists began to engage behavioral researchers. One milestone was *Nature Climate Change* being the first *Nature* journal to welcome social science, including invited papers in its 2011 inaugural issue.[32] *Nature Energy* followed suit in 2016.[33] Since then, climate communication research has exploded, although most remains within disciplines, without a bonding strategy.

One notable exception is the Climate Advocacy Lab.[34] Founded to bring social science to bear on climate change advocacy, it experimented with different models for internal and external communication, before settling on a satisfactory one. For example, the Lab's readable, authoritative guide to social science communication design principles did not leave advocates confident in using it. We participated in three subsequent experiments, none of which proved effective: a column on new studies, an online research seminar for designing and testing messages, and collaborative fieldwork with advocates, with the hope of later publications. Eventually, the worlds of research and practice proved too dissonant, and the Lab created workshops led by its own staff, who were familiar with the research and experienced at hands-on advocate support, along with a lively website and social network. In terms of the bonding strategy, the experience was a failure. No academic team emerged with adequate staffing, internal, or external communication.[35] Fortunately, the Lab found a way to get along without us.

Better Stories

In the context of communications, the decision science arc entails analyzing decision makers' information needs, describing their existing beliefs, and intervening to bridge critical gaps, creating needed information if necessary. In my experience, the first step is the hardest: narrowing the fire hose of

---

[30] Morgan, M. G., & Dowlatabadi, H. (1996). Learning from integrated assessment of climate change. *Climatic Change*, 34(3), 337–368.
[31] Dryden, R., Morgan, M. G., Bostrom, A., & Bruine de Bruin, W. (2018). Public perceptions of how long air pollution and carbon dioxide remain in the atmosphere. *Risk Analysis*, 38(3), 525–534.
[32] Pidgeon, N., & Fischhoff, B. (2011). The role of social and decision sciences in communicating uncertain climate risks. *Nature Climate Change*, 1(1), 35–41.
[33] Wong-Parodi, G., Krishnamurti, T., Davis, A. L., Schwartz, D., & Fischhoff, B. (2016). Integrating social science in climate and energy solutions: A decision science approach. *Nature Climate Change*, 6(6), 563–569.
[34] https://climateadvocacylab.org (accessed August 23, 2024).
[35] There were parts of two dissertations.

138 Bounded Disciplines and Unbounded Problems

information that would be nice to know to the thin, focused stream that decision makers need to know. The foci of those analyses might range from estimating a single critical fact to bringing order to an unruly domain. Two examples will give a feeling for the versatility of the analytical toolkit.

Understanding single factors. At one extreme, a single fact, once understood, could affect a decision. For example, a policy maker deciding whether to require smart electricity meters might want to know the expected change in consumers' electricity use. A driver deciding whether to buy a plug-in hybrid vehicle (PHEV) might want to know the emissions from generating the electricity that they plug into. A policy maker might want to know what drivers believe about those emissions. Each decision maker would also want to know how good the evidence is.

In the early 2010s, we collaborated with a major electricity company to answer the first of these questions.[36] As a natural first step, we reviewed existing studies.[37] We found thirty-one, almost all in the gray literature of technical reports, with uneven review processes. To evaluate the quality of their evidence, we applied a version of the Cochrane Collaboration criteria for evaluating medical clinical trials (see Box 5.3). Figure 9.3 shows our ratings of the trials on six Cochrane criteria. Light gray indicates cases where researchers did not report what they had done (e.g., sequence generation for randomization), leaving decision makers to guess. Medium gray indicates high risk of an admitted bias (e.g., using volunteers, letting participants select their condition).

There are so many medical clinical trials that researchers have been able to estimate the impact of some biases, by comparing results from studies with and without them. We assumed (a large assumption) that each bias would have the same impact on smart meter trials. Correcting for those biases, trials that on average reported a 3 percent reduction in energy consumption no longer reported a statistically significant reduction. The effect of meters on peak-shaving—reducing consumption during periods of greatest demand (e.g., hot, muggy summer days)—was roughly halved.[38]

---

[36] The purchase, installation, and management of smart meters had, I believe, been justified, in part, by claims regarding their impacts on consumers, as well as savings from laying off meter readers and improving grid management. It would be interesting to know what evidence was used to support those claims.

[37] Our study owed its existence to the anomalous inclusion of a requirement for behavioral science as part of the funding for smart meters in the America Recovery and Reinvestment Act, following the 2008 financial industry collapse that threatened the entire economy. Our company partners gambled, correctly, that allocating a small portion of their budget to our research would increase their chances of having a winning proposal.

[38] Another analytical study used propensity score analysis to assess how volunteers for such studies differed from the general population, as a way to provide more relevant adjustment factors.

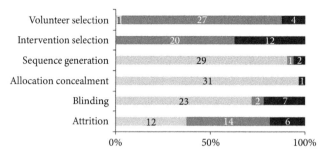

Figure 9.3 Quality of evidence in consumer electricity consumption trials
Distribution of studies that meet the criteria for high, low, or unknown risk of bias.
Source: Davis, A. L., Krishnamurti, T., Fischhoff, B., & Bruine de Bruin, W. (2013). Setting a standard for electricity pilot studies. *Energy Policy*, *62*, 401–409.

Another study in the project directly assessed the impact of another potential bias: the Hawthorne effect, behavior change due to knowing that one is in a study.[39] We sent a large random sample of consumers a postcard a week, for four weeks, saying that they were in a study of electricity consumption.[40] Over that month, they used about 2.5 percent less electricity than would otherwise be expected. That observation offers a baseline for assessing the impact of more elaborate one-month interventions.[41]

The overall message from our research was negative. There was little evidence that interventions using smart meter data promoted energy conservation.[42] Gentle reminders might be enough. We had suggestions for better designs, but without supporting field trial data.[43] Our electric utility partner had little absorptive capacity for behavioral science and limited access to its senior decision-making echelons. As best we could tell, it did the minimum required by the Public Utility Commissions (PUCs) regulating its subsidiaries. Also lacking absorptive capacity for behavioral evidence, the PUCs relied on their (differing) intuitions regarding the critical single factor that we analyzed, requiring interventions in one jurisdiction, but not an adjoining one. In bonding strategy terms, the project had good staffing and internal discourse, but ineffective external discourse.

---

[39] Schwartz, D., Fischhoff, B., Krishnamurti, T., & Sowell, F. (2013). The Hawthorne effect and energy awareness. *Proceedings of the National Academy of Sciences*, *110*(38), 15242–15246.
[40] It included an opt-out option, which few selected.
[41] Another empirical study attempted to predict how much more effective smart meters might be if the displays communicated real-time energy use more effectively,
[42] Although there was evidence of impacts on peak-shaving, those effects had also been found with "kill-a-watt" programs, dating back many years.
[43] Krishnamurti, T., Davis, A. L., Wong-Parodi, G., & Wang, J. (2013). Creating an in-home display: Experimental evidence and guidelines for design. *Applied Energy*, *108*(10), 448–458.

Understanding multiple factors. At the other extreme, decision makers are unsure which of many factors deserve detailed attention. Influence diagrams are a management science tool for that analysis, identifying the factors relevant to predicting valued outcomes. For example, the influence diagrams for malaria[44] and H5N1[45] focus on disease risks, but with different granularity in the drivers, outcomes, and roles of public health capabilities (Figure 5.2; Figures 7.1 to 7.3).

Climate modeling involves complex computed models, combining possible values of multiple variables to predict aggregate outcomes (e.g., mean temperature, sea-level rise, GDP). For people making decisions (as opposed to people worrying about the fate of the world), climate modelers *downscale* the models for specific locales, as much as their data and computer power allow. In the mid-1990s, colleagues at the Battelle Pacific Northwest National Lab (PNNL) asked for help in translating climate model outputs into terms useful for decisions related to managing the Columbia River dams, built for power, irrigation, and tourism, on the viability of salmon populations.

To that end, we created the influence diagram shown in Figure 9.4.[46] It synthesizes biological models of salmon survival that use historical data in ways that can accommodate climate-induced changes. We then created influence diagrams for how climate change effects on seasonal temperature and annual precipitation would affect survival rates at different salmon life stages (e.g., fry-molt), through intermediary processes (e.g., river temperature, snowpack runoff). Given the novelty and complexity of these interactions, we did not conduct a formal expert elicitation.[47] Rather, we worked with fishery experts to think through the potential (and interacting) impacts on salmon life stages,[48] for plausible temperature and precipitation estimates (from climate models).

With that foundation, we interviewed mid-level managers in four major policy-making organizations regarding decisions that could be informed by our analyses. We identified ten nonroutine decisions with clearly defined decision makers and decision-making processes. To illustrate the approach, we settled on the decision set out in Figure 9.5, as being well defined, immediate, and with relatively complete data: managing the water level on Lake Pend Oreille, behind one of the dams. Its primary valued outcomes were effects on

---

[44] See Figure 5.2.
[45] See Figures 7.1 to 7.3.
[46] The research was the dissertation of Sharon Jones, currently Vice Provost for Research at University of Washington Bothell.
[47] See Box 5.3.
[48] As an example of the complexity, reduced survival at one stage can reduce competition and increase survival at a later stage.

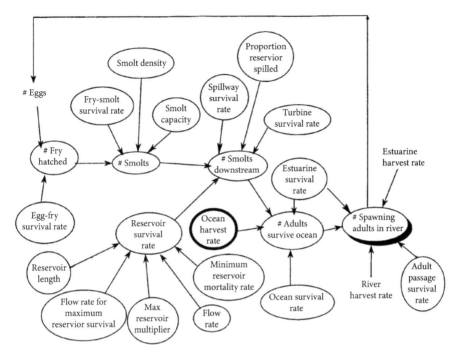

Figure 9.4 An influence diagram for factors affecting the viability of salmon populations

Source: Northwest Power Planning Council (1992). *System planning model documentation update version 5.10*.

the viability of salmon runs and economic benefits (calculated separately). Its inputs reflected the range used in this policy arena. Our analyses found that, using historic data, economic benefits dominated, leading to high reservoir levels and low stream flows (and salmon habitat). Adding in climate change reversed the decision, so that the reservoirs were managed to ensure salmon survival.

These analyses were conducted just one degree of separation from the decision makers, and with tightly coupled intermediaries (PNNL). Nonetheless, they had no discernible impact.[49] We concluded that our approach had addressed two common barriers to making science useful: *relevance* to specific decisions and *compatibility* with official decision-making models. It had not overcome two other barriers: *accessibility* to decision makers, in these complex, multiparty deliberations, and *receptivity* of those processes to new kinds of evidence. In bonding strategy terms, the project had good staffing,

---

[49] The article containing the technical details has four citations by people other than the authors, according to Google Scholar: Jones, S., Fischhoff, B., & Lach, D. (1998). An integrated impact assessment for the effects of climate change on the Pacific Northwest salmon fishery. *Impact Assessment and Project Appraisal*, 16(3), 227–237.

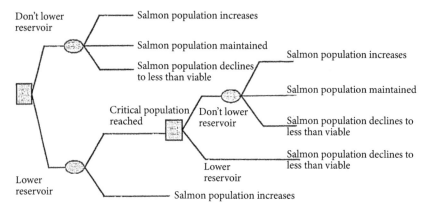

Figure 9.5 Decision tree for managing Columbia River reservoirs

Source: Jones, S., Fischhoff, B., & Lach, D. (1999). Evaluating the science–policy interface for climate change research. *Climatic Change, 43*(3), 581–599.

internal, and external discourse, in a situation where analysis alone could not carry the day. We predicted that climate science would not affect policy without enough sustained contact between researchers and policy makers to affect the decision-making processes.[50]

Reflection

Both cases, smart meters and salmon viability, had conditions for bonding bounded disciplines around a common cause. We had the freedom to define the problems broadly. We had the informal networks needed to staff our work with diverse experts. We had work settings that promoted the candid internal consultation needed to let the work evolve. Our colleagues facilitated direct and indirect external consultation with decision makers, helping us to tailor the work to their needs, as well as providing absorptive capacity for its results. The analytical methods, all drawn from the management science toolkit, served as platforms for collaborative work and communications. The limited practical impact was out of our collective hands. There must have been enough chance for them to ask for our help, hoping that the stars would be aligned when the answers arrived.

---

[50] This reflection and summary had ninety-five non-self-citations, per Google Scholar: Jones, S., Fischhoff, B., & Lach, D. (1999). Evaluating the science–policy interface for climate change research. *Climatic Change, 43*(1), 581–599.

Conclusions

Like any satisficing account, the usefulness of the bonding strategy depends on how well it helps explain past experiences and plan future ones. The examples in this chapter involve cases where I had some opportunity to implement some aspects of the strategy. They benefit from my fluency in its constructs, drawn from management science, as well as my participant-observer status in the applications. That status could also prejudice the accounts, as could hindsight, outcome, and confirmation bias.[51] Thus, they are surer representations of what could happen than of what did happen. As with the other examples in the book (and lectures), the bonding strategy provides a template for interpreting and organizing complex projects. Box 9.1 offers some heuristics for implementing this satisficing strategy, comprised of boundedly rational elements.

Box 9.1 Heuristics for Applying the Disciplinary Bonding Strategy

Have a general contractor with the broad management science expertise to coordinate the application.

Seek terms of engagement that give the greatest opportunity for applying the theory of change (e.g., getting everyone around the same table).

Offer properly qualified advice as it comes into view, to sustain engagement and get feedback; complete the research asynchronously.

Practice slow science, taking the opportunity to take everything in.

Share the model, to create an intellectual commons.

Assess collaborators' ability to create a functioning community, given their internal dynamics, incentives, etc.

Assess collaborators' absorptive capacity for requesting and using management science expertise.

Look for existing relationships, as a basis for initial trust; promise enduring relationships, as a basis for sustained trust.

---

[51] Hindsight bias is believing that one could have known in foresight things that were only apparent in hindsight. Outcome bias is evaluating a decision by how things turned out, rather than by the thought that went into deciding. Confirmation bias is either looking for information that will affirm existing beliefs or exploiting ambiguity in information to interpret it as affirming.

Chapter 10
Management Science as a Bonding Discipline

Any communication carries an obligation to use its audience's time well. For my lectures and this book, I envisioned an audience with a common challenge: applying the knowledge of necessarily narrow scientific disciplines to inherently complex practical problems. I envisioned that audience as including management scientists, specializing in elements of applications; other scientists, hoping to make themselves more useful, with management scientists' help; practitioners, hoping that management science can help them to navigate the maze of experts; and onlookers, wondering about society's return on investment in science and students' return on investment in education.

I propose a strategy for *bonding bounded disciplines*. As mentioned, like other theories of change, it is not a theory in the boundedly rational sense of making directly testable predictions. Rather, it is an organizing construct for identifying satisficing solutions consistent with disciplinary knowledge. Thus, it is *theory informed*, but not *theory driven*. Its primary commitment is to the problems, not the research. It is, however, *theory informing*, in psychology's *construct validity* sense. Each application tests the usefulness of the theories that it tries to employ. Successful applications increase faith in each constituent; unsuccessful ones reduce that faith. Both help disciplinary scientists situate their work in the world and among the disciplines.

Management science plays several central roles in this strategy. The organizing graphics are drawn from its analytical methods. Its statistical and expert elicitation procedures can be used to estimate model parameters. Its preference elicitation procedures can identify and balance valued outcomes. Its empirical disciplines can create trusted communication channels and messages for sharing beliefs, concerns, and solutions. It can be the general contractor, employing its organizational frameworks to coordinate the disciplines, contributing their expertise as subcontractors.

Fulfilling this vision requires organizational settings that are faithful to the problems and to the science. Those settings could be schools of management with slow science philosophies, confident that such collaborations will prove theoretically productive, while fulfilling the duty to serve. Those settings could also be consultancies that stay abreast of the science, even when serving clients who cannot tell how sound the science is.

Schools of management science create absorptive capacity for the strategy, by training people familiar with the analytical and empirical methods central to it. Those graduates practice management science every day. They can apply the science that they have mastered and get help when specialized help is needed. They can translate their organization's problem into terms recognizable by management scientists and translate those scientists' advice into terms recognizable by their organization.

Decision Science

In this account, decision science,[1] my management science, plays five roles. One is as a unifying platform for denotative aspects of complex decisions. Given its Bayesian roots, decision science can accommodate any kind of expert or nonexpert belief and preference. Given its cognitive roots, it has procedures for eliciting beliefs and preferences that include measures of their success. Given its psychological roots, it has links to topics outside its disciplinary bounds, including affective, social, and physiological processes.

A second role is as part of the conceptual world that management science graduates carry to their workplaces. Decision science's analytical, descriptive, and intervention research has found its way into most management schools. Today, any graduate will know that judgments can be biased and that preferences can depend on how choices are framed. Many will have some feeling for decision trees, expert elicitation, multi-attribute utility analysis, and risk communication. Some will try their hand at these methods, recognizing the marginal utility of even sketched versions for clarifying complex domains, and seek expert help for more detailed work.

A third role is illustrating its vision of the wisdom that is an emergent property of any boundedly rational discipline. That wisdom reflects the breadth of disciplinary training, affording graduates diverse methods and perspectives (e.g., psychophysics for eliciting numerical estimates, nonverbal communication for avoiding unintended cues). It reflects the rigors of apprenticeship in graduate research seminars that sweat the details of study

---

[1] As mentioned, the field is also known as behavioral decision research, which can be confused with behavioral economics, which draws on some of the same psychological research, as well as the disciplinary resources of microeconomics.

design, anticipating the harsh light of peer review. It also reflects internecine struggles that focus scientists on a topic (e.g., probability vs. frequency representations), revealing limits to methods and results, as protagonists dispute one another's studies.

A fourth role is illustrating the kinds of challenge that any discipline faces in playing its part in the strategy. For decision science, the primary challenge is implementing the full analysis–description–intervention arc needed to treat a topic thoroughly. That means sustained two-way interactions with decision makers and experts, iterating through the stages until the decision and decision makers are well enough understood to be helpful. Not everyone has the time, patience, and resources for such engagement.

A fifth role is showing how disciplines can advance by addressing such challenges. Like much of management science, decision science began as a boundary busting enterprise. Those boundaries were the ones separating analytical, behavioral, and intervention research.[2] Ward Edwards, Howard Raiffa, Herbert Simon, James March, and others all had variants of the insight that the norms of sound decision-making processes, as captured in decision theory axioms,[3] were a bounded aspiration rather than a reality. Building on work by Bernoulli, Boole, Ramsey, Allais, and others,[4] these founders of decision science recognized that descriptive research could reveal how well behavior approximates these aspirations and how well interventions can bring it closer.

From a Multidisciplinary Field to an Interdisciplinary Platform

In order to become a discipline, an emerging field must set its bounds. For decision science, the primary bound was decisions with an analytical representation that allowed behavior to be evaluated. The bookbag-and-poker chip studies[5] readily met those requirements, even if it took some imagination to link the tasks with real world ones.[6] Fortunately for the field, there were funders who saw the links. They were mostly military research branches with the freedom to gamble on projects with distant payoffs. Moreover, these

---

[2] Or, as Ward Edwards named them, normative, descriptive, and prescriptive.
[3] For example, one axiom is comparability: for any two objects, a rational person, in this sense, prefers one or the other, or is indifferent between them.
[4] Kyburg, H. E., & Smokler, H. E. (Eds.) (1964). *Studies in subjective probability*. Wiley.
[5] Chapter 3.
[6] As researchers might have argued.

funders structured their programs to bridge the "valley of death" that can separate research and applications.

One notable initiative was the 1970s US Department of Defense Advanced Research Projects Agency (DARPA) Advanced Decision Technology Program. It had disciplinary scientists with boundary-breaking interests that spanned the analysis–description–intervention arc, with leads at Harvard (Howard Raiffa), Stanford (Ron Howard), the University of Southern California (Ward Edwards), and Decision Research (Paul Slovic, Sarah Lichtenstein, and me). They met two or three times a year, at meetings that included reports on applications like decision aids for assessing combat readiness and allocating defense budgets. One paper in the 1977 annual report was on "the use and abuse of formal analytic methods in public policy decisions and critical assessment of the state-of-the-art of decision analytic methodology and its application."[7]

All scientific publications also appeared as technical reports with executive summaries extracting their practical implications.[8] In one, we reported that "Such overconfidence may lead to premature cessation of information gathering and to ineffective decision making. No generally effective way to combat it is available."[9] These meetings and executive summaries were strange exercises for disciplinary scientists. However, they forced the kind of internal and external consultation needed to bond bounded disciplines. The program also supported basic research without other funders. For scientists with faculty positions, that support made the research easier.[10] For scientists on soft money, like Paul Slovic, Sarah Lichtenstein, and me, it made the research possible.[11]

For obscure reasons, an early Reagan administration move ended even the limited funding for decision-making research.[12] When the National Science Foundation (NSF) established its Decision Risk and Management Science program in 1982, management science was quick to see the opportunities

---

[7] https://apps.dtic.mil/sti/citations/ADA058478 (accessed August 23, 2024); quote on p. iv.

[8] Remarkably, some of the technical reports from that program are available online, such as: https://apps.dtic.mil/sti/tr/pdf/ADA101986.pdf (accessed August 23, 2024). Also published as: Lichtenstein, S., Fischhoff, B., & Phillips, L. D. (1982). Calibration of probabilities: State of the art to 1980. In D. Kahneman, P. Slovic, & A. Tversky (Eds.), *Judgment under uncertainty: Heuristics and biases* (pp. 306–334). Cambridge University Press.

[9] https://apps.dtic.mil/sti/tr/pdf/ADA059147.pdf (accessed August 23, 2024), p. ii. Also published as: Fischhoff, B. & Slovic, P. (1980). A little learning …: Confidence in multicue judgment. In R. Nickerson (Ed.), *Attention and performance, VIII* (pp. 779–800). Erlbaum.

[10] They include Amos Tversky and Daniel Kahneman, some of whose publications on judgment under uncertainty and prospect theory include acknowledgments.

[11] Our subcontract was administered by the Office of Naval Research, with a wonderful program manager in Marty Tolcott, who reminded us to tell a story "for the admirals."

[12] In pockets like the NSF cognitive psychology program.

in its interdisciplinary vision. Box 10.1 has excerpts from an early workshop report.[13] They are consistent with the bonding strategy. They also presage the challenges to interdisciplinary collaboration, when disciplinary reviewers serve as gatekeepers. DARPA initiatives are time-limited, allowing them to jumpstart, but not sustain, research programs.[14] NSF programs can provide such support, hoping that academic institutions provide positions for researchers who follow those new paths.

Box 10.1 Conditions for Interdisciplinary Decision and Management Science Research

> Decision and Management Science is a multi-disciplinary area. The need is for real hybridization, not just a collection of disciplines. Interdisciplinary research, however, requires participants who have reasonable familiarity with one another's fields, including not only matters of the language in which problems are discussed, but also the goals and "world views" of the various practitioners. Such familiarity is not easily acquired across disciplinary boundaries. Encouragement notwithstanding, it is difficult for researchers from non-overlapping specialties to come up with interdisciplinary proposals without some preliminary interaction.
>
> Two ways to foster such speculative interaction are (1) to develop support (i.e., for released time, administrative costs, etc.) for potentially interdisciplinary groups at campuses where the right mix of people already exists, but where no mechanisms exist to make it easy for such people to become acquainted and (2) to fund postdoctoral appointments or extended visits of DMS researchers from one field to laboratories where research from some other DMS field is being done. In both cases the intent is to make access to people in other fields easier than is currently the case.

Source: Little, J. C. (1986). Research opportunities in the decision and management sciences. *Management Science*, 32(1), 1–13, quote from p. 12.

An Interdisciplinary Platform in a Multidisciplinary World

As with any field, the evolution of decision science reflects its institutional homes. The logical candidates have been psychology, economics,

---

[13] Little, J. C. (1986). Research opportunities in the decision and management sciences. *Management Science*, 32(1), 1–13. It still makes good reading, to see who was at the table and talking to one another.

[14] Fuchs, E. R. H. (2020). Rethinking the role of the state in technology development: DARPA and the case for embedded network governance. *Research Policy*, 39(9), 1133–1147.

and management science departments. What follows is my incompletely informed sense of how it has fared in those three settings, leading to the conclusion that management science offers the best fit.

Psychology

Psychology departments turn over faculty slowly, typically refilling specialty slots. When decision science arose, few departments had mathematical psychology programs, a natural home for research requiring both analytical and behavioral skills. Almost all departments had social psychology programs, with long-standing interests in human failings. As a result, research shifted in that direction, boosted by Richard Nisbett and Lee Ross's influential *Human Inference: Strategies and Shortcomings of Social Judgment*.[15]

That shift led to research with imaginative tasks, potential new biases, and social consequences. Chapter 4 describes some of that explosion of new research. However, without the analytical foundation, it was sometimes unclear how distinct the biases were, and sometimes whether they were biases at all.[16] Moreover, social psychology's historic concern for social biases (e.g., racism) naturally encouraged manipulative interventions (e.g., reducing prejudice) rather than empowering ones, the default in decision science.

As an establilshed field, comfortable in its boundaries, social psychology largely pursued its own path, studying biases that met its normative standards and pursuing its favored paths for correcting them. The Ross and Nisbett sequel, *The Person and the Situation: Perspectives of Social Psychology*, focused on that progress, with little attention to decision science.[17] Conversely, decision science rarely pursued issues raised by social psychology research, although it still enjoyed the flow of replications and extensions. The paucity of mathematical psychologists limited the chances for the casual conversations that can lead to bringing disciplines together.

Decision science has also had little connection with psychologists who study specific decisions (e.g., health, careers, voting) with simple linear models. As described in Chapter 3,[18] these models sum measures of good and bad outcomes, weighted by their importance, and then predict that people

---

[15] Nisbett, R. E., & Ross, L. (1960). *Human inference: Strategies and shortcomings of social judgment.* Prentice-Hall.
[16] See Chapter 4, which also discusses the slow progress on individual difference measures, despite most departments teaching them and the central role of psychometrics. Fischhoff, B. & Beyth-Marom, R. (1983). Hypothesis evaluation from a Bayesian perspective. *Psychological Review*, 90, 239-260.
[17] Fischhoff, B. (1992). Review: A social perspective on psychology [comment on *The person and the situation: Perspectives of social psychology*, by L. Ross & R. E. Nisbett]. *Psychological Inquiry*, 3(1), 85–89.
[18] Repeating some material so that the passage is self-contained.

will choose options with higher scores. Variants of the health belief model, expectancy-value models, and the theory of reasoned action follow this strategy. Their success reflects investigators' insight into which outcomes matter—insight that comes from their immersion in a domain. However, the "robust beauty" of such models ensures some predictive success for researchers with that insight.[19] It limits what can be learned from regression weights on those predictors, as many sets of weights (including equal weights) will have similar success.[20] Rather than reflecting importance, the weights depend on technical issues, such as multicollinearity, sample restrictions, and measurement quality.

As a result, decision science rarely uses such models for explaining *how* people make decisions, while still acknowledging their value for predicting *what* decisions people make. The resulting disconnect between the fields has, arguably, left simple linear model users unproductively deliberating chance differences in weights. It has left decision scientists unproductively missing the insights of linear model researchers immersed in specific decisions and decision makers.[21]

Recently, these worlds have come together in studies of when people believe misinformation. That research requires both substantive understanding of the issues and analysis of how much difference misinformation makes. The former needs domain specialists (e.g., in health, careers, voting, or social decisions). Decision science can provide the latter. These collaborations have produced theoretically and practically relevant findings. One such result is that people judge the quality of scientific evidence by its perceived precision.[22] Another is that communicating uncertainty well, by explaining its sources, can increase the credibility of evidence.[23] A third is that programs reducing the effects of climate change do not reduce commitment to avoiding it.[24]

---

[19] Dawes, R. M. (1979). The robust beauty of improper linear models in decision making. *American Psychologist, 34*(7), 571–582.

[20] Jaccard, J. (2012). The reasoned action model: Directions for future research. *Annals of the American Academy of Political and Social Science, 640*(1), 58–80.

[21] The same arguments apply to other fields that use such models, not realizing that, in the hands of insightful researchers, they always have some indistinguishable predictive value.

[22] Broomell, S. B., & Kane, P. B. (2017). Public perception and communication of scientific uncertainty. *Journal of Experimental Psychology: General, 146*(2), 286–301.

[23] van der Bles, A. M., van der Linden, S., Freeman, A. L., & Spiegelhalter, D. J. (2020). The effects of communicating uncertainty on public trust in facts and numbers. *Proceedings of the National Academy of Sciences, 117*(14), 7672–7683; van der Bles, A. M., van der Linden, S., Freeman, A. L. J., Mitchell, J., Galvao. A. B., Zaval, L., Spiegelhalter, D. J. (2019). Communicating uncertainty about facts, numbers and science. *Royal Society Open Science, 6*(5), Article 181870.

[24] Mark, C., & Wagner, G. (2024). Presenting balanced geoengineering information has no effect on mitigation engagement. *Climatic Change, 177*(1).

Economics

Economics slowly at first, then explosively, adopted decision science results and tasks. In a story well told in Richard Thaler's *Misbehaving*[25] and Daniel Kahneman's *Thinking, Fast and Slow*,[26] economists troubled by seemingly nonrational behaviors found support in psychology's ready acceptance (even pursuit) of such behavior. David Grether and Charles Plott created an empirical bridge between the disciplines with their experiments examining alternative explanations of the preference reversals documented by Sarah Lichtenstein and Paul Slovic.[27] They followed experimental psychology's boundary testing strategy: manipulate a variable and see how that affects responses (see Box 1.2).

As with social psychology, decision science found its way into economics through a few tasks that readily fit the adopting discipline. Preference-reversal tasks had such a fit. They came with instructions that economists could follow, directly observing individuals make inconsistent choices. They had been refined through a trail of studies, in expert experimentalists' hands, to provide reliable results and rule out alternative explanations.[28] They did not, however, come with decision science's accompanying wisdom regarding the range of reliable replicability and the methods for testing it.

Although Grether and Plott's article appeared in a top economic journal, it seems to have provided proof of principle, rather than launching an era of collaboration with behavioral researchers. One missing ingredient was an account that fit the disciplinary norms of economics, which prize formal models.[29] Prospect theory provided that bridge between the disciplines.[30] It offered a simple linear model, in expectation form, with elements roughly analogous to those of expected utility theory—even if expressing very different versions of those constructs.

As with social psychology, these initial adoptions by disciplinary leaders were followed by a period of internal consolidation, digesting the possibility

---

[25] Thaler, R. (2017). *Misbehaving*. W.W. Norton.
[26] Kahneman, D. (2011). *Thinking, fast and slow*. Farrar, Straus & Giroux.
[27] Lichtenstein, S., & Slovic, P. (1971). Reversals of preference between bids and choices in gambling decisions. *Journal of Experimental Psychology, 89*(1), 46–55. Lichtenstein, S., & Slovic, P. (1973). Response-induced reversals of preference in gambling: An extended replication in Las Vegas. *Journal of Experimental Psychology, 101*(1), 16–20.
[28] Or at least weaken the case for those alternatives.
[29] Producing such models provides a return on the enormous investment in statistical methods required by the discipline's credentialing process. Thaler, R. H., & Shefrin, H. M. (1981). An economic theory of self-control. *Journal of Political Economy, 89*(2), 392–406.
[30] Kahneman, D., & Tversky, A. (1979). Prospect theory: An analysis of decision under risk. *Econometrica, 47*(2), 263–292.

that people are not always the rational actors that economics had assumed. Some of that work, economists needed to do on their own, such as exploring ways to reformulate the utility theory axioms to accommodate behavioral anomalies. Also, as with social psychology, economists interested in anomalies eventually formed their own subdiscipline, creating their own version of decision science. At times, they independently discovered methodological lessons that psychology had learned through its long history. At other times, they missed those lessons, creating tasks that left psychologists uneasy.[31]

One class of such tasks embodied some economists' insistence on *incentive-compatible* rewards, intended to induce people to reveal their true beliefs and preferences. That imperative gave economists license to ignore psychological research, as just observing "cheap talk." It gave psychologists license to ignore economic research, as forcing people to express themselves in arcane ways, leading to untrustworthy responses.[32] Some psychologists were also uncomfortable with some economists' innovative experiments in poor countries, where a fixed budget for rewards could go much further than in wealthier places. For psychologists, these studies were a large leap from their own studies, changing so many things at once that it was hard to interpret them, compared to their strategy of painstakingly varying individual factors.

As economics consolidated its approach, in *behavioral economics*, it sometimes engaged psychologists in choice architecture (nudge) interventions.[33] Intended to steer people toward better outcomes than they could achieve on their own, these manipulations are justified by claims that people cannot fend for themselves, due to personal or market failings.[34] They are a natural fit for behavioral researchers eager to see if lab results replicate in the world. They are a poorer fit for decision scientists uncomfortable about assuming that any one behavior is right for everyone.

Management Science

Decision science arose in management science units in business schools, complementing case studies (e.g., Harvard, Duke, Michigan, Cambridge,[35]

---

[31] See Chapter 6.
[32] See Chapter 7.
[33] Johnson, E. J. (2022). *The elements of choice*. Penguin Random House.
[34] Perhaps even imagining that people lived in a world with efficient markets that reduced the computational burden by providing easily digested information about restricted sets of plausible options.
[35] In Cambridge, this process started in the engineering department, which then became the foundation of what is now the Judge School of Business, led by Stephen Watson.

Carnegie Mellon) or in engineering schools, complementing engineering economics (e.g., Stanford, Southern California, Technion, Virginia, Carnegie Mellon). Given their goal of supporting professionals, these schools seek to empower autonomous decision making, the default for decision science.

For independent actors (people or organizations), that goal means having *informed* choices, based on *articulated preferences* and *value awareness*. Informed choices would not change with any additional information that currently exists or could reasonably be created. Articulated preferences would not change with any additional perspectives on how to think about what matters. Value awareness reflects a stable decision-making process, balancing cognitive, affective, and social aspects, so that decision makers can be as rational as they want to be.

For interdependent actors, that goal means having *fewer, but better conflicts*.[36] Avoid disagreements due to unintended misunderstanding or disrespect, by promoting proactive, two-way communication. Focus on legitimate disagreements, which might be resolved by new information, options, or deliberative processes. Acknowledge power differentials that allow parties to restrict the flow (or creation) of information and to impose their preferences on others. Avoid brushing aside disagreements by claiming that opposing parties do not understand the issues, hence should be disregarded or coerced into compliance—as often happens when nonexperts dispute experts' claims.

Assessing success in achieving these goals requires much slower science than does assessing success in achieving behavior change. In principle, it means knowing each individual's preferences and circumstances well enough to tell whether they are making informed choices and are engaged in productive conflicts. Those assessments require researchers skilled in probing how people think about their wants and their world, and about the realities that constrain them.

Management schools have people with the expertise to address these goals and assess their success.[37] Whether they are drawn to discipline-bonding collaborations will depend on how they see the intrinsic and extrinsic incentives. The former reflect the personal and intellectual benefits of working with other disciplines, learning about new domains, and helping people to articulate preferences that might disagree with their own. The latter reflect the rewards that their employer and discipline provide for work that is theory informed, and theory informing, but not theory driven.

---

[36] Here I have used some repetition of earlier passages so that the chapter will be self-contained.
[37] Engineering schools do not.

The incentives that individual faculty see will depend, in turn, on those seen by their employers and disciplines. Do they see intrinsic rewards in engaging other disciplines, domain experts, and decision makers? Or do they fear losing the quality control found within disciplinary bounds? Do they see extrinsic rewards from marketing these innovations and protecting themselves against charges of insularity? Or do they fear gambling resources on ventures with slower, if potentially much larger, payback?

Strategic Gambles

Thus, management schools are well positioned to take these strategic gambles, and bond bounded disciplines. They have faculty with analytical and empirical skills. They have units dedicated to decision-making processes (e.g., strategy, organizational behavior, accounting) and decision-making outcomes (e.g., marketing). They have students seeking skills that will help them change the world, for public or private good. They have more flexibility than disciplinary departments and clients who expect them to innovate. My sense, as a sympathetic outsider, is that the main barrier to collaboration is faculty members' disciplines.

Academic institutions need experienced disciplinary scientists who have the wisdom to assess whether junior colleagues have the technical skills to create evidence that can withstand conventional peer review. However, those disciplinary experts need not have the wisdom to evaluate work beyond those bounds. Indeed, they may intuitively deprecate such work, if their human capital resides in having mastered, and perhaps even having set, disciplinary standards. They can assess how strongly research tests disciplinary boundaries, but not the legitimacy of the gamble, its degree of success, or the value of its failures.

These concerns also apply to the gatekeeping function of publication in top disciplinary journals. Absent unusual editorial leadership, these journals prefer the most accomplished research on topics of current disciplinary interest. One imperfect response is publishing in journals that consider only technical competence (e.g., *PLOSOne*), letting the community decide what is interesting. A second is publishing in journals where technically trained professional editors make that community judgment (e.g., *Nature*), without allegiance to current tastes. Such journals may also be more willing to recruit reviewers with diverse disciplinary expertise (and not just diverse positions on theory and method).

Relying on publications is a risk-averse strategy for evaluating faculty. The more conventional the criteria (e.g., top five journals), the greater the aversion, both to downside risks (faculty who cannot perform to disciplinary standards) and to upside ones (faculty who can innovative beyond them).[38] The risks of such risk aversion are recognized by institutions that hire faculty who have taken successful career gambles elsewhere or have long tenure clocks to encourage such gambles. Yet even they run the risk that disciplinary insularity will create intellectual common mode failure.

Psychology's reproducibility crisis reflects such a failure: a normalized pathology of repeating studies or analyses in different ways until an expected result emerges. Researchers then convince themselves that the "successful" study and analysis were the right ones all along.[39] However, because that trial and error process capitalizes on chance, results often fail to replicate. Studies claiming to demonstrate judgment biases and priming effects have been prominent failures.[40]

Disciplinary psychology has mounted a vigorous response to the crisis. Journals increasingly emphasize how well studies are done, rather than just how interesting their outcomes are. Those new practices include *preregistering* methods and analyses, limiting the opportunities for selective reporting; encouraging *replications*, reducing editors' inclination to reject them as uninteresting; promoting *multisite replications*, evaluating robustness in different hands; and *meta-analyses*, combining all related studies, weighted by measures of their quality.[41]

While improving research within disciplines, these practices may dampen research across them. The novelty of interdisciplinary studies means that their analyses are "exploratory," hence need to be observed again in preregistered replication studies in order to be taken seriously. Interdisciplinary projects often involve complex, collaborative applications, so unique that they cannot be repeated, much less be subject to meta-analysis. The construct validity of their results depends on wisdom from other disciplines.[42] Disciplinary studies spun out of them may take time to begin[43] and time to refine.

---

[38] One telling study found that influential papers in economics often did not appear in the "top five" journals, which are often the criterion for professional advancement. Heckman, J., & Moktan, S. (2020). Publishing and promotion in economics: The tyranny of the top five journals. *Journal of Economic Literature, 58*(2), 419–470.

[39] Fischhoff, B., & Davis, A. L. (2014). Communicating scientific uncertainty. *Proceedings of the National Academy of Sciences, 111* (Suppl. 4), 13664–13671, and references therein.

[40] "Falsification" is sometimes used to describe such poor science, as distinguished from "fabrication," involving deliberate deception. Reporting just the last study has been called the "file drawer problem." Reporting just the last analysis has been called "p-hacking." If those final results are real, reporting them as "shown" would better capture their status as demonstrations of things that can happen, rather than "found," implying that they happen routinely.

[41] The incoming editor of *Psychological Science*, a journal that was a hotbed of replication failures, declared transparency as its new norm.

[42] See the face mask story in Chapter 9.

[43] What I have called asynchronous.

Rather than evaluating faculty solely by their work output, academic institutions could evaluate them by their work process. The bonding strategy provides templates for those evaluations. How completely were their research teams staffed? How well did they perform needed internal connections? How consistently did they create and maintain needed external ones? How cognizant were they of the missing elements and their impact on results?

The weight given to that process assessment, alongside conventional output assessment, would depend on an institution's willingness to take the risks. To what extent does it believe that the future belongs to bonded disciplines? To what extent will it accept slower rates of disciplinary publications, as needed with asynchronous pursuit of complex, novel projects? To what extent does it expect the gamble to attract talented students and faculty, as well as decision makers with interesting projects? To what extent does it expect funding agencies to honor the effort?

Funders have powerful leverage for overcoming the intrinsic inertia of disciplinary science. However, they need explicit criteria for wielding that power effectively and transparently. Otherwise, they risk supporting proposals that make bold but vague promises, with the ingredients for grand collaborations, but not the mixing instructions for a proper recipe.[44] Disciplinary bonding offers such criteria. Funding agencies that adopt the strategy would require proposals to include:

An influence diagram, showing the outcomes that the research hopes to affect, the primary factors believed to affect those outcomes, and the sources of that knowledge on the research team—allowing funders to assess whether researchers have a coherent picture of their domain and the elements that they are addressing (and missing).
A network diagram, showing how members of the research team will consult with one another and with what level of engagement (e.g., parallel, sequential, or co-designed projects)—allowing funders to assess their plan for internal collaboration.
A consultation diagram, showing how researchers and decision makers will interact throughout the process, regarding research priorities, plans, progress, and changes of plan—allowing funders to assess whether decision makers want the help that the researchers hope to create and will receive it in a timely, usable fashion.

---

[44] See the National Network for Critical Technology Assessment: https://www.nncta.org (accessed August 23, 2024).

Requiring these plans could enable collaborations that would not otherwise happen, however much researchers might want them. Proposal writers need to feel that "We can't get the money unless we include [expertise that might be ignored], co-design projects with the community [rather than just work in parallel], and have stakeholders review plans before starting [rather than assume their approval]." Having these management plans could help funders defend their sciences' social license to operate (and secure public resources), by showing projects' roadmap for achieving their goals, and not just hopes of somehow helping someone someday.[45]

In this light, funding agencies are essential change agents. They can send a clear signal that sustained support for such collaborations is now policy, reassuring junior faculty that engaging in them is a reasonable career gamble and helping senior faculty convince their institutions to create positions requiring both disciplinary and collaborative excellence. Implementing that strategy might begin with a time-limited DARPA-like initiative to jumpstart the research and cultivate examples. Successful models could then frame the sustained funding needed for career planning and creating stable research groups.[46]

Conclusions

Disciplines accrete their wisdom slowly, as illustrated by the evolution of decision science. Its analytical core has taken centuries to evolve. Its empirical methods have roots in nineteenth-century psychophysics, adapting natural science methods to behavior, while borrowing from hard-won developments in other specialties, known to decision scientists through their broad training. Its innovations needed extended, rigorous, open-minded peer review to mature, with some dead ends along the way. Its internecine disputes reflect the focus possible when participants agree on the bounds of discourse.

My Clarendon lectures, and this book, have asked how bounded disciplines can apply their wisdom to unbounded problems. I propose a bonding strategy that respects the disciplines' wisdom, as essential to solving complex practical solutions, and their need for such challenges. The proposal protects

---

[45] Drummond, C., & Fischhoff, B. (2022). Assessing broader impacts of funded research: The United States National Science Foundation vs. Rep. Lamar Smith. *Science and Public Policy, 49*(2), 313–323.

[46] It is my sense that cognitive neuroscience has succeeded in this regard. An account of the fate of the nascent field of conflict resolution can be found in Harty, M., & Modell, J. (1991). The first conflict resolution movement, 1956–1971: An attempt to institutionalize interdisciplinary social science. *Journal of Conflict Resolution, 35*(4), 720–758. An alternative funding model is initiative-based, as in computer science, where funders see gaps and soft money researchers apply to fill them.

society by providing auditing templates for seeing whether it is getting the science it needs.[47] It protects science by structuring collaborations so that they advance the contributing sciences. It protects both by strengthening the bond between them.

Schools of management are natural places to implement the strategy. They have the analytical and empirical expertise for the structured empathy at its core: identifying, organizing, and delivering information that decision makers need. They seed the world with professionals who provide their organizations with absorptive capacity. They know how to organize major projects, with general contractors coordinating individuals, information, and resources. Their standard toolkit includes variants of the three organizing templates: influence diagrams, network analyses, and consultation charts. They can, if they wish, embrace the slow science that arises when fast science disciplines work with one another and with those they hope to serve. They can, if they wish, reward faculty for collaboration, which might involve publishing outside their home discipline and cultivating external relationships, ready for opportunities for joint action.

I believe that the world is looking for such leadership. I hope to have offered a practical strategy for making it happen. Pursuing the strategy would, I believe, contribute to intellectually vibrant schools and disciplines, helping them to recruit and retain students and faculty who both love science and want to change the world. It would strengthen the commons of public goodwill needed to support our work.

I am grateful for the opportunity that the Clarendon Lectures provided to articulate this vision, addressing a problem that has been on my mind throughout my career in science and before—when deciding whether to have such a career: How can scientific disciplines pursue their self-contained dreams, while making themselves useful? In my view, the wisdom of disciplinary science lies in the uncommon turn of mind that comes with trying to get to the bottom of things. That bounded rationality confers an unusual ability to ask very hard questions about very narrow topics. Practical collaborations offer structured opportunities to refine those bounds, while working on projects that are intellectually, personally, and socially rewarding. I have had many such opportunities in my career. I hope to have shown ways to create them for others.

---

[47] As in the unsupported claims of bias.

Index

For the benefit of digital users, indexed terms that span two pages (e.g., 52–53) may, on occasion, appear on only one of those pages.

A

absorptive capacity 24*b*, 24, 34, 129, 139, 145
adversarial collaborations 9
AIDS-related survey 64, 67
ambiguity 2–3, 62, 64–66, 67–69, 71, 131
articulated preferences 80, 89–90, 153
auxiliary assumptions 6
availability bias 42
availability heuristic 7–8, 39–40
avian flu (H5N1) 78–79, 100–101, 101*f*, 102*f*, 104*f*, 115, 116*f*

B

ball-and-urn research 36–38, 47
Bayesian belief networks 72
Bayesian framework for descriptive decision science research 44*b*
Bayesian inference 36–38, 47
Bayesian reasoning 43–44
behavioral economics 50, 145 n.1, 152
beliefs (slow science)
   context 62
   of experts 74–79
   face validity of answers 67–70
   face validity of questions 63–67
   study conclusions 79
benefits, defining 85–88
bias
   ability to correct for 7–8
   attrition 76*b*
   availability 42
   in Bayesian hypothesis evaluation, potential sources of 44*b*
   and competence 58–60
   confirmation 43–44, 143
   in consumer electricity consumption trials 138–139, 139*f*
   debiasing 60
   and decision-making competence 48–50
   and decision science 58–59, 94
   in descriptive research 50
   at epicenter of psychology's reproducibility crisis 59–60
   experts receiving training to reduce 32
   in fatalities studies 40
   growing with distance between disciplines 107
   in heuristics-and-biases framework 38, 45
   hindsight and outcome 143 n.51
   in protocol of summarizing scientific uncertainty 76*b*
   and psychology 149
   response 36–37
   rush to judgment producing unsupported claims of 45
   selection 76*b*
   "umbrella" 78–79
bias heuristic 42–45
bonding bounded disciplines
   barriers to 97–98
   boundary organizations for 122–125
   strategy for 98–111, 113, 120–121, 125, 128, 143, 144, 157–158
boundaries *see* disciplinary boundaries
boundary disputes 9–12
boundary organizations 121–125
bounded accounts of preference reversals 11*b*, 151
bounded disciplines *see* bonding bounded disciplines
bounded rationality
   conferring ability to ask hard questions about narrow topics 158
   as consequentialist 4
   of disciplines, science progressing through 126
   expert elicitation and climate models 32
   heuristics 3
   within matrix 3

160 Index

bounded rationality (*Continued*)
  normative analysis, psychological insight, and prescriptive potential 45
  and processing of stimulus 6
  of scientists 97, 103
  as strategy for dealing with complexity 3–4, 12, 96
bounds
  decision science flourishing within 36–37
  out-of-bounds observations 38–39

C

calibration 38–39 n.22, 78–79
certainty equivalents 90–91, 91*f*
civility 8
climate change
  as complex problem 25–26
  in context of decisions 132–142, 150
  disciplines of 26–28
  effects on malaria 72–74, 73*f*
  expected impacts of global warming (1992) 135*f*
  expected impacts of measures (1992) 136*f*
  failure to create community of practice 99–100
  human dimensions of 25–34
  lessons learned 32–34
  management science tasks 29–32
  psychological dimensions, research projects 29*b*
  report extract 27*f*
  summary 13, 34
  surface temperature change 33*f*
coding
  frequency 7, 38
  mental model approach 74
  reliability 74
Cognitive Bias Codex 43
coherence 37, 78, 81, 94
collaboration
  in adolescent decision making study 69–70
  adversarial 9
  of analysts and decision makers 109*f*
  analytical methods serving as platforms for 142
  barrier to 154
  bonding bounded disciplines strategy required for 120–121, 157–158

Broader Impacts and Intellectual Merit 122
community of 110
cross-disciplinary, projects requiring 29*b*, 32
and decision science 62
and disciplinary departments 123
DOE-AAAS 27, 32, 125, 135
economists and psychologists 10
experts rewarded for specialization rather than 61
facilitated by qualitative formal models 113–114
factors determining success 24*b*
and funding agencies 156–157
institutional incentives for 123–124
interdisciplinary 59–61, 69, 106*f*, 107*f*, 147–148, 155
with people being studied 81
practical 158
professional 112
and psychology's reforms 59–60
at root of decision science 35, 45, 47
and schools of engineering 125
and schools of management 124–125, 153, 158
and slow scholarship 67
struggles with 97–98
Committee on Equitable Allocation of COVID-19 Vaccine *see* NASEM Committee
common cause 23, 24*b*, 32, 142
communication
  analytical methods serving as platforms for 142
  carrying obligation to use its audience's time well 144
  on climate change 28 n.33, 31–32, 99–100, 132–138
  efficient, within disciplines 74–75
  fixed 119
  on health matters 8, 20, 24, 102*f*, 104*f*, 129
  "just the facts" 129
  model for two-way, in project management 108–110, 109*f*
  with one another (internal consultation) 105–108, 126
  with other stakeholders (external consultation) 108–110, 126

between people and models 114
persuasive or manipulative 133–134
recommendation to promote proactive, two-way 153
risk, mental model approach to 99
of uncertainty 150
communities, creating 116–120
community of consultation 108–110, 114, 120–121, 126, 130
community of discourse 105–106, 110, 112, 114, 120, 126, 128, 130
community of practice
creating 112, 114, 120–121, 128, 130
purpose 105–106
in bonding bounded disciplines strategy 98–100, 110, 126
competence
avoiding rush to judgment 45, 49–50, 61
and bias 58–60
context 48–49
and discipline of decision science 50–51
individual differences 54–58
"literacy" tests 53–54
and scientists 60–61
structured empathy 51–53
study conclusions 61
complexity
confronting 2
coping with 3–4, 12, 96
as inherent to challenging problems 1
rewards for embracing 95
sciences in 4–8, 98, 126
complex problems
of climate change 13, 25–26
of COVID-19 vaccine allocation 13–16
and engineering sciences 112–113
individual scientific disciplines unable to solve 13
and management science 113
need for diverse views when solving 16–17
need for slow scholarship 113
requiring best available science from multiple disciplines 34
compliance 102f, 103, 104f, 105, 108–109, 116–117, 131, 153
comprehension 103, 104f
computable models 72–74, 110–111, 113, 117, 125
confirmation bias 43–44, 143

conflicts 116, 125, 153
see also boundary disputes
consequentialism 4, 50
construal processes 66
constructed preferences 94
construct validity 39–40, 55–56, 69–70, 78, 87–88, 94, 144, 155
consultation diagrams 156
contingent valuation 85–86, 87–88, 92–93
Coombs, Clyde 80, 90
coordination 3, 13
correspondence 78, 81
COVID-19 vaccine
as complex problem 13–16
disciplines 16–25
equitable allocation of 14–25, 34, 99, 119, 127–129
lessons learned 23–25
management science tasks 20–23
in relation to change 127–129
see also face masks; movie studios

D

decision aids 45–46, 147
decision analysis 49–50
decision making
adolescent, study of 69
complexity as great challenge of 2
descriptive research characterizing 35
heuristic way of thinking about 4–5
overconfidence leading to ineffective 147
in relation to climate change 135, 139–142
and schools of management 152–154
sound, normative model defining 36, 146
and value awareness 153
decision-making competence (DMC)
affecting how people fare in world 48
importance of information on risks 52
and individual differences 54–58
and intervention research 50
prevalence of poor decision outcomes for people with high and low scores of 57b
psychometric tests for individual difference measure of 55b
decisions
climate change in context of 132–142, 150
elements 2
interrelated steps to studying 35
types of 36

Index

decision science
- aka 'science of human frailty' 58–59
- analytical 49
- apprenticeship 94
- arc of normative, descriptive, and intervention research 50–51, 61, 62, 137–138, 145–146
- Bayesian framework for descriptive research 44b, 47
- bias heuristic 42–45
- and business schools 123
- courses in 118, 121
- definitions 34, 36
- descriptive 49–50
- and economics 151–152
- emergence 35, 47
- evolution of 148–149, 157
- as flourishing within bounded world 36–37
- and focus on process 50
- interdisciplinary platform in a multidisciplinary world 148–154
- and management science 125, 152–154
- from multidisciplinary field to interdisciplinary platform 146–148
- and normative analysis 51–52, 61, 95
- out-of-bounds observations 38–39
- primary bound of 146–147
- providing common language for experts 100
- and psychology 149–150
- pushing heuristic bounds 39–42
- relation to pathology 48
- requiring interdisciplinary collaboration 61
- research on beliefs and preferences 81
- roles played by 152–154
- simple models or simple processes 45–47
- standard gamble 92
- synthesis of elements 38–39

decision scientists 47, 49–50, 59–60, 135, 150, 152, 157
decision trees 51–52, 127
descriptive decision science 49–50
descriptive research
- Bayesian framework 44b
- characterizing decision making 35
- in decision science arc 50–51, 61, 62, 137–138, 145–146
- in fatalities study 40–41
- in heuristics-and-biases framework 38

detail 7–8
dilution effect 43–44
disciplinary boundaries
- academic institutions 154
- burrowing within 5–7
- collaboration across 32
- communication for revealing 107
- consequences of neglecting 59
- continuing interaction increasing permeability of 120
- disputes within 9–12
- expanding 105
- and familiarity with one another's fields 148b
- impact of delineating 79
- leap of faith required to cross 120–121
- probing 105
- separating analytical, behavioral, and intervention research 146

disciplinary departments 112, 123, 154
disciplinary mentoring 4–5
disciplined empathy 51–52
disciplines
- and legitimacy 12
- potential benefits of consultations 24–25
- in relation to climate change 26–28
- in relation to COVID-19 vaccine allocation 16–25
- scheme for characterizing state of knowledge 75b, 75–76
- slow accretion of wisdom 157
- see also bonding bounded disciplines

discrete choice methods 90–91, 91f, 92–94
DMC see decision-making competence (DMC)
drinking and driving interpretive task 65b, 66–67
drinking and driving studies 82
Drug Facts Box 8

E

economics
- advanced econometrics as lingua franca of 12
- behavioral 50, 145 n.1, 152
- and decision science 151–152
- experimental 9–10
- as grounded in rational actor models 81

economists 9–12, 23, 26, 69, 83, 88, 151–152

Edwards, Ward 12 n.28, 35, 38–39 n.22, 146
emergent properties 74, 145–146
emotion 8, 50, 67–68
epistemic uncertainty 69–70
event-driven organizations 122
events
   and availability heuristic 7–8, 39–40
   and complexity 2
   as element of decision making 2
   epistemic uncertainty 69–70
   learning frequency of 5–7
   options and outcomes 2, 36
   and teenagers' estimation of risk 69
existence value 85–86
expert elicitation 32, 33*f*, 77–78, 114–116, 116*f*, 144
experts
   behavior of 32
   beliefs of 74–79
   and computable models 113
   and mental models 72–74, 99
   methods for assessing beliefs 114–115
   motivation of 34
   need for common language 100
   and network diagrams 113
   and nonexperts 1, 31–32, 72–75, 79, 108–110, 113–114, 116–117, 120, 122, 135, 153
   in psychological dimensions of climate change research projects 29*b*
   two-way communication between 108
   two-way interactions with decision makers 146
   use of models in general 117
   working together 61
external consultation 99–100, 108–110, 112–113, 129, 131–132, 135, 142, 147

F
face masks 14–15, 36, 129–131
face validity
   of answers 67–70, 88–92
   definition 63
   and fast science 94
   mental models research addressing 73–74
   as primary test of preference measurement 81
   of questions 63–67, 70, 81–88
factors
   multiple, understanding 140
   single, understanding 138
fatalities studies 40–42, 70–71
feasibility 103, 104*f*, 105
"fifty-fifty" answers 69–70, 93
fluency 118, 143
food and drink contamination 52–53
frequency encoding 7, 38
frequency learning 6
frequentists 38
funding agencies 156–157

G
general contractor
   complex projects requiring 125
   for construction projects 13
   heuristic for disciplinary bonding strategy 143*b*, 144
   management science as 112–114
   in schools of management 158
grounded theory 74, 115 n.8

H
Hawthorne effect 139
heuristics 3–4
   for applying disciplinary bonding strategy 143*b*
   availability 7–8, 39–40
   bias 42–45
   and claims of competence 48–49
   for disciplinary science 5*b*, 5
   in judgment 7
   as often lumped in with biases 50
   pushing heuristic bounds 39–42
   satisficing 3, 96, 110
   teaching, as beneficial to mathematical problem solving 50
heuristics-and-biases demonstrations 45
heuristics-and-biases framework 38

I
incentive-compatible proper scoring rules 154
incentive-compatible rewards 152
incentive-compatible tasks 9–10
incentives
   for candor 78–79
   climate scientists 99–100
   for collaboration 123–124, 153–154
   creating 120–122
indigenous technical knowledge 109–110

individual differences
and competence 54–58
psychometric tests for DMC 55*b*
infectious disease 100–103, 101*f*, 102*f*, 104*f*, 105, 108
inference
Bayesian 36–38, 47
testing web of 39–40
influence diagrams 72, 100, 103–105, 107–108, 110–111, 113, 140
for behavioral interventions to control infectious disease 102*f*, 103
criteria 98–99
for factors affecting viability of salmon populations 140–142, 141*f*
and funding agencies 156
for pharmacological interventions to control infectious disease 100–101, 101*f*
predicting effects of climate change on malaria 72, 73*f*, 140
for roles of compliance and communication in behavioral interventions to control infectious disease 103, 104*f*, 105
informed choices 153
integrative approach 12
intellectual commons, creating 114–115
interdisciplinary decision and management science research, conditions for 148*b*
internal consultation 105–108, 112–113, 127–128, 131, 135, 147
internal validity 55–56, 126
interpretation 63–67, 65*b*, 68–70, 86–88, 95
intervention research 42, 50, 61, 145, 146
see also prescriptive research
irrelevance 62

J
judgments
affecting definitiveness of results 31
avoiding rush to 45, 49–50, 61
Bayesian model of inference for 47
biased 39, 43, 145, 155
and construct validity 70, 78
correspondence 78
coherence 78
and expert elicitation 32, 33*f*
heuristics in 7
limited insight into factors shaping 47
numerical 36–37, 41–42
probability 10, 37, 70, 78–79
regarding avian flu 77–79, 83
simple regression models predicting 46
testing robustness of 41–42

L
leadership 13–14, 33, 124, 126–127, 158
"literacy" tests 53–54

M
management schools *see* schools of management
management science
boundary organizations for bonding bounded disciplines 122–125
conditions for interdisciplinary research 148*b*
creating communities of practice, discourse, and consultation 116–120
creating incentives 120–122
creating intellectual commons 114–115
and decision science 125, 152–154
disciplines recommended for intelligence community 119*b*
as general contractor 112–114
strategic gambles 154–157
roles in bonding discipline 144–145, 157–158
roles in vision 112, 125
roles in climate change 29–32
roles in COVID-19 vaccine allocation 20–23
manipulation checks 10, 64, 70, 87–88
manipulative communication 133–134
manufacturer responsibility 52–53
matrix 3, 10, 11*b*
medical clinical trials 31, 76*b*, 130, 138
medical malpractice 52
mental models 28, 71–74, 78, 99, 115–116, 134–135
meta-analysis 76*b*, 76–78, 130–131, 155
metaphors 117
misaggregation 37
misperception 37
misunderstanding 62, 116, 153
moderation 24*b*, 24, 128
movie studios 131–132

N

NASEM
  COVID-19 vaccine allocation 15–16, 127–129
  bringing decision science into intelligence analysis 118–119, 119b
  disciplines 16–25
  factors determining collaboratory success 24b
  lessons learned 23–25
  management science tasks 20–23
  members 17b
  recommendation for phased approach to COVID-19 vaccine allocation 22f
  in relation to face masks 129–131
  statement of task 19b
network analysis 105–107, 106f, 107f
network diagrams 106f, 107f, 113, 156
nonexperts
  and experts 1, 31–32, 72–75, 79, 108–110, 113–114, 116–117, 120, 122, 135, 153
  methods for assessing beliefs 115
  testing COVID-related understanding 132
normalized pathology 12, 74–75, 155
normative analysis 35–36, 50
  benefits of 95
  in decision science arc 50–51, 61, 62, 137–138, 145–146
  of fatalities 40–41
  as foundation of decision science process 51–52
  and heuristics 45
  structured empathy of 51–52, 61
normative rules 37, 43–44
normative standards 36, 38–39, 47, 149
novel problems 96
numeracy tests 54
numerical probabilities 68f, 68–70
NUSAP (Numerical Unit Spread Assessment Pedigree)
  applying assessment element of 76b, 76
  characterization of the pedigree of statistical evidence 75b, 75–76

O

options
  climate change 29b, 134, 135f
  complex 2
  continuous 3, 36, 49
  discrete 3, 36, 49
  and discrete choice methods 90, 94
  evaluating 80
  events and outcomes 2, 36
  in influence diagram 100–101, 101f
  for people facing ambiguous questions 66
  as rows in matrix 3
  and satisficing heuristics 3
outcomes
  in breast cancer screening 94
  in climate modeling 140
  as columns in matrix 3
  and complexity 2–4
  and decisions 36, 49–50, 56–57, 57b, 90, 149–150
  as element of decision making 2
  in infectious disease control program 108–109, 109f
  in influence diagrams 100–101, 101f, 110–111, 113, 140, 156
  in management science tasks 21
  in protocol of summarizing scientific uncertainty 76b, 77–78
  "tangible" 125

P

pathology
  analogy to decision science 48
  normalized 12, 155
  pessimism 59
pattern recognition 3, 38
peak shaving 31, 138, 139 n.42
persuasive communication 133–134
precipitation forecasts 78–79
preference reversals, bounded accounts of 11b, 151
preferences (slow science)
  context 80
  face validity of answers 88–92
  face validity of questions 81–88
  ostensibly simple tasks 80–81
  slowing down to provide answers 94–95
  study conclusions 95
  whether the questions have answers 92–93
prescriptive research 35, 50
  in decision science arc 50–51, 61, 62, 137–138, 145–146
  and heuristics 45
  see also intervention research
probability

probability (*Continued*)
　of accidents while drinking and driving 65*b*
　as element of decision making 2
　frequency representations 145–146
　in normative model 36
　President Truman interpreting 67
　related to climate change 33*f*
　related to COVID-19 risk 21, 132
　related to avian flu 78–79, 115, 116*f*
　of traffic accidents, factors affecting 81–82, 82*f*
　see also judgments: probability; numerical probabilities; subjective probabilities
professional schools 123
propositional knowledge 71
prospect theory 68–69 n.17, 151
prudential algebra 46, 49 n.3
psychologists 9–12, 38–39, 54 n.23, 88, 149–150, 151–152
psychology
　clinical 46–47
　cognitive 5–6, 47, 63, 71
　and decision science 35, 149–150
　disciplinary 155
　and face validity 63
　heavy reliance on readily available research participants 105
　prompting revolution in safeguards 59–60
　reproducibility crisis 38–39 n.24, 59–60, 75–76, 155
　social 9, 50, 63, 149, 151–152
psychophysics 36–37, 40–41, 145–146, 157
publication in journals 121, 154–156

R
reactive measurement 49–50, 94
recognition 98–99
regression models 45–47
reliability 55–56
requisite variety 98–99
research monoculture 39
respectful ways of interacting, methods for creating 119–120
response biases 36–37
revealed preference 82
risk communication 133
risks
　comparing estimates of aggregate 82*f*
　defining 81–84
　hazards as sources of 83–84
　two-factor space defined by qualitative aspects of 85*f*

S
satisficing
　as approach to dealing with complexity 3, 96–97
　and bounding bonded disciplines 144
　as consequentialist 4
　for practitioners 97–98
　in scientific disciplines 4–5
satisficing heuristics
　for determining when to revisit or abandon processes 110
　as holistic and hard to describe 3
　showing where to look and when to stop 96
schools of management
　as beneficial for collaborations 124–125
　and bonding strategy 144–145, 158
　and decision science 145
　having expertise to address goals and assess success 153
　as well positioned to take strategic gambles 154
science communication 133
science education 53–54, 117, 133
sciences
　complexity 4–8, 98, 126
　criteria for assessing strength of 76*b*
　disciplinary 97–98, 144, 147, 154
　engineering 112–113, 125
　see also beliefs (slow science); preferences (slow science)
scientific disciplines
　and bounded rationality 96, 158
　coping with complexity through bounded rationality 12
　unable to solve complex problems individually 13
scientific uncertainty 76*b*
scientists
　balancing acts 49–50
　bounded rationality of 97, 103
　climate 31–32, 99–100, 132–133, 136–137
　dealing with problems 30–31
　and decision makers 120
　distinguishing from consultants 5
　as only human 60–61

organizational 107, 109–110
and practitioners 98, 103
scope insensitivity 86–87
search facilitation 98–99
service-driven organizations 123
shared problem space 24*b*, 24, 33
shared ways of thinking, methods for creating 116–119
simple models or simple processes? 45–47
'sitting at same table' 24*b*, 24, 32–33, 143*b*
slow scholarship 62, 63–64, 66–67, 69–70, 74–75, 79, 113–114
slow science *see* beliefs (slow science); preferences (slow science)
social resilience 102*f*, 103, 104*f*
speech act 108–109
speed–accuracy trade-off 10
staffing 99–103, 108, 110, 126–128, 131–132, 135, 139, 141–142
standard gambles 90–92
statistical frequency 36
statistical power 38–39, 94–95
stimulus range effects 36–37
strategic gambles 154–157

structured empathy 45, 49–50, 51–53, 59, 61, 158
subjective probabilities 36, 38

T

technical proficiency 118
theory informed, theory informing, theory driven 144, 153
theory of change 97, 126
think aloud protocols 63–64
tokens 6, 8
transactions, framework for specifying 87–88, 89*b*
trust 103, 104*f*, 105, 108–110, 114, 117–118, 143*b*

U

utilities 36, 92
utility curves 90–91

V

value awareness 153
value-of-information analysis 101
verbal quantifiers 67–69, 68*f*
voluntariness, double standard for 83–84
voluntary risks 83–84